The Cleaner Plate CLUB

The Cleaner Plate Club

Beth Bader &
Ali Benjamin

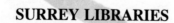

Storey Publishing

Dedication

For our daughters,

with thanks to those who encouraged and inspired us:
our spouses, dear friends, and the farmers who grow our food.

*The mission of Storey Publishing is to serve our customers by
publishing practical information that encourages
personal independence in harmony with the environment.*

Edited by Margaret Sutherland, Nancy Ringer, and Sarah Guare
Art direction, photography, and illustrations by Dan O. Williams
Text production by Jennifer Jepson Smith and Dan O. Williams
Indexed by Christine R. Lindemer, Boston Road Communications

Storey Publishing
210 MASS MoCA Way
North Adams, MA 01247
www.storey.com

Printed in China by Toppan Leefung Printing Ltd.
10 9 8 7 6 5 4 3 2 1

Library of Congress Cataloging-in-Publication Data

Bader, Beth.
  The cleaner plate club / by Beth Bader and Alison Wade Benjamin.
    p. cm.
  Includes bibliographical references and index.
  ISBN 978-1-60342-585-8 (pbk. : alk. paper)
  1. Cooking. 2. Food. 3. Children—Nutrition. 4. Dinners and dining.
  I. Benjamin, Alison Wade. II. Title.
  TX643.B33 2011
  641.5—dc22
                    2010030060

contents

▬▬ **Introduction** 1

▬ # Chapter 1
Getting Started: Bringing a Family Together with Food 9
Food Preferences 12 • Stop Fighting 18 • Portion Distortion 20
The Nutritional Gatekeeper: 72 Percent Ain't Bad 23
It's Not Always About Food 25

▬ # Chapter 2
Shopping Strategies: Stocking Up Without Breaking Down 27
Aisle by Aisle: Navigating the Supermarket 30
Six Simple Words = A Lifetime of Better Health 38
Say "Yes" for a Change: Farm-to-Consumer Venues 45

▬ # Chapter 3
Meet Your Vegetables: How to Fall in Love with What's Good for You 57
Alliums 62 • Asparagus 66 • Beets 68 • Broccoli 70 • Brussels
Sprouts 72 • Cabbage 74 • Carrots 76 • Cauliflower 78 • Chard 80 •
Cucumber 82 • Eggplant 84 • Herbs 87 • Kale 89 • Lettuces 92
Peppers 96 • Potatoes 98 • Root Vegetables 101 • Snap Beans 105
Spinach 107 • Summer Squash 109 • Sweet Potatoes 112 •
Tomatoes 114 • Winter Squashes 119 • The "Un-Vegetables" 122
More Vegetable-Rich Side Dishes 130

▬ # Chapter 4
Mealtime: Recipes to Make It Work 155
Breakfast 159 • Lunch 170 • Dinner 174

▬ # Chapter 5
Snacks and Sweets: Taking the Fight Out of Kids' Favorite Foods 235
Dips and Chips 238 • Sweets and Desserts 248 • The Real Scoop
on Sugar 266

▬▬ **Epilogue What's Next: A Road Map for the Journey** 275
▬▬ **Resources** 292
▬▬ **Index** 297

"Pull up a chair.
Take a taste.
Come join us.
Life is so
endlessly delicious."

Ruth Reichl, "Teach Your Children Well,"
Gourmet, March 2007.

introduction

In a way, this book began with a box of chicken nuggets.

ALI CAN STILL REMEMBER THE BOX; it was bright red, accented with yellow and blue, its brand name displayed in a rippling banner across the top. The name made it sound like the food inside — frozen, breaded hunks of processed meat — was a feast fit for royalty.

Ali's older daughter was a toddler at the time, still relatively new to eating but already demonstrating a remarkable resistance to any food that didn't come out of a box. Although Ali had mastered a handful of recipes in college — carrot-ginger soup from her Moosewood cookbook, a spinach pie from the Greek mother of a roommate, one-bowl brownies from the back of the Baker's chocolate box — her daughter was willing to eat just one of these options: the brownies, of course.

On that afternoon, Ali popped the nuggets into the toaster oven, and then looked at the fine print on the packaging. That's when she noticed that the brand was owned by a huge agribusiness corporation notorious for food recalls and unethical practices. Just months before, this company had been implicated in what was at the time the second largest meat recall in history. She looked at her daughter, watching curiously from her high chair just steps away, and sighed. *I have to do better than this*, she thought.

In another way, this book started on a Missouri farm in the 1970s. That's where Beth grew up. In Beth's childhood, eggs came from under the neighbor's ill-tempered chickens (probably explaining Beth's lifelong fear of chickens). Beef came from a great-uncle's pasture. She picked strawberries in June and dragged five-gallon buckets of tomatoes up the hill from the garden in July. August and September brought trips to the local orchard for peaches and apples. Her parents worked long hours, and Beth was helping to cook family dinners by the age of ten. Fast food? It took longer to drive to a fast-food restaurant than to cook a four-course meal.

As an adult, Beth became passionate about — okay, *obsessed with* — food. She signed up for culinary classes, working by day, cooking by night. She began reading nonstop about food politics, production systems, and the environmental and social issues of industrial-scale agriculture. Beth saw the small-scale family agriculture of her youth under constant siege from agribusiness. When her own daughter was born, all these issues became galvanized around her child's health and wellness.

A FEW YEARS LATER, the two of us met online. We met over a kale recipe — the recipe that eventually became the Salt and Vinegar Kale Chips on page 241. Since that fateful encounter with the red-boxed nuggets in her kitchen, Ali had begun cooking more, learning about industrial food production, meeting her nearby growers, working with fresh-from-the-farm ingredients, and constantly striving to find new ways of preparing vegetables that her family — her older daughter was now school-age, and a second daughter was in the mix — would enjoy. She wasn't always successful — in the beginning she had tried at least nine green bean recipes before making something edible from them (hint: When picking beans yourself, choose ones that are thin and tender, not fat and stringy). We recognized right away all that we had in common: a commitment to sustainability, a desire to opt out of our hyperprocessed food system, a hope of passing on a healthier world to our kids, a love of a good glass of wine while cooking, and an exasperation with "airplane games" and other shenanigans to encourage kids to eat dinner.

We also recognized that we had much to learn from one another. From Beth, Ali learned things that made her a better cook: that garlic turns bitter when burnt, the value of a really good roux, and that "sweating" onions does not mean placing them in your sports bra while jogging. At the same time, Ali was able to share what it's like to shift a child's diet midstream from nuggets to nutritious, her perspective on the help that a new cook really needs, and a sneak preview of life with a school-age kid's newfound food independence and on-the-go schedule.

SWEATING
ONIONS

Eventually, we realized that we had the makings of a really good book, one that could help real families eat well without the battle and within the budget.

COOKING REAL FOOD ISN'T DIFFICULT — the truth is, when you're working with quality ingredients, simpler is usually better. But it does take a little know-how. That knowledge goes beyond a book full of recipes. Particularly if you're eating locally, you don't necessarily know in advance what you'll be bringing home. You might go to the farmers' market armed with an asparagus recipe only to find that the asparagus harvest has ended, and you're now staring down a heap of baby spinach. Or you discover a delicious recipe for string beans and find yourself wondering, "Can I make the same thing with zucchini?"

There are other challenges, too. If you're accustomed to meals that can be microwaved in three minutes, you'll need to make some adjustments — a little more prep time, a little more planning ahead. Most of all, you must get used to working with food that doesn't come with its own directions.

That is why we provide more than just recipes in this book. In the following pages, you'll find templates that will allow you to cook delicious meals from whatever you have and whatever's in season. You'll also discover ways to substitute ingredients for each other, and you'll learn building blocks for sauces, soups, and sides that can be used with any vegetable combination. Our philosophy is simple: use what's in season, and get the most from whatever you have.

Along the way, we'll show you how to eliminate food waste, get the most out of the time you spend cooking, plan for the efficient use of leftovers, stretch your food dollar, present food in ways that are appealing to kids, and quit fighting with your children — at last — about food.

Consider this book the directions that don't come with real food.

THIS IS MORE THAN A COOKBOOK, however. We begin, in chapter 1, by examining why children eat what they do — how their food preferences are created through a complex alchemy of genetics, culture, modeling, and exposure. We also look at the state of children's health and offer tips for encouraging kids to try new flavors and textures.

In chapter 2 we explore shopping strategies — the best way to navigate a supermarket with kids, how to find alternative shopping venues like farmers' markets and Community Supported Agriculture organizations (CSAs), and ways to bring home healthful foods without going into debt.

In chapter 3 we present in-depth profiles of dozens of our favorite vegetables, each with nutrition information and tips about selection, storage, and preparation. For each vegetable, we present at least one kid-tested recipe . . . a total of 50 great recipes.

Chapter 4 examines meals — breakfast, lunch, and dinner, with 45 main-course recipes. These include meat dishes, fish dishes, and "meatless mains." Many can be prepared within minutes; others allow you to cook once and reuse ingredients throughout the week. Some convert easily from a side dish to a main course with just the addition of an ingredient or two.

In chapter 5 we take a fresh look at the foods that might otherwise launch battles between you and your kids: snacks and sweets. We present healthful snacks, terrific whole-food desserts, and tips for eating well between meals.

Throughout these chapters, we present research, advice from experts, and an array of innovative ideas about feeding children well. Feeding a family doesn't have to be a mystery; there are literally hundreds of experts who study what kids need and which strategies work best. We've highlighted the studies that we found most helpful to arm you with practical information.

Finally, in the epilogue, we point you toward resources where you can learn more and get more involved with healthy food systems at the community, state, and national level.

FOR THE PURPOSE OF THIS BOOK, we define "healthful" broadly. We don't count calories, we don't fear fat, and we're not spooked by carbohydrates. Our recipes are based on whole foods — foods that contain just a single ingredient rather than a dubious cocktail of mass-produced items like preservatives and additives. Whole foods offer a diverse range of nutrients and micronutrients. Most recipes, including the snacks and sweets, have fresh produce at their base. Because we try to eat seasonally, these fruits and vegetables tend to be ones that you can find at farmers' markets, often for less money than you'd spend at the grocery store. Many of them can easily be grown in a backyard garden or in rooftop pots. If you're interested in eating locally, we even provide a seasonal index of recipes (see page 288).

This approach is healthy not just from a family perspective but also from an environmental and social perspective. Working with real food — whole ingredients, grown locally where possible, and heavy on the vegetables — brings an array of external benefits: robust local economies, healthier soil, lower carbon emissions, and reduced agricultural runoff. As Barbara Kingsolver wisely wrote in her book *Animal, Vegetable, Miracle*, "Food is the rare moral arena in which the ethical choice is generally the one more likely to make you groan with pleasure. Why resist that?"

THIS IS A FAMILY GUIDE TO REAL FOOD, but we didn't dumb down any recipes. After all, we don't want to eat 100 different variations of macaroni and cheese; we figure you don't either. This is food you'll be glad to eat — and to share with others. And yet every recipe in this book has been a hit with at least one child, and most recipes have been happily gobbled by a number of children.

Make no mistake: our children are not alien beings who reject French fries for foie gras. Our offspring are regular kids who will dive happily into a ketchup-saturated platter of chicken strips when given the opportunity. But they've learned the same lessons that we have: that even children enjoy real food when it's prepared well.

We also know that every child is different, with different tastes. That's why we've presented a range of options, from curries to coleslaw, from soups to scallopine, and from ratatouille to risotto. Many of the recipes include a hint of sweetness; studies show that children are more likely to try new foods if they are presented with a sweet edge. Others, though, are good choices for kids who prefer foods to be sweet *or* savory, not both. We present a couple of options for stealth nutrition — for example, the incredible beet brownies on page 259 — but mostly we present fruits and vegetables front and center, in colorful ways that appeal to young taste buds.

We didn't give our recipes cute names, although we encourage you to do so if you think it will help . . . and if your children are young, it just might. Research shows that when young children are presented with "X-ray vision carrots," they eat twice as many as when they're presented with regular ol' carrots, even if the carrots themselves are the same. We've been known to turn an Asian slaw into "happy confetti salad" or a tomato-bread soup into "pizza soup." Whatever works.

WE'RE REAL MOMS, both working in other fields, who simply do our best to put good food on the table, meal after meal. Most of the recipes were created by Beth, the lifelong cook, so you know they're good. They have all been tested and approved by Ali, the more recent kitchen convert, so you know they're simple and easy to follow. We made them in our real kitchens, in the middle of real life — as phones rang and dogs barked and small children clung to our legs. We wrote this book between work deadlines, soccer games, dance classes, trips to the library, fevers and ear infections, swimming lessons, PTA meetings, birthday parties, heaps of laundry, far too many bills, piano lessons, car inspections, and all the other tiny details that fill up real lives, sometimes to exhaustion.

If we can do it, you can, too.

Even if you adopt only some of the strategies recommended in this book, you'll probably notice some important things happening. You might stop thinking about food as the enemy or as a constant source of conflict in your family. You might begin to reject what we call the "mega meal–diet pill dance" in favor of something more positive and health-affirming. You might start to enjoy food again, to sit down as a family a little more often. One day, you might look around and notice vegetable-packed soup bubbling away on your stove top, filling your kitchen with mouthwatering aromas. Maybe you and the kids will even have picked some of the ingredients yourselves. In that moment, you might realize that this soup — and the life changes that came with it — are just so much more satisfying, so much more life-enriching, than peeling back the plastic film on a microwaveable frozen dinner ever could be.

From a box of frozen chicken nuggets to a tastier, healthier way of life: If you ask us, it's a journey worth taking.

Change your own eating habits for the better and your kids' habits will likely change, too.

An increase of one fruit or vegetable serving per day in a parent is associated with an increase of half a fruit or vegetable serving per day in his or her child.

Source: D. Haire-Joshu, M. B. Elliott, N. M. Caito, et al.
"High 5 for Kids: The impact of a home visiting program on fruit and vegetable intake of parents and their preschool children."
Preventive Medicine 47(1):77–82.

CHAPTER ONE
GETTING STARTED

Bringing a family together with food

what did children eat before boxes of macaroni & cheese came along?

Take a look at any children's menu at virtually any restaurant and you might get the idea that kids' stomachs are gastronomically programmed to digest only a small handful of items: processed meats, pasta, fried potatoes, and melted cheese. Yet considering the human species was kicking around some 200,000 years before the invention of dehydrated cheese powder, it's a reasonable assumption that somewhere along the line, children were willing to eat *something* else. If you've picked up this book, chances are good that you're interested in that something else, and that you'd like to give your family something other than deep-fried potatoes and processed grains.

Here's the good news: It's possible. It is possible to feed your family well, to encourage your kids to enjoy kale, or tomatoes, or squash, or beans, and to instill in them lifelong healthy habits. It is possible to teach them that chickens don't have fingers and that the very best foods don't come emblazoned with cartoon characters. It is possible to serve food that brings your family together, helps children thrive, and gives your kids the roots they need to someday have healthy families of their own.

It's even possible to do all this without a fight.

But if you're reading this, you probably know something else: eating well in a fast-food world can be a struggle. The struggle follows us everywhere we go. Take the kids to the community center for swimming lessons or gymnastics classes and there's a good chance that on the way in you'll pass vending machines filled with junk food and soda. Lollipops are passed to children through car windows at the gas station and through teller windows at the bank. Candy is offered as a reward for good behavior at school. A simple trip to the grocery store can be like a minefield, with 17,000 new processed foods introduced yearly, many of which are positioned right at children's eye level, with their favorite TV characters on the packaging.

Most parents agree that in moderation these treats are fine. Yet these same parents often feel besieged by the very foods that they don't mind in moderation. And therein lies the problem: not with any one food item, but with the accumulation of them, all of those junk food encounters, one on top of another, moment after moment, day after day after day. Add to these encounters the food on children's menus at restaurants (94 percent of which is extremely high in calories and devoid of essential vitamins and minerals), unhealthy cafeteria lunches, well-meaning relatives, an endless stream of birthday parties, and those evenings when you need to throw dinner on the table fast. Soon, you might find that your child's diet is more high-fructose corn syrup than high nutrition. Somewhere in there, moderation skipped town.

At what moment, exactly, does moderation become excess? Where does a harried parent draw the line in the sand? When do "some" treats become too many? What *should* kids be eating, anyway?

When you cut through all the noise — all the marketing messages, the packaging, the whining, the crying, and the cajoling — the answer to the last question is pretty simple. It's the same advice you'll hear from any experts worth their salt, the same advice you've heard since you were a child. Children need lots of fruits and vegetables. They need whole grains, healthy proteins, and a certain amount of healthy fats. They need vitamins and minerals and micronutrients. The best place to get these things, of course — in fact, the only place to get many of them — is through good food.

food preferences

So what makes children prefer one food over another? How are children's food preferences formed, anyway?

We wish we could tell you that there was a simple formula, that if you just do *these things*, then your child will embrace the right foods, all of them, forever. Yet food preferences are like every other aspect of your child: they don't lend themselves easily to any kind of formula. Like one child's penchant for wearing a cowboy hat with a ballerina tutu, or another's inexplicable need to wear T-shirts and shorts in February, food preferences result from a strange and sometimes mysterious interplay of many factors.

To be sure, genetics plays some role. Most children are born with a few basic taste preferences: an aversion to bitterness, which translates into a low tolerance for vegetables like broccoli, and an affinity for sweet and fatty foods. Children can also inherit a tendency to avoid new foods, known as neophobia (a.k.a. "vegephobia" by some).

Then there's plain old personal taste. In food, as in anything else — clothing, art, books, hobbies, hairstyles — people are individuals, predisposed to enjoy some things more than others. Parents of multiple children often marvel at how siblings can have wholly different experiences of the exact same foods. Surely you've seen this: Same parents, same home environment, yet one child loves a particular food — say, strawberries — while her sibling scowls and clamps her lips at the mere sight. Some preferences you just can't explain at all. Your kid licks the trash can at the grocery store but then refuses the carrots you just bought in the produce section. It's no wonder we parents are confused.

There's no question: Innate tendencies toward different tastes, textures, and flavors play an important role in shaping food preferences. Still, genetic factors are hardly the only factors at work. Ever heard of a child in India who refuses curries? Or an Inuit child who can't stand fish? Not likely. That's because in addition to innate food preferences, children's tastes are influenced by external factors: exposure, culture, and modeling.

Exposure

CHILDREN ENJOY THINGS that are familiar. That's why the single most valuable way to encourage a child to eat well is through repeated exposure to good food. When we say "repeated," we mean it. Research shows that it can take as many as *15 tries* before a child accepts a new food. Sure, it sounds like a hassle, but consider how many times you must repeat everything else with your kids. Yep, that much.

Exposure doesn't have to mean a fight. In fact, research shows that forcing children to eat a given food has the opposite effect: too much cajoling, and children end up liking the food *less* than they did before. Exposure means simply that: learning several different ways of making a food taste good, then offering that food repeatedly, simply, and without a fight.

The key, of course, is *making the food taste good*. There is a world of difference between waterlogged, army-fatigue green beans out of a can and a pan of freshly roasted green beans, drizzled with a touch of balsamic vinegar or fresh lemon juice. Compare a mealy pale tomato, in the dead of winter, with a garden-fresh, juicy summer variety and you can begin to understand why so many people swear they don't care for tomatoes: because they've never had one that tastes good.

Ideally, you can start exposing your children to new foods and flavors in early childhood. These are foundation years for food preferences and food-related behaviors. By age two, kids already have formed strong preferences and resist new foods. But if your kids are

13

abnormal norms

No, you're not crazy. That's the good news.

If you think it's harder than ever to raise a kid with a healthy attitude toward food and wellness, you are definitely not crazy. After all, if your child's friends and classmates eat like most kids in the United States, they are getting too much of the wrong stuff and too little of the right stuff.

Chances are good that your child's peers are eating too many fats, too many of the wrong kinds of fats, and too many added sugars. In fact, by the time they're teens, they will probably be consuming twice the recommended amount of sugar — much of it through sweetened beverages. Then there's sodium. And empty carbohydrates. And calories.

Even while they're getting too many calories, your child's peers are not getting enough of the foods that they really need. If they are between six and eleven years old, a whopping 80 percent of them don't meet the daily requirements for vegetable intake, and nearly 75 percent don't get enough

fruit. They're probably not drinking enough milk, and they are surely not getting enough calcium.

It's probably no surprise, then, that your child's peers are fighting some pretty serious diseases. About 16 percent of children are now obese, with another 15 percent of children at risk for obesity; in total, the childhood obesity rate has more than tripled in the past four decades. If they're typical, the girls in your child's classroom now have a 40 percent lifetime risk of being diagnosed with type 2 diabetes; the boys' risk is only slightly lower, at 30 percent. Should they develop that disease, they will be at increased risk for blindness, coronary artery disease, stroke, and kidney failure. Even when they look healthy on the outside, there's a good chance that blood tests reveal early signs of heart disease.

So, no, you're not crazy. It's definitely hard to raise a healthy child in a world where these things are the norm. To give up, though — to shrug and say that the norms are probably good enough — now, *that* would be nuts.

past the early childhood years, don't worry: familiarity is still the name of the game.

So, take a deep breath, find some recipes you enjoy, and start serving up the good stuff.

Cultural Influences

PERHAPS YOU LIVE in one of those rarefied bubbles where children never see refined sugars, where a Whopper ain't nothing but a really good story, and where your children wouldn't recognize Ronald McDonald if he bit them on the leg.

Most of us don't live there. Instead, we are raising children in a world where it's simply expected that kids have their "own" foods, wholly distinct from the world of adult eaters. None of these items can be prepared at home, at least not without the aid of specially marked frozen dinners and boxes and cans with cartoon characters.

And, uh, sometimes these foods are *neon blue.*

Such is our food culture, the messages that society gives us about what foods are normal and acceptable. Here in twenty-first-century America, the message that kids should eat only "kid food" is reinforced in grocery store displays, in television advertisements, in the homes of friends and family members, in school cafeterias, at parties, and every time a child is handed a separate menu at a restaurant.

It wouldn't be so troubling, of course, if the culture of kid food wasn't taking such a toll on children's health. But the vast majority of children's foods are filled with things that are bad for them: trans fats, added sweeteners, and/or chemical additives. Vegetables, the very things kids need to be eating in abundance, are an afterthought, at best.

The culture of kid food is pervasive enough that parents who present their children with whole foods, real food, are often considered "fringe." Tell the world your kid eats kale, and you'll be dismissed as a hippie, or overprotective, or an elitist, or merely smug.

So right about now, you might be asking the question that's been asked by millions of parents (including us): How do I live in the real world and still serve my kid real food? How, precisely, can we swim against the ever-rising tide of Pop-Tarts and froot snacks and 40-ounce Slurpees?

The key is shaping your environment so that your children are simply less exposed to junk foods and the characters that pimp them — by turning off the television, cooking at home more often, and getting food directly from farmers when possible. We've also found it helpful to keep kids active so that they work up a real appetite; good food invariably tastes better to hungry children. Having fun with food helps, too — allowing kids to see food as an adventure.

There's also another, extremely important step: showing them day in, day out, what a healthy eater looks like.

Modeling

SURE, THERE ARE MANY INFLUENCES on your child's diet. But the most important influence is you. The strongest predictor of fruit and vegetable consumption by children ages two to six is the amount of these foods that their parents eat. The influence remains even as children get older: teens whose parents eat five servings of fruits and vegetables daily are significantly more likely to do the same than kids whose parents eat less produce. On the other hand, teens whose parents drink soda every day are 40 percent more likely to drink soda than teens whose parents don't drink it.

By modeling, you teach your kids what real food is, that new foods can be fun, that it's important to take care of your body, and that good foods are enjoyable.

Modeling shouldn't be a chore, though. Good food *tastes good*. There are endless ways to prepare food, endless ways to enjoy the bounty. Good food offers flavor, texture, and variety. When you model good eating, you have the potential to enjoy two of life's great pleasures: eating good food and sharing this food with loved ones.

Sure, you'll hit stumbling blocks. Take comfort in this: Research shows that parents and their children share 76 to 87 percent of food likes. Yet only 19 percent of shared likes occur among adolescent friendships. Most of these preferences are for snacks.

FACT: The National Health and Nutrition Examination Survey (NHANES-III) showed that the diets of 78 percent of school-age children showed a need for improvement. Only 6 percent of children had a "good diet," while 16 percent had a "poor diet." These rates were similar across all income levels.

Source: U.S. Department of Agriculture and *Food Marketing to Children and Youth: Threat or Opportunity?* Institute of Medicine report (December 2005).

"The basic principles of good diets are so simple that I can summarize them in just ten words: eat less, move more, eat lots of fruits and vegetables. For additional clarification, a five-word modifier helps: go easy on junk foods."

Marion Nestle, *What to Eat*, North Point Press, 2007.

"Having a child who's a picky eater is not and never will be your problem. If it's a problem at all, it's the child's to deal with, when he or she decides she's ready. Your job is putting the food down on the table. The child's job is eating it."

Ann Hodgman, *One Bite Won't Kill You: More Than 200 Recipes to Tempt Even the Pickiest Kids on Earth and the Rest of the Family Too*, Houghton Mifflin Harcourt, 1999

"How we handle picky eating is so simple that I call it the Second Rule of Baby Food. . . . The rule is, when I put the food down in front of [my daughter] my job is done. I don't also hold myself responsible for making sure it gets into her mouth — no cajoling, no airplane game. I have been known to say things like, 'Iris, this kale is awesome,' but I say that to everyone."

Matthew Amster-Burton, *Hungry Monkey: A Food-Loving Father's Quest to Raise an Adventurous Eater*, Houghton Mifflin Co., 2009.

DID YOU KNOW? A bagel 20 years ago was 3 inches in diameter and had 140 calories. Today, the typical bagel weighs in at 350 calories — two and a half times more than it used to have.

17

stop fighting

One of the wisest pieces of parenting advice we ever heard was this: Don't pick a fight with your child. When it comes to food, we take this to heart.

There will be many issues over which you must battle with children, like safety and schoolwork. But food? Food can be something that sustains a family and brings its members together. If the family meal has become a family feud, then perhaps it's time to shift gears and try a new approach.

Mind you, we know exactly how challenging it is to feed kids well in a world where you can't take a step without bumping into a rack of Cheetos or a box of Krispy Kremes. We simply don't think fighting helps very much.

It sure can backfire. Multiple studies show that when certain foods are restricted, children desire more of those foods (and eat more of them when given the chance) than their peers who were not restricted from eating those foods. The opposite is true, too; when children are cajoled into eating certain foods, they like those foods *less* than children who weren't pressured.

Seen in one light, this body of research can leave a well-intentioned parent immensely frustrated. *You're damned if you do, damned if you don't.* We suspect, though, that there's a more hopeful way to see the results: over the long haul.

The ultimate goal here, after all, is to raise a healthy child, one who will grow into a healthy adult. While we wish that this goal could

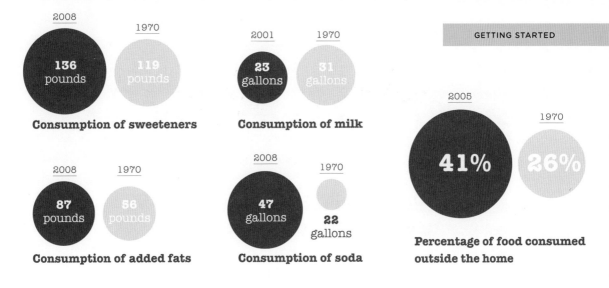

2008 **1970**
136 **119**
pounds pounds

Consumption of sweeteners

2001 **1970**
23 **31**
gallons gallons

Consumption of milk

2005
41%

1970
26%

2008 **1970**
87 **56**
pounds pounds

Consumption of added fats

2008 **1970**
47
gallons
22
gallons

Consumption of soda

**Percentage of food consumed
outside the home**

be neatly achieved in a given meal, or a single snack, or a day, or even a year, it can't. It is a long-term goal if ever there was one. In the end, the point isn't *this* radish, or *that* green bean, or even that cookie or bag of chips. It's about the big picture, of kids' diets over time.

Your children don't have to enjoy every vegetable, they don't have to eat everything with a smile, and they don't have to detest sugary snacks. Your purpose, as their parent, isn't to make them into models of eating perfection, and it's not to ensure that no corn chip ever passes their lips. It's to help them understand, over the long haul, that good food can taste good, that it will nourish a healthy body, and that it will make their lives — and their world — better.

Don't get us wrong. By suggesting that you don't pick a fight, we aren't saying that you need to cave in to your child's every desire. It means only what's implied: not fighting. Your mission, should you choose to accept it, is to offer up good food. Find some recipes that you all enjoy, and make those. Try some new ones. If your kids don't like a given recipe, find another. Or make it again and see if they like it better the second time, or the third. (They often do.) Take the kids berry picking once in a while, or bring them to a farm stand or farmers' market. Invite them into the process: Plant some herbs together. Cook a meal with them. Bake from scratch. Tell them why you make the choices you make. Set boundaries, be consistent, keep serving the good stuff, and keep the faith.

But whatever you do, don't make it into a fight. If you feel the urge to control something, try portions instead.

Overall, Americans are consuming more sweeteners, added fats, and oils each year. Milk consumption has decreased and soda consumption has increased. Americans are also eating 15 percent more meals outside home — over 40 percent of their meals.

Source: USDA Economic Research Service.

19

portion distortion

Portions are bigger than they used to be. You name the food, the average portion size has increased dramatically in a generation.

A typical serving of pasta with meatballs now weighs in at more than 1,000 calories — more than twice as much as a few decades ago. A typical serving of fries has tripled in size and calories during that time. From soda to spaghetti, from muffins to milk shakes, our portions have increased significantly. But portion distortion hasn't just happened at restaurants; it's also occurred in our own kitchens. Somehow, we've forgotten what an actual portion looks like.

The typical plate used to be a mere 10 inches in diameter. Today, in many homes, plates are 12 inches. In case you've forgotten your high-school geometry, that's a whopping *44 percent more area* to fill with food — a sure sign that we're dishing up more food than ever before.

"So what?" you might say. "After all, just because portions are bigger doesn't mean we have to eat more." While that's technically true, you should be forewarned that if your family doesn't eat more as a result of bigger portion sizes, you're pretty much the only humans for whom that's true. Study after study confirms that when we're served more, we eat more. It's true for adults, and it's true for kids. It's true for men and women alike. It's true for even the healthiest of individuals. We eat what we're served, or a large percentage of it anyway.

According to a study published in the *American Journal of Clinical Nutrition*, by age five, serving size makes a critical difference to

a growing plate...

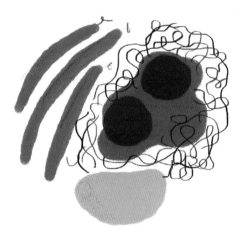

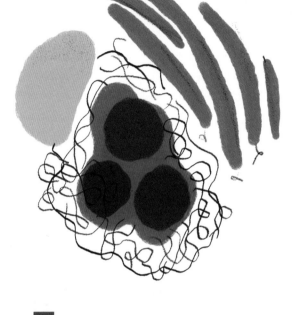

Spaghetti and meatballs: 12 ounces
1 slice garlic bread: 4 ounces
Green beans: 1 cup

10" plate:
564 calories

Spaghetti and meatballs: 16.6 ounces
1 slice garlic bread: 5.6 ounces
Green beans: 1.4 cups

12" plate:
790 calories

consumption. The researchers gave different serving sizes of macaroni and cheese to children aged three and aged five. The three-year-olds ate the same amount regardless of how much they were given. The five-year-olds ate 26 percent more when given the larger portion.

Remember those 12-inch plates? Why not replace them in your own home with the 10-inch variety? Unless, that is, you're serving a heaping amount of vegetables.

exercise, of course...

Whenever we talk about children and food, we always stumble across someone who rolls his or her eyes and declares that food isn't the problem. The argument always goes something like this: "When we were kids, we ate candy/guzzled soda/bathed in milk shakes. So food's not the problem. The problem is that kids today aren't getting enough exercise."

To which we say this: "Yeah, that too."

We agree. Children are moving less today than they ever have before, and this is an enormous problem. Even with the most healthful diet, kids cannot achieve optimal health if they're sitting in front of a television or computer screen every afternoon, or if their eyes never stray from video games or the computer screen.

Exercise is critical. Not only does exercise help kids use the calories they've taken in, but the more children exercise, the better they are able to absorb the nutrients in their foods. Not to mention that getting outside allows them to receive vitamin D right from the sun's rays, helping them absorb the calcium they need for strong bones, a healthy heart, and transportation of nutrients across the cell membranes.

We'll say it again. Exercise: yes, yes, yes.

But just because exercise is critical, that doesn't make the quality of food *less* important. The fact is, today's lack of exercise comes precisely at a time when children are eating more than ever before and when there are more of the wrong kinds of foods available than ever before. In a single generation, it seems, we've replaced milk with soda and home-cooked meals with fast food, and we've increased the portion size of absolutely everything, from cartons of French fries to bagels with cream cheese. None of these things help our kids get off the sofa, run fast, enjoy backyard baseball games, or even climb a tree. The words *vicious cycle* come to mind.

Exercise? Yes, of course. And good food? Yes, that too.

the nutritional gatekeeper:
72 percent ain't bad

So, what happens when your friends or family members don't share your food values?

What can you do when loved ones feed your children soda, sugary cereal, or candy in excess? What about play dates, or trips to a favorite aunt's house?

As with everything, *it depends*. Sometimes you can speak with these loved ones and express your concerns. Grandparents, for example, often don't have a clear sense of how dramatically the food landscape has changed since the days when they were raising children. Simply talking with them and explaining your struggle can sometimes be enough to rally their support for a more healthful lifestyle.

Sometimes, though, these individuals look at you like you have three heads. *"Oh,"* you can feel them thinking, *"so you're one of those parents."* When that happens — when you feel like your food concerns might create a wedge between you and other people who love your children — try to relax. It's true that you can't control everything your child eats in all of those different settings. But research shows clearly that it's your influence that matters most.

Food experts have a term for the person who does most of the shopping and meal preparation in the home: the nutritional gatekeeper. By buying and preparing the household food, the nutritional gatekeeper determines what's for breakfast, lunch, dinner, and snacks, day after

23

day after day. According to Brian Wansink, a Cornell University researcher in the psychology of eating, surveys of nutrition experts and parents alike suggest that the nutritional gatekeeper — that's you — is responsible for about 72 percent of a family's diet. If you're a good cook, that percentage is probably even higher.

No, 72 percent is not everything. But it's not bad, either, especially when you consider that not *all* of the remaining 28 percent is likely to be junk food. So take heart, relax, and keep doing what you're doing. As the nutritional gatekeeper, you're the most important influence.

it's not always about food

We parents have all heard it: the dreaded phrase "I do it!"

When children are young, this phrase can be the backdrop to a table-side power struggle that is sometimes more about control than food. Whether it's the weeklong strike against anything but macaroni and cheese, the sudden refusal of a favorite fruit, or a newfound dislike of all things green, new food behaviors might simply be your child's way of exerting control.

As children get older, their desire for control exerts itself in other ways. "I do it!" gives way to eye rolling or a disdainful, "I don't *like* this," before they even taste what you've prepared. Knowing the real source of the conflict — control — can help with your frustration level.

Don't play the control game

- Have a couple of options, and allow your child to choose between them.

- Let children choose items from the produce section or the farmers' market and help decide how that food will be prepared.

- Start a garden with your kids; children are more likely to enjoy a new item if they helped grow it.

- Limit foods available at home to healthy options.

- Have your child help prepare a meal with age-appropriate tasks.

25

▪ Prepare foods in a way that makes them taste good, but don't make a big deal out of it if your efforts are rebuffed. Try different preparations of the same foods, or try the same recipe on a different day.

▪ For young kids, think about nutrition over the course of a week rather than during a given meal or even an entire day. Many pediatricians note that young children fill their nutritional requirements over a weeklong period.

▪ Don't bargain for bites. Pressuring kids to eat or negotiating for a few more bites makes them *less* likely to choose healthy foods.

▪ If children occasionally choose to skip a meal, let them. As long as they're healthy and growing, skipping a meal is usually okay.

▪ Keep in mind that this, too, shall pass. Most kids go through phases during which they refuse certain foods.

And then there's *your* health. It seems like having kids would make adults healthier. After all, once kids come along, there's that much more reason to turn the house into a No-Fry zone. But many parents notice that something different happens. You get tired. There's so much laundry. It's harder than ever to make ends meet. Some days, food that's fast and mindless and inexpensive is about all you can handle. Meanwhile, kids are hungry. They're hungry all the time, to a bewildering degree. And when they eat, you eat. Just a little. Maybe just finish off their plates so that nothing gets wasted.

Sound familiar? If so, you're not alone. It turns out parents eat less healthfully than other adults. According to a 2007 report published in the online *Journal of the American Board of Family Medicine*, adults with kids under the age of 17 eat the equivalent of a full pepperoni pizza's worth of added saturated fat each week compared to those without kids.

So there's another reason to get your kids eating healthfully: for your sake. Even if you're not worried about their health — *They're young! They exercise! They have the metabolism of a hummingbird!* — you deserve better, too.

CHAPTER TWO

SHOPPING STRATEGIES

stocking up without freaking down

it sounds like a simple enough plan...

You'll stop by the grocery store and pick up a few items, like a gallon of milk, a roll of paper towels, maybe some toothpaste or a quart of yogurt. You plan to dash in, grab things you need, use the express checkout, and then make a fast exit.

Somehow it all falls apart. Perhaps your child spies a box of cereal with her favorite cartoon character on the front. Or he notices the snack bars that his friend eats daily at school, and he begins to beg. You see some new products that pique your curiosity — packages that blare "Omega-3s!" or "Made with Real Fruit!" You round the corner and come face-to-face with a two-for-one special on crackers. These go in the cart. Passing the macaroni and cheese, you stock up on a couple of boxes. You know you should stop lingering, but . . . oh look, a favorite ice cream brand is on sale for almost half its regular price. By this point your child is wailing with hunger, so you hand her a quick snack from the bakery section — anything to quiet her down. But now it's later than you expected, and you realize you won't have time to make dinner; an eight-piece fried chicken special from the deli counter seems like a pretty good deal.

By the time you complete your shopping, your cart is filled to the brim with items you hadn't planned to buy, you're dragging an exhausted, chocolate-smeared child after you, and your plans for a healthful dinner have been replaced by a box of deep-fried chicken wings.

You also forgot the milk.

Sound familiar? It sure does to us. The problem here is not that you're an inefficient shopper; it's simply that someone *else* gave far more thought to your trip to the grocery store than you did. What for you is merely a necessary stop for groceries is to others the culmination of decades of research and billions of dollars' worth of marketing efforts. Every one of those dollars and years was spent with one simple goal: to make sure you fill your cart with things you hadn't planned on buying. This chapter presents the "counter intelligence" you need to resist the urge to splurge.

DID YOU KNOW? According to a recent study undertaken at the UCLA School of Public Health, 80 cents of each American food dollar pays not for the food itself but for processing, distribution, labor, packaging, marketing, and transportation. In 2008 U.S. consumers spent $1,165,251,000,000 for food, so that 80 cents really adds up. Minimally processed foods such as fresh fruits and vegetables provide lower profits, so they're not heavily marketed or branded. With their high nutrition, limited marketing budget, and superior taste and quality, they just might be the best-kept secret in the grocery store.

FACT: An investigation into 1,474 possible kids' menu choices at 13 top chain restaurants revealed that 93 percent were too high in calories, 45 percent were too high in saturated and trans fats, and 86 percent were too high in sodium.

Source: "Kids' Meals: Obesity on the Menu," August, 2008, Center for Science in the Public Interest, by Margo G. Wooten, D.Sc., Ameena Batada, Dr.P.H., and Elizabeth Marchlewicz, CSPI, and in cooperation with the California Center for Public Health Advocacy.

aisle by aisle: navigating the supermarket

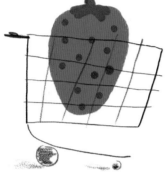

First, understand that food marketers have a goal that is the opposite of your own.

While you hope to get in and out of the supermarket quickly, with healthful food that didn't cost very much, food marketers are trying to get you to stay as long as possible and to buy as much as possible, without much regard to whether the items are healthful or not. If you ever hope to get in and out of the supermarket without ruining all hopes for good health, you should understand some of the strategies at work as you shop.

Some of the tactics are sensory, like the bakery-fresh smell that is piped into the store to attract your attention to the doughnuts, or the slow music that encourages shoppers to unconsciously linger in the aisles. Some tactics are about exposure, which is why food companies often pay hefty "slotting fees" for prime real estate, like the towering displays at the end of each aisle and eye-level space on the shelves. Then there is the layout of the store itself, of course — the way staples like milk and eggs are placed in the far rear corner of the store, so that you pass as many products as possible on your way to them, invariably putting some into your cart.

But the marketing strategies also operate at a much deeper level. Long before you stepped into the store, food companies hired

supermarket battle plan

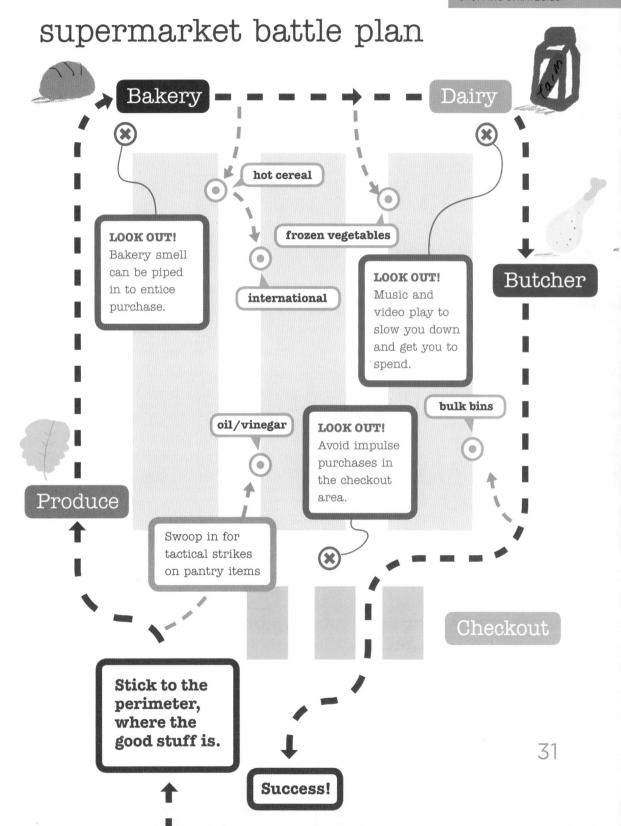

Bakery

Dairy

hot cereal

LOOK OUT!
Bakery smell can be piped in to entice purchase.

frozen vegetables

international

LOOK OUT!
Music and video play to slow you down and get you to spend.

Butcher

bulk bins

oil/vinegar

LOOK OUT!
Avoid impulse purchases in the checkout area.

Produce

Swoop in for tactical strikes on pantry items

Checkout

Stick to the perimeter, where the good stuff is.

31

Success!

sociologists, anthropologists, psychologists, and child development specialists with the sole purpose of identifying the triggers that make you and your children unconsciously reach for certain foods. These triggers involve naming, packaging, image licensing, advertising, and stealth marketing. They are even intended to exploit weaknesses in the parent-child relationship (known within the industry as "pester power").

"Oh, come on," you might think, offering up a healthy dose of skepticism. "People are just not that gullible. These strategies can't possibly work." Amazingly, study upon study confirms that they do. That's why 70 percent of shoppers bring lists into supermarkets, but a mere 10 percent stick to them. For every item on the list, shoppers pick up an average of *two* items they hadn't planned to buy.

The research clearly indicates that just about everyone — including the "experts" who spend their lives studying these very food marketing strategies — are influenced by food marketing. What's more remarkable is that nobody ever thinks it works.

Speaking personally, this is one of the reasons we prefer to visit farmers' markets instead of supermarkets whenever possible. It's a relief, we've found, not to have to steel ourselves to resist an environment that encourages us to buy, buy, buy. It's nice not to have to fight like David against a billion-dollar marketing Goliath.

However, it's hardly practical to give up supermarkets altogether. After all, even if you are fortunate enough to be able to buy most of your staples directly from the farmer year-round, chances are you'll need to stop by a supermarket for laundry detergent or light bulbs, at least once in a while.

Strategies for shopping healthfully and frugally

Shop the pantry at home first. Planning meals around the ingredients you have on hand helps keep the list short, and it also keeps your grocery bill lower than your mortgage payment.

look at home

make a list

have a snack

stick to the perimeter

- **Plan ahead, then stick to your list.** Plan your meals in advance. If you begin planning meals while you're in the grocery store, you'll probably get overwhelmed. Knowing what you need before you enter the store is critical. But sticking to a list is even more important. It can also help to set a budget before you go, and then to keep a running tally on a calculator as you add items to your cart.

- **Don't go hungry.** If you enter the supermarket on an empty stomach, you'll make more impulse purchases.

- **Never bring children who are hungry or tired.** Trust us on this one: It is always a mistake. Fill them up with good food before you arrive. When in doubt, stop by the deli area for some sliced cheese that you can feed to your child as you go.

- **Stick to the outer aisles.** The healthiest items in the store are almost always on the periphery — the produce, dairy, fish, and frozen sections. With few exceptions — dried beans and rice, olive oil, and seasonings among them — the center aisles are filled with highly processed, nutrition-poor alternatives.

- **Beware of anything making health claims.** A health claim emblazoned on a box is, ironically, usually the telltale sign of something you probably *don't* want to eat. Fresh broccoli doesn't brag about its high iron and fiber content, and you'll never find apples boasting about their calcium levels.

- **Bulk up.** If you're lucky enough to shop at a store with a bulk aisle, you'll find delicious, healthful whole-food options, *without* the extra packaging, at a great price. From quinoa — an amino acid–rich seed that can be cooked like rice — to whole-grain flours, dried beans, and nuts, most bulk products are good for your health, your wallet, and the planet. (See page 40 for more information.)

- **Explore the produce aisle.** If there's one place to get adventurous or to make impulsive purchases, it's the produce aisle. This section is a smorgasbord of health-boosting phytochemicals, vitamins, minerals, fiber, and great tastes. If your kids are young, bring along a copy of Louise Ehlert's *Eating the Alphabet* and let the kids choose a new

be adventurous with produce!

try the bulk aisle

33

fruit or vegetable to try. Or play a game of I-spy to help a child learn the difference between an eggplant and a kiwifruit.

Know what you're up against. While you're shopping, remember that every step you take and every thing you see, hear, and smell has been carefully choreographed by some of the world's savviest minds to make you buy more, and to do it unconsciously. Your best chance, then, is to be conscious about what you purchase. Before an item goes in your cart, ask yourself, "Do I really need this today?" If the answer is no, put it back on the shelf.

Pantry Goods and Staples

ONE PROBLEM WITH TRYING NEW RECIPES is that they sometimes require buying ingredients you use only once. Unused leftover ingredients are a waste of money and food. For this reason, most of the recipes in this book draw from a basic set of pantry goods, with only a few extra items for some recipes. Using staples you already have on hand reduces waste and prevents you from trying to plan your week's meals while standing in the middle of the grocery store. You can also plan ahead and buy pantry items when they are on sale, because you know you will use what you are buying.

The Downside of 30 Percent More

ALMOST ANYONE OFFERING ADVICE about how to save money on groceries will suggest that you buy greater quantities in order to get a better unit price. Indeed, entire companies thrive on this business — chains, like Costco, allow you to stock up on the items you use the most. Seems like a great deal all around, except for one fact: you could eat away at the money you save. Literally.

Cornell University researcher Brian Wansink has tested how package and portion size affect consumption. His research is unequivocal: the more there is, the more people consume.

a well-stocked pantry

Oils
Olive oil
Canola oil
Butter

Vinegars
Balsamic
Cider
Red wine
White wine or white
    balsamic

Spices and extracts
Allspice
Ancho chile powder
    (milder for kids than
    regular chili powder)
Bay leaf
Black pepper (whole,
    to be ground fresh)
Cayenne pepper
Cinnamon (ground
    and stick)
Cloves
Coriander
Crushed red pepper
    flakes
Cumin
Curry blend
Fennel seed
Garam masala blend
Ground ginger

Herbes de Provence
    blend
Nutmeg/mace
Orange extract
Paprika
Turmeric
Vanilla extract

**Herbs, fresh and
dried***
Basil
Chives
Cilantro
Mint
Parsley
Rosemary
Sage
Thyme

Aromatics
Garlic
Onions
Shallots

Nuts
Almonds
Pecans
Pine nuts
Walnuts

Flour
White
Whole wheat

Salt (kosher)

Baking powder

Baking soda

Cocoa powder

Soy sauce

Dijon mustard

Dairy
Feta cheese
Goat cheese
Half-and-half
Milk
Parmesan cheese
Plain yogurt

Sweeteners
Brown sugar (light
    and dark)
Granulated sugar
    (organic if possible)
Honey
Maple syrup
    (grade B)

Bouillon
Low-salt chicken
    broth
Low-salt vegetable
    broth

Pasta
Spaghetti
Whole-grain penne
    or other small
    macaroni

Dried fruit
Blueberries
Cranberries
Raisins

Bread crumbs
Panko
Whole-grain

Grains
Basmati rice
Brown rice
Couscous
Quinoa
Steel-cut oats

Dried legumes
Beans (black, pinto,
    white, and so on)
Lentils
Split peas

Canned goods
Beans (black, cannel-
    lini, garbanzos,
    kidneys, and so on)
Coconut milk
Diced tomatoes
Tomato paste

* With herbs, fresh is always best. Most are easy to grow yourself,
  indoors year-round or outdoors during the warm months. To substitute
  dried herbs for fresh in a recipe, use half the amount of the fresh herb.

35.

Wansink has tested this across an array of products, from spaghetti dinners to vegetable oil. For almost all breakfast, lunch, and dinner foods, people who are given food in bigger packages eat 20 to 25 percent more than those who are given the same food in smaller packages.

It is even worse for snack foods. Wansink tested how many M&M's people ate from either a half-pound or a full-pound bag while watching a movie. Those who had the full-pound bag ate almost twice as much as those with the half-pound bag. A similar study showed that moviegoers

▬ Coupons: Healthy or Not?

When is a bargain not really a bargain? When you pay for it with your health.

It's true that coupons can be great money-savers. If you use coupons for already discounted items, or if you visit a store that doubles or triples coupons, they certainly can make a big dent in your grocery bill — as long as you were going to purchase those things anyway.

But you don't have to look much further than your average Sunday circular to realize that most coupons are offered for foods that you probably want to avoid in the first place. Sure, you can find coupons for healthful items like yogurt, bagged salads,

cans of beans, and frozen vegetables. You just need to be prepared to sift through pages of coupons for packaged products that are highly processed and filled with sugar, additives, and trans fats.

Another concern with coupons is that they can lead to purchasing greater quantities of foods, which means you're likely to eat more. Research is clear: the more you have, the more you eat. So if you get three boxes of cinnamon graham crackers for the price of one, you'll probably wind up eating more graham crackers at each sitting.

Many natural food product manufacturers will send you coupons if

you request them. If you buy a product frequently, be sure to contact the company and ask whether someone can mail you coupons. Many food cooperatives also offer their own coupon books, which often offer good deals on more-healthful, less-processed items. Also, you can check online sites like www.coolsavings.com to search for deals on items you purchase frequently.

The bottom line? Make sure you're using coupons only for items that you really want to eat.

who were served fresh popcorn in large tubs ate 45 percent more than those given fresh popcorn in medium containers.

It's not true merely for food. Whatever the product, we consume more if we're given big packages. It's true for dog food, for plant food, for shampoo and laundry detergent. Wansink tested the theory with a total of 47 products and found only one for which package size did not affect consumption: liquid bleach.

The amazing part? People who receive both the large and small packages report having eaten about the same amount — meaning those who consumed twice as much didn't get any more satisfaction than those who ate less. Also, while most people acknowledged that portion or container size could influence others, they wrongly believed that they themselves had not been influenced. This suggests that the increased consumption is completely unconscious — which is what makes it so dangerous.

Savvy parents can use this information to their advantage: Give a child a big bowl of carrots or cucumbers, and she'll likely consume more than if she'd been given a small bowl. Give her a smaller bowl of dessert, and she'll consume less. Buy more spinach for the household, and you'll likely eat more spinach. Buy prepared desserts in small packages, and you'll all eat a little less sugar and saturated fat.

▬ "Smart" Choices Not Always Healthy

The nation's largest food companies launched a program called "Smart Choices" [in 2009], designed to "help shoppers easily identify smarter food and beverage choices." Foods that represented a smart choice would be labeled with a big green check mark on the packaging.

Some of the Smart Choices seemed kind of dumb. Among the foods that could be spotted sporting the Smart Choices symbol were Froot Loops and Lucky Charms cereals, Fudgsicles, and Fruit Roll-Ups. Some of the products were 40 to 50 percent sugar, and many of them were choices that

Walter Willett, a physician and chair of the Harvard School of Public Health, dubbed "horrible."

The lesson? Turns out that it's smart to be skeptical of food claims — very, very skeptical.

six simple words = a lifetime of better health

We could summarize this book in six simple words: *fewer processed foods, more whole foods.*

A whopping 90 percent of the money that Americans spend on food is spent on processed foods — food that has been altered in some way from its natural state. Not all processing is bad for your health, of course; frozen vegetables are officially processed, simply by freezing. Even all-natural yogurt is milk that has been processed, through the addition of healthy bacteria. Most processed foods, however, have been processed well beyond their natural state . . . and well beyond anything that's good for your family's health. These foods are often jam-packed with salt, sweeteners, and trans fats. They have been bleached, emulsified, artificially flavored, and hypersweetened, and they are filled with any combination of thousands of chemical additives currently on the market.

Simply trying to pronounce some of these ingredients — butylated hydroxyt-*what?* — can be enough to bring us down. So we weren't surprised when we learned that a 2009 study in *The British Journal of Psychiatry* found that people who ate a diet high in processed foods

38

were 58 percent more likely to experience clinical depression than those who ate more whole foods.

Ready to ditch the processed stuff? When you're shopping, look for foods that have minimal ingredients. When it comes time to compare products, choose the one with fewer, more pronounceable ingredients. In fact, some of the best, most healthful foods don't even need an ingredient label, because they contain just one ingredient: themselves.

By choosing whole foods over highly processed foods, you'll avoid a whole host of chemical additives and artificial sweeteners. You will control what types of fats you consume and how many. You will keep the good nutrition that otherwise gets stripped during processing — the fiber, vitamins, antioxidants, and other health-boosting micronutrients. By eating whole foods, you will develop a taste for the foods that promote health rather than detract from it. Best of all, you won't have to jump on the latest food bandwagon to stay healthy. Low-carb? Low-fat? High-protein? Grapefruit only? Say goodbye to all that; whole foods allow you to feel great without fads.

Fortunately, whole foods don't have to be expensive. In fact, sometimes the least-processed foods are the best deal of all . . . for example, the bulk bins.

39

A Dozen Must-Try Bulk Items

Let's face it: The bulk bin aisle can be intimidating. The items there aren't wrapped in colorful packages, they don't come stamped with directions, and — yikes! — how much of this stuff are you supposed to buy, anyway? Then, when you finally get up your nerve to try something, you place the bag beneath the bin incorrectly, and an avalanche of rice scatters all over the floor.

Sure, it can be scary. But it's worth conquering any fears you might have. The bulk aisle offers a fantastic array of health-boosting goodies, typically at rock-bottom prices. It doesn't matter whether you buy a cup or a gallon; there's no need to purchase excess food and spend more to "save." From nutrient-packed heritage grains to healthier baking supplies, you'll find foods that are tasty, that are packed with vitamins and minerals, and that can be prepared for pennies. It's not difficult, it just takes a little know-how.

As for the items scattering all over the floor? We recently asked a store manager how often this happens. He said it happens twenty times a day. The store is used to it. So relax. Go ahead. Buy something.

1. Barley

Barley is one of the best-loved whole grains; it is mild, versatile, and tasty. Cook and writer Lorna Sass called it the "chicken of the grain world" because it goes with just about everything. Chef and *New York Times* food writer Mark Bittman suggests that barley is probably the best grain to use when making soup. There are several types of barley. Whole barley is like brown rice; it retains its hull and bran. Because of this, whole barley takes much longer to cook, and it never becomes fully tender. "Naked" barley, or hull-less barley, has had its hull removed but maintains the bran. It has a nice chewiness. Pearled barley, which is most common, has had its hull and bran removed; it cooks faster than whole barley and becomes slightly chewy when cooked. Barley grits are whole or pearled grains cut into uneven sizes. Below are instructions for pearl barley.

Ratio: 1 cup pearl barley to 3 cups liquid.
Cooking: Combine pearl barley, water, and a pinch of salt in a medium saucepan. Bring to a boil over high heat. Reduce heat to low, cover, and cook for about 45 minutes or until barley is tender and most of the liquid is absorbed. Fluff grains with a fork.
Proportion: 1 cup dry equals 3½ to 4 cups cooked.

2. Beans

Dried beans are nutritious, tasty, and economical. With dried beans as a foundation, you can prepare a delicious, healthful meal for mere pocket change. Their downside is that they require some preparation; unless you have a pressure cooker, beans must be soaked in advance, and even then they generally require at least an hour's cooking to become tender enough to eat. Once you get the hang of it, though — once you master the rhythm of soaking beans before bed, or simmering them on the stove top while you and the kids run around the backyard — you'll find that dried beans are a tasty, frugal alternative to meats, as well as to their canned brethren. Because they can take a while to prepare, consider making a large batch of beans and then freezing them in parts for later use.

Ratio: After soaking, you will need 3 to 4 cups of water for every 1 cup of beans.

Cooking: Soak beans first, either for 8 hours in cold water or by bringing to a rapid boil, then turning off the heat and letting them sit for 1 hour. Drain and rinse soaked beans, add water, bring to a boil, and then simmer until tender (do not boil). Most beans require 1 to 1½ hours simmering. Others, like soybeans, take longer. *Note: With a pressure cooker, cooking times for most beans can be reduced to 10 minutes or less.* Do not add salt or vinegar until beans are tender. Depending on your water conditions (hard or soft), this can prevent beans from becoming tender.

Proportion: 1 cup dry beans generally equals 3 cups cooked, depending on the type of bean.

3. Bulgur

This grain is made by parboiling wheat kernels, which are then dried and cracked into different sizes. The result is a quick grain, one that is generally soaked instead of cooked. Although it looks bland, it has a surprisingly robust, nutty flavor. It is often used in grain salads; perhaps its most common use is in tabbouleh — a combination of bulgur, tomato, parsley, cucumber, and mint. Bulgur can be coarsely ground, medium-ground, or finely ground. Typically, what you find in the supermarket is a medium variety.

Ratio: 1 cup bulgur to 2 cups liquid.

Cooking: Bring water to a boil, pour over bulgur in a heatproof bowl, and then let sit until water is absorbed, about 20 minutes.

Proportion: 1 cup dry equals 3 cups cooked.

4. Couscous

Couscous is like miniature kernels of pasta, and is incredibly easy to prepare. Couscous picks up the flavor of whatever it's cooked with. All you have to do is mix it with boiling water plus a little butter or olive oil and let it stand for a few minutes. Fluff the grains with a fork, and serve it as a side.

Ratio: 1 cup couscous to 2 cups liquid.

Cooking: Bring liquid to a boil, stir in couscous, and then cover and remove from heat. Let sit for 5 minutes, until liquid is absorbed.

Proportion: 1 cup dry equals 2½ cups cooked.

5. Lentils

Though one of the smallest members of the legume family, lentils pack a powerful nutritional punch. They're packed with fiber, minerals, and B vitamins, including folate, and they contain 26 percent protein — higher than almost any other legume. They also have twice as much iron as other legumes. They cook faster than other legumes, require no presoaking, and readily absorb flavors of whatever they're cooked with. Because of their versatility, their beautiful range of colors, and their ease of use, lentils form a healthy blank canvas for your culinary adventures. Use them in soups, curries, Mexican dishes, or vinaigrette salads.

Ratio: 1 cup lentils to at least 3 cups liquid.
Cooking: Bring water to a boil, add lentils, cover, and simmer for 20 to 30 minutes, or until tender; drain.
Proportion: 1 cup dry equals 2½ cups cooked.

6. Millet

Millet is one of the most healthful whole grains, and it is a staple food for one-third of the world's population. It's a treasure trove of magnesium, B vitamins, iron, calcium, and zinc. Yet amazingly, in most Western countries, millet is used primarily in bird seed . . . even as our Western diet is increasingly for the birds! It can be cooked up into a sweet porridge, can be used as a grain for savory side dishes, and can add thickness and texture to stews. When it absorbs excess water, it can even take on the creamy consistency of mashed potatoes, which many people enjoy as an alternative to traditional spuds.

Ratio: 2½ cups liquid to 1 cup millet.
Cooking: Toast millet before cooking for best flavor. Add water and salt, bring to a boil, and then simmer, uncovered, for 20 minutes. Cover and let sit off the heat for 10 minutes. Fluff before serving.
Proportion: 1 cup of dried millet equals 4 cups of fluffed millet.

7. Quinoa

Though often treated as a grain, quinoa is technically a seed. This accounts for its high protein content; indeed, quinoa is a complete protein, meaning it contains all the essential amino acids. It is also rich in iron, fiber, calcium, and potassium. Quinoa can be treated like rice or couscous, but it is nutritious enough to serve as the basis for an entire meal. Quinoa was historically cultivated in the Andean region and probably dates back as far as 5000 BCE. It is nutty, with a satisfying crunch.

Ratio: 1 cup dried quinoa to 2 cups liquid.
Cooking: Rinse quinoa before using to remove the bitter saponin that coats the seeds. Bring to a boil, then simmer for 20 minutes, until seeds have split. They should have a soft texture with a slight crunch.
Proportion: 1 cup dried quinoa makes 3 to 4 cups cooked.

8. Rice

There are tens of thousands of varieties of rice, but all fall into one of two general categories: long grain or short grain. Long-grain rice is the most common rice in the United States; it cooks into separate kernels. Short-grain rice tends to be moister and stickier.

Basmati rice is a delicate, fragrant long-grain variety. Jasmine is another aromatic long-grain rice, although it is moist and sticky enough to seem like a short grain. Arborio rice, the rice often used in risotto, and sushi rice are both short grain. Brown rice can be long or short grain; it is simply rice with an intact bran layer. This makes it more nutritious than white rice, but it takes longer to cook, and it never becomes as tender as white rice.

Arborio

Ratio: 1 cup rice to 3 cups liquid (add liquid incrementally for risotto).

Cooking: Simmer for 20 minutes, until tender.

Proportion: 1 cup dry equals 2½ cups cooked.

Basmati

Ratio: 1 cup rice to 1½ cups liquid.

Cooking: Simmer, covered, for 15 minutes for white, 40 to 45 minutes for brown.

Proportion: 1 cup dry equals 2½ cups cooked.

Glutinous (sweet or sushi)

Ratio: 1 cup rice to 1 cup liquid.

Cooking: Simmer, covered, for 15 minutes.

Proportion: 1 cup dry equals 2 cups cooked.

Long-grain

Ratio: 1 cup rice to 1½ cups liquid.

Cooking: Simmer, covered, for 15 to 20 minutes for white, 30 to 45 minutes for brown.

Proportion: 1 cup dry equals 2½ cups cooked.

Medium- and short-grain

Ratio: 1 cup rice to 1½ cups liquid.

Cooking: Simmer, covered, for 20 minutes for white, 40 minutes for brown.

Proportion: 1 cup dry equals 2½ cups cooked.

9. Split Peas

Split peas can be green, red, or yellow. Unlike most dried legumes, they can be prepared relatively quickly from their dried state, taking just 30 minutes to cook. They contain a rich, earthy flavor and have been a staple of inexpensive, nutritious meals throughout human history (fossilized pea remains have been found at archeological sites dated as far back as 9750 BCE). Pair them with onions, garlic, carrots, and herbs for a simple split pea soup. The yellow and red varieties pair especially well with curries.

Ratio: 1 cup split peas to 3 cups liquid.

Cooking: Bring to a boil, and then simmer for 30 minutes, until soft.

Proportion: 1 cup dry split peas equals 2 cups cooked.

FACT: In 2008, the average supermarket contained 46,852 items.

Source: Food Marketing Institute, Industry Overview 2008.

10. **Steel-Cut Oats**

Most people are familiar with rolled oats, which are hulled grains that have been literally flattened by steel rollers. Steel-cut oats, less ubiquitous in this country, are simply the whole grain (including the bran, germ, and endosperm, the sources of all the good nutrition) cut into small pieces with steel blades. They look like little kernels of brown rice, and they are delicious. They are chewier than regular oats, with a nutty texture and full flavor.

Ratio: 4 cups water or milk to 1 cup steel-cut oats.

Cooking: Bring to a rolling boil and then simmer uncovered for about 20 minutes. Add a touch of salt, and then serve with milk, syrup, and/or fruit. You can cut the cooking time to about 5 minutes if you soak the oats in water overnight. Alternatively, you can put the water, salt, and oats in a slow cooker before bed — the oats will be done by morning.

Proportion: 1 cup uncooked steel-cut oats equals 3 cups cooked.

11. **Wheat Berries**

These beauties are the whole-grain kernels of the wheat plant. Typically ground up into flour, wheat berries can also be cooked whole; when cooked, they have a chewy, slightly nutty texture, with a touch of sweetness that makes them a great addition to salads, soups, and chili. They have an unusually long shelf life as well, making them a great pantry staple (as well as a favorite among survivalists). Because

they take an hour to prepare, make a large batch at one time, and then use them throughout the week.

Ratio: 1 cup dried wheat berries to 3½ cups liquid.

Cooking: Bring to a rolling boil, add a pinch of salt, and then reduce heat, cover, and simmer for 60 minutes.

Proportion: 1 cup uncooked wheat berries equals about 2½ cups cooked.

12. **Wild Rice**

You've probably heard this before, but wild rice isn't rice at all. It's actually a grain belonging to the grass family, and humans were eating it as far back as prehistoric times. Cooked wild rice is nutty and earthy, with a chewy, satisfying texture. It is rich in minerals, B vitamins, niacin, zinc, and protein, and it contains many times more folic acid than long-grain brown rice. It is notoriously difficult to cultivate and harvest, so it tends to be more expensive than most grains.

Ratio: 1 cup of grain to 3 cups of liquid.

Cooking: To remove any hulls or unwanted storage debris, place the grains in warm water and stir; discard any particles that float to the top. Repeat. Combine water or broth, wild rice, and salt to taste in a saucepan. Bring to a rolling boil. Reduce heat and simmer for 45 minutes; grains are cooked when they open, revealing their inner portion.

Proportion: 1 cup dry equals 3½ cups cooked.

Say "YES" for a change: farm-to-consumer venues

Want an alternative to slick supermarket merchandising?

CONSIDER PURCHASING FOODS directly from the people who grow them. Farm-to-consumer venues include **farmers' markets**, which take place at a specific time and place, usually weekly; **farm stands**, which typically take place at or near the point of production; **CSAs**, which allow consumers to purchase a "share" of a farm's bounty for the season; and **food cooperatives and buying clubs**, in which a group of people come together to purchase in bulk directly from a farm or farms. There are also numerous locally minded food markets that, while not direct-to-consumer, strive to connect their customers with an array of healthful, local, and otherwise ethical foods.

There are many reasons to purchase food directly from farms. For harried parents, the lack of sophisticated food marketing strategies can be chief among them. It's a relief to go somewhere where most choices are good ones and where no one ever hired a child psychologist specifically to determine the best ways to encourage our kids to pester us for junky food.

Certainly you can still make impulsive purchases in these venues, but these are different in both quality and scale. Since the farmers' markets tend to be cash economies, it's rare that you walk out with

45

three times as many items as you intended. Besides, if you're going to pick up an impulse purchase, wouldn't you much rather it be radishes, or a few bunches of chard, than sugary cereal? Even when there are less-healthful choices available — for example, a small-scale baker offering homemade cookies — these tend to be more wholesome than their supermarket alternatives because they're not filled with trans fats, dyes, preservatives, and other additives.

In a world where more than a billion dollars go toward marketing junk food to children every single year, it's a relief simply to be where almost all the alternatives are good ones.

Farmers' Markets

IN THE 15-YEAR PERIOD between 1994 and 2009, the number of farmers' markets in the United States more than tripled, from 1,755 markets to 5,274. Consumers now spend roughly $1 billion at farmers' markets annually, with about three million consumers visiting farmers' markets on a weekly basis. And you can find farmers' markets in some surprising places, from inner-city communities to hospitals and health care centers, mall parking lots, and the premises of stores like Target and Home Depot.

There is one simple reason for the rise of farmers' markets: People love them. Why? Because they offer an array of benefits:

■ Keeping Real Food Real Easy

One way to save time in the kitchen is to double recipes, then use the leftovers to create different meals for the rest of the week. Roast chicken is a perfect dish for this. For the first night, serve Lemon-Herb Roast Chicken (see page 195) as the main course. Then cut up the leftover chicken, removing the bones and skin, and use it as the base of a chili, salad, wrap sandwich, or soup that will work for weeknight dinners and lunches. Our Chicken Chili (see page 196) or Red Grape, Blueberry, and Almond Chicken Salad (see page 194) would both make short work of leftover roast chicken.

The appeal of farmers' markets

Great, healthful food. Farmer's markets are literally overflowing with good-for-you foods, from basil to bok choy, from eggplant to free-range eggs, and from peppers to parsnips. These are the foods that will boost your family's health, give you energy, and help you all look and feel your best.

Fresher food. Most of the time, farmers' market produce has been picked within 24 hours — a far cry from the cross-country journey taken by most supermarket produce. Because produce loses nutritional value the longer it sits uneaten, this freshness also means better health. In addition, farmers' market produce is typically harvested at the peak of freshness, whereas many supermarket fruits and vegetables are picked early and ripen (or not) during their journey. The shorter trip to market also allows your local farmers to produce some of the more delicate and flavorful varieties of fruits and vegetables, items that would not survive the cross-country or cross-continent trip to the store.

More vibrant experience. Farmers' markets offer a refreshing antidote to all the antiseptic, corporate spaces that dominate so much of our lives. They are wholly sensory, filled with colorful foods — from purple basil to rainbow chard — and often even more colorful individuals. Sometimes they offer live music or craft activities, as well.

Greater diversity. A diversity of farmer backgrounds and ethnicities might allow you to find ingredients from a wider range of cultures than you can find in the typical megamart. Look for Asian greens, Italian heirloom squash, or unusual flavorings like lemongrass.

Community. Farmers' markets create gathering places for a community, allowing shoppers to meet neighbors, catch up on news, and feel more grounded in a community — a feeling that you don't often find in a big box grocery store. Brian Halweil, senior researcher at Worldwatch Institute, notes that shoppers are ten times more likely to have a conversation at a farmers' market than at a supermarket.

47

■ **A chance to meet your growers.** In an era of food recalls — of salmonella, *E. coli*, mad cow, and mercury — farmers' markets allow you to establish loyalty and trust with those who provide you with food.

■ **Support for the local economy.** Farmers' markets boost the local economy. Retailing at farmers' markets can increase farmers' profits by 40 to 80 percent over what they would otherwise earn by wholesaling or through other marketing methods alone. And when they're situated in downtown areas, farmers' markets provide a critical mass of activity in districts that sometimes struggle to draw customers.

■ **A chance to say "yes."** If you're tired of food being a wedge between you and your kids, or if you're tired of thinking about food as an enemy that threatens your health, the farmers' market is the place for you. At last, here is a place where you can say "yes." Over and over again, you can say it: "yes." It's refreshing to let your defenses down for change.

How to Shop a Farmers' Market

IF YOU'RE ACCUSTOMED to giant supermarkets, visiting a farmers' market can be a refreshing — or daunting — experience. Here are a few tips to help you get the most out of your market experience.

■ **Take cash.** Most farmers' markets are cash only, though an increasing number are figuring out ways to make it easier for people on nutrition assistance programs to shop there. Do the farmers a favor and take smaller bills, as well.

> **FACT:** A study in Massachusetts found a direct correlation between the shelf space devoted to high-calorie snack products in stores and the body mass index of area residents.
>
> Source: Rose D, Hutchinson P. L., Bodor J. N., Swalm C. M., Farley T. A., Cohen D. A., Rice J. C. "Neighborhood food environments and Body Mass Index: the importance of in-store contents." *American Journal of Preventive Medicine.* 2009; 37(3):214–9.

- **Get the lay of the land.** When you first arrive, don't start buying right away. Walk around a bit and see what's being offered. Otherwise, you might spend all your money at the first couple of booths, only to find with disappointment that you've run out of money before you noticed the really spectacular-looking cherries or the zebra-striped tomatoes.

- **Take sturdy bags that are comfortable to hold.** It seems obvious, but it's easy to forget. You'll need bags, and you'll want them to be comfortable when weighed down with produce.

- **Ask questions.** Can't tell a radish from a rutabaga? No clue how to prepare collards? Not sure how to store leeks? Ask the farmers — after all, they're the experts. You can also ask them how to store their produce, how to prepare it, and what pairs well with it. Ask them about their farms and their growing practices. Do it politely, of course, and do it when there's not a line of 15 customers waiting behind you. But don't hesitate to ask.

FACT: Eighty percent of candy purchased at the supermarket is bought on impulse.

Source: Weir, T. "Rethinking the front end." Progressive Grocer, 2003; 82(12), referencing Front End Focus study, conducted by Dechert-Hampe & Co., 2003.

FACT: In 2008 alone, food manufacturers introduced 22,850 new food and beverage products in the United States. The largest share of these new products were candy, gum, and snacks; beverages; condiments; and processed meat.

Source: Economic Research Service, United States Department of Agriculture, Food Marketing System in the U.S.: New Product Introductions, November 3, 2009.

▪▪▪ **Don't assume organic is the only way to go.** Many farmers who use sustainable practices haven't had the time, personnel, or money to become "certified organic." Others are in the process of converting farmland to organic standards. Don't pass up a great sustainable farmer simply because there's no sign that says "organic."

▪▪▪ **Take the kids.** Even the most skeptical child can find that the farmers' market is way more fun than hanging out in aisle 11. Take them from booth to booth, and let them pick a few items themselves. Take a little extra cash for a ready-to-eat item, and if the market offers children's entertainment, plan to spend a little extra time.

▪▪▪ **Shop early . . . or late.** Some of the hard-to-find items get snapped up early, so you'll have the best selection (and the shortest lines) if you arrive before the crowds. On the other hand, some of the best deals are found just before the market closes, because many farmers prefer not to take their produce home with them.

▪▪▪ **Do not pass go.** Now that you have such gorgeous vegetables, it would be a shame to allow them lose nutrition and flavor by letting them sit in a hot car. Take your produce straight home to the refrigerator, or take a cooler to keep things fresh.

Are Farmers' Markets a Better Value Than Supermarkets?

FARMERS' MARKETS sometimes have a reputation as being expensive. While you certainly can find farmers' markets that charge a premium, many are no more expensive — and are often less expensive — than grocery store fare.

Sam Breach, who writes the popular blog Becks and Posh, compared the same items, pound for pound, purchased from his local Safeway supermarket and the San Francisco Ferry Plaza farmers' market. He discovered happily that shopping for fresh produce at the farmers' market over two weekends saved a full 29 percent on what he would have spent on the same or inferior items at Safeway.

Working with an undergraduate class, Seattle University economics professor Stacey Jones compared prices for organic produce at

51

that city's Broadway farmers' market with prices for the same items at a local supermarket chain and at the cooperatively owned Madison Market. The farmers' market was slightly less expensive, pound for pound, for 15 different staple items — apples, red potatoes, carrots, spinach, and salad mix among them.

It's worth noting that these studies compared price only and did not take into account the quality, freshness, or flavor of the produce; the experience of shopping at either place (most people enjoy farmers' markets much more); the total amount spent at each location; the number of nonessential impulse buys that are often part of the supermarket experience; or the multiplier effects of spending locally.

Can you go broke at a farmers' market? Sure you can. But plenty of people find quite the opposite. And as a bonus, you get a few riches money can't buy.

▬ Farmers' Market Shoppers Eat More Fruits and Veggies

Researchers at UCLA tracked the eating habits of 602 women who received nutritional assistance through the federal Women, Infants, and Children Program (WIC). Some of the women were given $10 in weekly vouchers for vegetable and fruit purchases at a nearby farmers' market or supermarket, while a control group received coupons for nonfood products in exchange for sharing information about eating habits.

After six months, women who shopped at the farmers' markets ate three additional servings of fruits and vegetables every day compared to the control group. Supermarket shoppers consumed one-and-a-half extra servings — more than the control group, but only half of what those who shopped at farmers' markets achieved.

More vegetables equals better health. That's just one more reason to love the farmers' market.

Community-Supported Agriculture

WITH CSA (community-supported agriculture) farms, community members buy "shares" of a given farm, paying for their membership before the start of a growing season. Whatever food is harvested during this season is shared among members.

In the CSA model, small farmers have both the start-up funds necessary to begin growing — for seeds, labor, equipment, and so forth — as well as a guaranteed market for their product when the harvest arrives. Meanwhile, consumers have easy access to heaps of healthful produce that's fresher, and easily more delicious, than anything they would find in the grocery store.

But for us, that's just where the benefits begin. There are numerous other advantages, like the pleasure of visiting the farm and forging a closer connection to the food you eat. There is only one thing better than picking a ripe, golden cherry tomato from the vine and then eating it when it is still warm from the sun: seeing your child do exactly that.

Then there's community. Each week, as you pick up your shares, you'll see the same faces. People are usually in a good mood — people being handed heaps of colorful vegetables, fresh herbs, and flowers generally are. Soon, you'll find yourself sharing recipes and getting to know people whom you might not otherwise meet — people of every generation, often of wholly different backgrounds. Over the course of the season, there's a good chance you will attend harvest festivals, barn dances, field days, potlucks, and more. In the end, maybe nothing connects people better than a bundle of chives and a homegrown pumpkin.

With a CSA, you also support your local economy. Gone is the middleman that takes three-quarters of every food dollar. When you join a CSA, your money stays within the community, helping to support a better quality of life for you and your neighbors.

The downsides to CSA farms have to do with seasonality. For those of us accustomed to eating blueberries during January's deep freeze

53

or dining on mangos imported from Pakistan, the rhythm of eating food from a single farm, week after week, takes an adjustment. One week, you might have heaps of bok choy and baby turnips. Another week, you'll take home tons of spinach and tomatoes. Once you get used to it, though, you might find a certain comfort and connectedness to that pattern. Plus, the food is so fresh, and so tasty, that the chances are good you won't miss those pale, out-of-season tomatoes.

How about cost? Membership costs vary from farm to farm, but they usually start at several hundred dollars. Unlike other food-buying experiences, however, you pay before the start of the season instead of paying for food as you go.

While clear price comparisons can be challenging (since harvests differ from year to year and from farm to farm), research shows that CSAs can save consumers money. In 1995, a University of Massachusetts study compared the costs of three different CSAs to the cost of an equivalent amount of produce (both organic and conventional) from retail stores; in every case, the CSA was less expensive than the stores.

The following year, a study from the University of Wisconsin–Madison Center for Integrated Agricultural Systems (CIAS) compared CSA produce prices to those at several other retail outlets.

Co-ops

Looking for a store that sells natural, healthy, local, and/or sustainable foods? Consider becoming a member of a cooperative grocery market. These markets are customer owned, but most allow all community members to shop there. These stores are growing in popularity, boasting combined sales of more than $1 billion annually. Visit the National Cooperative Grocers Association (www.ncga.coop) to find a cooperative market near you.

"Would I spring out of bed with sheer joy at 7am on a Saturday morning to go to Safeway? Absolutely not. But for the Farmers' Market? Of course, even with a hangover. There has to be something to it."

Sam Breach, Becks and Posh blog, May 20, 2007.

54

Although the study found that sometimes the CSA produce was less expensive and sometimes it was more expensive, the comparison wasn't exactly apples to apples. Unlike the CSAs studied, the supermarket produce was not organic and was only rarely local. But more important, the study did not include pick-your-own produce, which we have found is a vast and important portion of a CSA's bounty.

Besides, would you *really* buy the equivalent amount of vegetables from a grocery store? Would you actually bring home piles of kale, a whole canvas bag filled with just-picked purple beans, or so many juicy tomatoes that you eat them whole, like an apple, for an afternoon snack? Would you serve fresh salads nearly every night of the week during warm months? Would you ever try mizuna greens, celeriac, or kohlrabi? In our experience, our families' vegetable consumption skyrocketed — both in quantity and diversity — when we joined our respective CSA farms.

More vegetables, and more kinds of vegetables: We're pretty sure that's just what the doctor ordered.

When you join, you might find yourself momentarily flummoxed by the process — after all, the whole experience is so unlike grocery-store shopping. Request a farm tour, ask many questions of the farmers and fellow members, and before you know it, you'll be waxing sentimental about the quality of your CSA carrots, too.

To find a CSA farm near you, check out Local Harvest (www.localharvest.org), a great online resource that can help you find sustainably grown food from your local family farms, farmers' markets, and other sources.

> **Nearly half of every dollar spent on food goes toward foods prepared outside the home.**
>
> Source: Economic Research Service, United States Department of Agriculture, Food CPI and Expenditures, June 17, 2009.

nutritional dilution

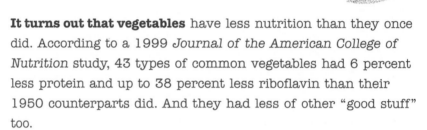

It turns out that vegetables have less nutrition than they once did. According to a 1999 *Journal of the American College of Nutrition* study, 43 types of common vegetables had 6 percent less protein and up to 38 percent less riboflavin than their 1950 counterparts did. And they had less of other "good stuff" too.

The research team narrowed the suspected causes for this drop in nutrition to a few variables. Contrary to popular thought, soil quality did not seem to be the culprit. It seemed to be more about the type, or cultivars, grown. In the past 50 years, large-scale growers have been selecting for varieties that grow quickly, grow larger, have higher yield, and ship well. Apparently nutrition suffers in this tradeoff. The older cultivars, ones not manipulated for rapid growth, size, or durability, had better nutritional contents.

It's a bit like the triangle production diagram, in which the three points represent *fast*, *good*, and *cheap*, and the caption instructs you to pick two for a realistic project. Conventional commercial growers have been selecting *fast* and *cheap*, leaving *good* (that is, full of flavor and nutrition) behind.

A conventional head of broccoli has the same amount of potential nutrition as that of its forebears, but it's spread more thinly as the plant gets bigger faster — what researchers call the "dilution effect." Also, conventional items are picked before they ripen to maximize shipping time and shelf life in the store, and as a result their nutritional content suffers. When you buy unique cultivars locally produced, you are buying produce that has been allowed to fully ripen on the plant. This allows them to attain peak flavor and nutrition.

CHAPTER THREE

MEET YOUR VEGETABLES

How to
fall in love
with what's
good for you

perhaps you were the kid who hid your mushy peas inside your napkin...

r maybe you waited out a plate of overcooked broccoli for hours after the rest of the family left the table. Or maybe you were the kid who downed carrots gladly and asked for more. You've had a long relationship with vegetables; has it been a good one?

Now you have your own family to feed, and you want to encourage them to eat vegetables. You know that while eating fads come and go, fruit and vegetable consumption remains the one wholly undisputed piece of food advice — the diet recommendation that has best stood the test of time. Kids who eat fruits and vegetables do better in school, get sick less often, and have a healthier body weight and image. In the long term, eating fruits and vegetables is directly linked to a lower risk of cancer, heart disease, and stroke. Getting at least "five a day" is key for optimal wellness.

Things might have seemed simpler in the past. If your kids didn't like fresh produce, you could throw some vitamin pills at them, or hand them some cereal fortified with vitamins and minerals, and

pea

napkin

then call it a day. Now, we know more. Vegetables and fruits contain not merely vitamins and minerals, but also phytonutrients: plant chemicals that boost immunity, prevent disease, and help regulate functions like the endocrine system. Phytonutrients — and there are literally thousands of them — hold the key to many of the health benefits that vegetables and fruits offer. And here's the kicker: The only way to get most of these phytonutrients is in their natural form. This means there's no way around it: Fruits and vegetables, in their whole form, are essential to good health.

Encouraging kids to eat fruit can often be as simple as handing them a slice of watermelon or a fresh summer peach. Vegetables, however, can be another story. But the story does have a happy ending: Vegetables aren't just good for you — they also taste good. Really good. Oh, sure, we've all experienced inedible vegetable dishes — drab heaps of watery spinach or squishy overcooked carrots. But we swear, it doesn't have to be that way. The key is buying the best vegetables, storing them correctly, and preparing them in a way that brings out their best flavor and texture.

Whether you have your own "vegephobia" to overcome or want to prepare family meals that everyone will eat, it's time to meet your vegetables all over again — and fall in love this time.

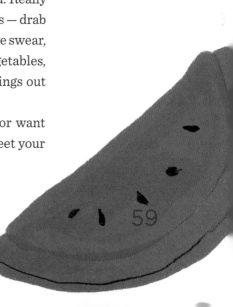

Let them eat Vegetables: tips to triumph over vegephobia

MAKE A SUN OUT OF CARROT AND TOMATO SLICES...

...OR TRY RED PEPPER STARS!

Looks matter.

Sometimes it *is* all about presentation. When vegetables are colorful, attractive, and fun, kids enjoy them more. For younger children, making "salad faces" on a plate, arranging carrot sticks like a burst of sunshine, or using a cookie cutter to make star-shaped red pepper bites can be a creative way to get past the "just one bite" barrier. As kids get older, adding special touches — garnishes, colorful plates, or other festive elements — can be the difference between a grimace and a grin.

Just dip it.

Like raccoons in the wild, kids have some kind of crazy attraction toward dunking their food before eating it. Use this behavior to your advantage by offering cut vegetables with healthful dips. Use anything from a natural ranch dressing to homemade Fig Balsamic Vinaigrette (page 95), Lima Bean Hummus (page 239), or White Bean–Pesto Dip (page 240).

Try again. And again.

Repeated offerings are the key to preparing a child to try a new food. Prepare an item different ways; there's a good chance that, with time, you will find one that works.

Go raw and cooked.

Textures play a significant role in kids' food preferences. Try serving vegetables in both raw and cooked forms. Often, the nutrition content varies between raw and cooked vegetables, just like the texture. Get the most nutritional benefit from each vegetable by serving it both ways.

Add a spoonful of honey (or cheese).

Research has proved that adding a touch of sweetness can help kids develop a taste for a new vegetable. We've seen a similar effect with adding cheese. Adding just a touch of these kid-pleasers may be all you need. Just be sure to keep the vegetable the main event rather than an afterthought.

Power to the (young) people.

Like all of us, kids want to feel respected and in control. Let them choose the vegetables that they want to try and let them be involved in deciding how they're prepared, or let them help cook. Studies show kids are far more likely to eat foods that they helped select, grow, and prepare.

What's in a name?

Giving food a tantalizing name can make all the difference. Ali once convinced a table full of skeptical preschool and early elementary school girls age four to seven to dive into a bowl of kale by naming it "Power Fairy Food" (they loved it).

61

alliums

ONIONS AND GARLIC are members of the allium family, along with chives, leeks, scallions, and shallots. We both confess to an abiding love of onion and garlic; Beth once even consumed several raw garlic cloves under a misguided attempt to fend off mosquitoes. The mosquitoes did not mind. Everyone else did.

Raw **onions** might be a bit much for most, but cooked onions are a foundation of many dishes, even the ones kids love best, like the tomato sauce on pizza and ragù on pasta. Caramelized onions (see recipe, page 65) make a great condiment as well as a lovely ingredient in other dishes, and the caramelization process brings out the sweet side of this pungent vegetable.

Garlic is the most pungent of the alliums, so much so that it is fairly pest resistant while growing. Raw garlic is great for pesto, but its flavor gets mellower and sweeter with cooking. Try not to burn it, though, as this imparts a bitter flavor.

Shallots are smaller than onions and have a sweeter flavor, somewhere between that of onion and garlic. They pair well with mushrooms and add an elegant flavor when used in place of onion. **Leeks** are another type of allium with a smooth, subtle flavor; they work well in soups, quiches, and casseroles. **Chives**, **scallions**, and **garlic scapes** (the edible stems of the garlic plant) complete the allium family. Scallions and garlic scapes are best used raw or lightly cooked. Chives are the most delicate allium, and they're almost always used raw.

Certain alliums are common kid-pleasers. Ali's daughter became hooked on chives when she first discovered them in ranch dressing. Today, she happily sprinkles chives on salads, baked potatoes, yogurt dips, soups, and more.

While alliums are generally used as ingredients in other dishes, there are some exceptions: Onions are terrific on the grill in summer, and simple sautéed leeks can make a colorful, unexpected side dish to any meal.

shallot

onion

chive
(and chive
blossom)

garlic
scape

leek

cut
shallot

scallion

garlic

63

Good for Your Family Because . . .

IN GENERAL, the more pungent the flavor of the allium variety, the more phytonutrients it contains, particularly the sulfur-containing compounds that research suggests have anticancer properties. Yellow onions offer more of these phytonutrients than white onions. Shallots contain the most of these compounds of all the alliums.

Alliums also contain chromium, which has been shown to help lower blood glucose levels and along with their phytonutrients may help prevent cardiovascular disease. Garlic, in particular, has been studied for its apparent cardiovascular benefits. Alliums also contain vitamins C and B$_6$, fiber, and minerals such as manganese, molybdenum, folate, potassium, phosphorus, and copper.

Selection and Storage

SWEET ONION varieties like Vidalias have a limited growing season, usually in early summer. Storage onions, garlic, and shallots have a longer growing season and store well, and they are generally available year-round. Onions, garlic, and shallots should have crisp, dry outer skins without any dark spots, soft spots, or openings at the stem end. Avoid buying onions, garlic, or shallots that are sprouting or show any sign of mold.

Leeks are in season in both fall and early spring. Smaller leeks tend to have the best flavor and texture. Choose leeks with firm, green stalks. Their deep layers can hold quite a bit of dirt, so be sure to wash them well: Rinse the leek, and trim it down to the white and tender green parts. Cutting lengthwise, slit the leek halfway through, so that you can unfold all the layers. Rinse well, from bottom to top, fanning the layers to allow the water to rinse between them.

Chives, garlic scapes, and scallions are generally available from spring through summer, and chives are easy to grow all year round in containers. They should have fresh, crisp green tops that are not yellowed or wilted. Look for a couple inches of white onion parts at the stem end.

Store onions, garlic, and shallots at room temperature in a cool, dry, well-ventilated place away from sunlight and heat. (Also store them away from potatoes, which emit ethylene gas, a substance that causes onions to spoil more quickly.) The length of time they will keep varies, with the more pungent varieties lasting longer than the sweeter ones. Chives, garlic scapes, leeks, and scallions should be stored in a bag in the vegetable crisper of the refrigerator, where they will keep for up to a week.

Quick Caramelized Onions

These onions are delicious as a side dish, and they're great on sandwiches and in other dishes (some of our other recipes use them).

1. Combine the oil, sugar, vinegar, and salt in a large skillet with a lid over medium-high heat, and stir until the sugar is dissolved. Add the onion and sauté for a few minutes to start the browning process.

2. Reduce the heat to low, cover, and cook for 10 minutes longer, stirring occasionally. Sprinkle with fresh herbs, if desired, before serving.

Makes about 1 cup cooked onions

1 tablespoon extra-virgin olive oil
2 teaspoons brown sugar
1 tablespoon balsamic vinegar
½ teaspoon kosher salt
1 large onion, thinly sliced
1 tablespoon chopped fresh thyme or rosemary, or 1½ teaspoons dried thyme (optional)

Caramelized Onions in Sandwiches

Caramelized onions are perfect for a healthful twist on grilled cheese. Use whole-grain bread, stone-ground mustard, cheddar, a few thin slices of apple, and a layer of the caramelized onions. Butter the outsides of the bread lightly. Grill the sandwich a few minutes on each side. The sandwich pairs well with soup or a side salad.

These also make for a great steak sandwich if you have leftover steak to use. Butter each slice of bread and place under a low broiler for a few minutes to toast. Spread on honey mustard, a layer of the onions, and steak, and top with sliced cheese. Place under the broiler for a couple of minutes longer until the cheese is melted and the sandwich is warm through.

65

asparagus

ASPARAGUS IS A PERENNIAL MEMBER of the lily family. The young shoots or spears begin to appear in early spring, and they are harvested soon after. The spears are usually green, though a sweeter-tasting purple variety also exists. (White asparagus is actually green asparagus that has been grown under cover to prevent chlorophyll from developing.)

Avoid canned asparagus if you want your kids to learn to love this vegetable. The canned variety is mushy, with a more pronounced sulfuric flavor, and lacks all the tender-crisp sweetness of the real thing. Asparagus is best when fresh, local, and in season. The easiest way to prepare this vegetable is by simply steaming or roasting it, but it also pairs well with eggs, pasta, and other spring vegetables.

Good for Your Family Because . . .

ASPARAGUS is high in folate, an important nutrient during pregnancy. Folate is also helpful for lifelong cardiovascular health. It is also a natural diuretic, giving your liquid emissions a distinctive, not-unpleasant odor. (The novelty of this can be used to encourage children to try the new vegetable, just to see what happens. Hey, whatever works.) Asparagus is also a good source of vitamins K, C, and A, and B_1, B_2, B_3, and B_6.

Selection and Storage

ASPARAGUS is a spring crop. Look for firm spears whose "petals" are tight to their stalks. The cut ends should not be too woody. Some people prefer asparagus pencil thin, though the purple variety is still tender and very tasty when picked much fatter. To prepare, snap the stalks by bending; the stalks will naturally snap at the point where they transition from tender to woody.

For storage, think about asparagus as you would cut flowers: keep them in the refrigerator, standing in a tall jar with enough water to cover the cut ends. If you do not have a shelf with enough headroom enough for this, lay the asparagus stalks diagonally in a container, cut ends down, with enough water to cover the cut ends. Stored this way, asparagus will keep for a few days.

Roasted Asparagus

This easy recipe gives the vegetable a tangy sweetness that children sometimes prefer to the flavor resulting from mere steaming. It works as well for green beans as it does for asparagus.

- 1 pound asparagus, woody stems removed
- 2 tablespoons extra-virgin olive oil
- 1 tablespoon balsamic vinegar
  Kosher or sea salt

1. Preheat the oven to 400°F.

2. Toss the asparagus with the oil and vinegar, and spread the spears out on a baking sheet. Sprinkle with salt. Roast for about 15 minutes, until they are lightly browned, watching carefully to be sure they do not overbrown.

Serves 6

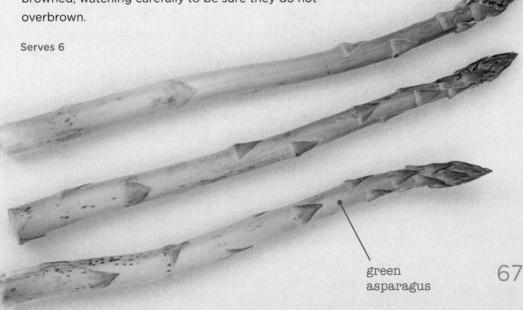

green asparagus

67

NOTHING QUITE STRIKES FEAR into the palate as much as canned pickled beet slices. Remember stacking these up on your plate instead of eating them? The real thing is much better. Deep purple-red is the familiar color, but you can also find mild-flavored golden and orange beets, as well as the sexy purple and white striped **Chioggia** beets.

Beets are terrific when roasted and dressed with a bit of olive oil and balsamic vinegar. Try incorporating roasted beets with kid-friendly orange sections or serving them with feta or mild, fresh goat cheese. Of course, there are also beet brownies (see page 259) for the tough cases. . . .

As a relative of chard, beets come with edible leafy greens attached. Bonus. The greens are tasty and can be prepared with a quick sauté, in a gratin, or in soup.

Good for Your Family Because . . .

BEETS are wildly healthful, true ruby gems of goodness. They are a very good source of folate and also offer some vitamin C, iron, and other minerals like potassium, but their real nutritional punch comes from an abundance of phytonutrients. Like red wine and red cabbage, the red-purple variety is high in anthocyanins, which are thought to have anticancer properties. Betaine, another beet compound, is an anti-inflammatory and is thought to explain beets' detoxifying effects.

Selection and Storage

BEETS are in season from late spring through October for most regions. For the best flavor, choose medium to small beets with firm, smooth-skinned roots and deep color. Be sure there are no bruised spots. If you are going to eat the greens — and they're delicious — make sure they are fresh and a vibrant green, not wilted or yellowed.

Beets for Breakfast?

Start your day with a huge serving of anti-oxidants and phyto-nutrients.
Blend together

- 3 beets, roasted, instructions at right
- 2 cups frozen blueberries
- 1 banana
- 12 oz. 100 percent fruit juice (black cherry or berry)

Makes 6 one-cup servings.

BEETS

To store, remove the greens, leaving about two inches of stem above the root. Store the greens separately in a bag, in the vegetable drawer of the refrigerator. Leaving the greens on will draw moisture from the root and accelerate spoiling.

For many recipes, you do not have to peel beets before cooking. Simply leave the outer skin, top bit of stem, and root end on, wash them well, wrap in foil, and roast in a preheated 400 degree F oven. The amount of time will vary according to their size, but they are done when a knife pierces them easily. When they are cool enough to handle, rub the outsides with a paper towel. The peel will slide right off.

Sometimes children are skeptical of this vegetable, and we're not above renaming it to encourage their tasting a beet-based dish. "Royal Ruby Jewel Salad," anyone?

range Salad

t orange sections and
ful, tasty introduction

t a 9-inch square baking

llots in the prepared pan.
sprinkle with salt and
for about 1½ hours, until
rature.

h the orange sections.
re, and garnish with mint,

2 large red beets, peeled and
cut into 1-inch cubes
2 large golden beets, peeled
and cut into 1-inch cubes
1 small fresh fennel bulb,
trimmed, cored, and cut
into eighths
2 shallots, peeled and
quartered
3 tablespoons extra-virgin
olive oil
2 tablespoons balsamic
vinegar
Coarse salt and freshly
ground black pepper
1 (15-ounce) can mandarin
orange sections, drained,
or 4 clementines, peeled
and sectioned
1½ cups coarsely crumbled feta
cheese
¼ cup chopped fresh mint
leaves (optional)

69

Chioggia beets

broccoli

TOPPING THE LIST as "most dreaded" of the green vegetables, broccoli deserves better. Most often, overcooking is the real problem, making the end result mushy and bitter and losing nutrition along the way.

Broccoli, with its branching structure and delicate florets, is a member of the cabbage family. Varieties include broccoli raab, with its sharp, mustard-green flavor; **broccolini**, which is a cross between broccoli and Chinese broccoli; and **broccoflower**, a cross between broccoli and cauliflower.

Cheese sauce is the number-one tactic parents use to get kids to eat broccoli, and it's a good one. The mac and cheese recipe on page 216 is made with broccoli and the gratin recipe on page 140 can be too. A pesto of broccoli and herbs (see recipe, page 224) tossed with pasta is also a good bet for kid-friendly meals.

Cruciferous Vegetables and Cancer Prevention

Researchers have found that greater consumption of dark green and cruciferous vegetables, especially broccoli and cauliflower, is associated with a decreased risk of several cancers.

Good for Your Family Because . . .

BROCCOLI is rich in phytonutrients shown to have anticancer properties. Broccoli, like many other cole crops, is rich in lutein and vitamins K, C, and A, as well as folate and fiber. It is also a significant source of phosphorus, potassium, magnesium, and the vitamins B_6 and E. Raw broccoli offers the most vitamin C and folate. Cooking broccoli makes more of its beta-carotene and phytonutrients available.

Selection and Storage

BROCCOLI is a spring crop in most areas. Some regions are able to have a second planting, ready for harvest in the fall. Look for heads of broccoli that have compact and firm florets. The head should be green, with no yellowing or opening flower buds. Store broccoli in an open bag in the vegetable crisper of the refrigerator. It will keep for several days but is best used as soon as possible.

Broccoli and Cauliflower Salad

Gold or purple cauliflower makes this salad even more stunning. The sweet-tart dressing, paired with nuts and bacon, brings out the best in crisp, raw broccoli.

1. Preheat the oven to 350°F.

2. Combine 2 tablespoons of the honey and the cashews, cayenne, and salt in a small bowl and mix well. Spread the mixture out on a baking sheet. Arrange the bacon strips on a separate baking sheet. Put both baking sheets in the oven to roast.

3. Roast the cashews for 8 minutes and set aside to cool. Roast the bacon for about 15 minutes, until crisp and browned, and set the strips on paper towels to absorb excess oil.

4. Cut the broccoli and cauliflower into florets (save the stems for use in soup). Combine the florets with the onion and currants in a large bowl, and toss well. Crumble in the bacon.

5. Make the dressing by whisking together the mayonnaise, remaining ⅓ cup honey, olive oil, vinegar, and soy sauce. Toss the dressing with the salad and refrigerate to chill.

6. Just before serving, chop the cashews and toss them into the salad.

Serves 8 to 10

2 tablespoons plus ⅓ cup honey
¾ cup unsalted cashews
⅛ teaspoon cayenne pepper
¼ teaspoon salt
½ pound bacon or turkey bacon strips
1 medium-large head broccoli
1 medium-large head cauliflower
1 red onion, chopped
⅔ cup dried currants or raisins
½ cup canola mayonnaise
¼ cup extra-virgin olive oil
¼ cup cider vinegar
1 tablespoon soy sauce

broccolini

71

brussels sprouts

LIKE BROCCOLI, Brussels sprouts are members of the cabbage family; indeed, many a keen-eyed child has observed just how much just they look like tiny heads of cabbage. Brussels sprouts grow along sturdy stalks, and you can sometimes find them sold in farmers' markets this way, lined up in rows on the stalks like tiny soldiers.

Brussels sprouts are terrific when roasted with olive oil and a touch of kosher salt. They also make a lovely braised dish, as in Cider-Braised Brussels Sprouts (page 73). Many people sing the praises of Brussels sprouts cooked with bacon; others prefer using lemon. *New York Times* food writer Mark Bittman once held a taste-off between the two methods and decided the lemony approach had won the day.

Good for Your Family Because . . .

BRUSSELS SPROUTS are nutritional powerhouses, boasting robust amounts of vitamins C, K, A, B_6, and B_1, as well as the minerals folate, manganese, potassium, iron, and phosphorous. Best of all, Brussels sprouts are rich in sulforaphane, a phytonutrient that appears to protect the body against disease and prevent DNA damage.

Selection and Storage

BRUSSELS SPROUTS are in season from fall through early winter in most climates. Look for small, firm Brussels sprouts that are still closed. Sprouts can be very different sizes; to ensure uniform cooking, pick sprouts that are of a similar size. Store fresh, unwashed sprouts in plastic bags in the vegetable bin of the refrigerator. For best flavor, cook within a few days of purchase. Brussels sprouts grow far above the ground, so they do not require intense cleaning. Because the leaves cook faster than the core, it's a good idea to notch a small X into the bottom of each sprout so that they cook evenly.

Cider-Braised Brussels Sprouts

This recipe uses the sweetness of autumn cider to mellow the flavor of the sprouts.

1. Cut the Brussels sprouts in half. Set them in a large saucepan, and add enough water to just cover the sprouts. Bring to a boil, then reduce the heat and simmer, covered, until the sprouts are bright green and tender but still firm, about 7 minutes.

2. Heat the oil in a large skillet over medium heat. Add the onion and sauté until translucent, 4 to 5 minutes. Add the garlic and sprouts and continue cooking until the garlic has softened but not browned, about 3 minutes.

3. Pour in the cider, increase the heat to high, and simmer until the cider is reduced by half and the sprouts are tender, adding a splash more water if necessary. Season with salt and pepper, and serve warm.

Serves 6

1½ pounds Brussels sprouts (about 6 cups), tough stems and outer leaves removed
1 tablespoon extra-virgin olive oil
½ small red onion, chopped
1 garlic clove, minced
⅓ cup apple cider
Salt and freshly ground black pepper

cabbage

Scientists at the ARS
Beltsville Human
Nutrition Research
Center identified 36
different anthocyanin
compounds in red
cabbage. Research
on these compounds
suggests that they
may provide cancer
protection, improve
brain function, and
promote heart health.

CABBAGE COMES IN SEVERAL VARIETIES, from the green and red types typically seen in coleslaw to Chinese cabbages such as **napa** (mild flavored, with light green leaves) and **bok choy** (dark green leaves with juicy white stems). A favorite is **choy sum**, or flowering bok choy, leafy greens, delicate stems, and yellow flowers.

While slaws are likely the most common way to enjoy cabbage, the vegetable is great in stir-fries, stews, soups, braised dishes, and meat dishes. Chinese types can be prepared more like greens, with a quick sauté. Overcooking cabbage can make for a less-than-appetizing smell. Slaws with a sweet dressing or cabbage and fruit dishes (such as Braised Red Cabbage with Blueberries, Raisins, and Goat Cheese, on page 75) have the most appeal for kids.

Good for Your Family Because . . .

THE NUTRITION content will vary depending on the type of cabbage. Red cabbage tops the list in nutrition, with a higher content of vitamin C and a high content of the phytonutrients called anthocyanins, which give red cabbage its color. Cabbages have shown some anticancer properties, and they are rich in vitamins C and K. Dark, leafy cabbages will be higher in vitamin A than light green cabbage.

Selection and Storage

CABBAGE is in season in spring, with a second season possible in the fall for many climates. Red and green cabbage heads should be firm, dense, and heavy for their size, with shiny outer leaves that are not cracked or bruised. Leafy types should have firm, not wilted, leaves. For the best nutrient content, buy cabbage whole, not preshredded. Heads of cabbage will keep for a week or more, in a bag, in the refrigerator crisper. More delicate leafy cabbages will not keep as long.

Braised Red Cabbage with Blueberries, Raisins, and Goat Cheese

Red cabbage gives this dish visual appeal and a nutritious punch. The subtle spice used here pairs well with sweet blueberries and raisins and gives the dish more kid-friendly appeal that adults will like as well. The creamy goat cheese makes a nice finish, but if you are watching fats, you can skip it and still have a delicious result.

1. Heat the oil in a Dutch oven or large pot over medium-high heat. Add the cabbage and onion and sauté until they wilt, about 3 minutes.

2. Add the apple juice, vinegar, blueberries, and raisins, and stir to combine. Add the bay leaf, cinnamon stick, cloves, and fennel seed to the pot. Continue to cook until the juice is absorbed and the cabbage is softened, about 10 minutes longer.

3. Season with salt and pepper. Remove the bay leaf and cinnamon stick. Serve warm, with the goat cheese crumbled on top.

Serves 8 to 10

2 tablespoons extra-virgin olive oil
1 head red cabbage, halved, tough core removed, and sliced into shreds
1 red onion, sliced
½ cup apple juice
¼ cup balsamic vinegar
¼ cup dried blueberries
¼ cup raisins
1 bay leaf
1 cinnamon stick
⅛ teaspoon ground cloves
⅛ teaspoon fennel seed
Salt and freshly ground black pepper
4 ounces fresh goat cheese

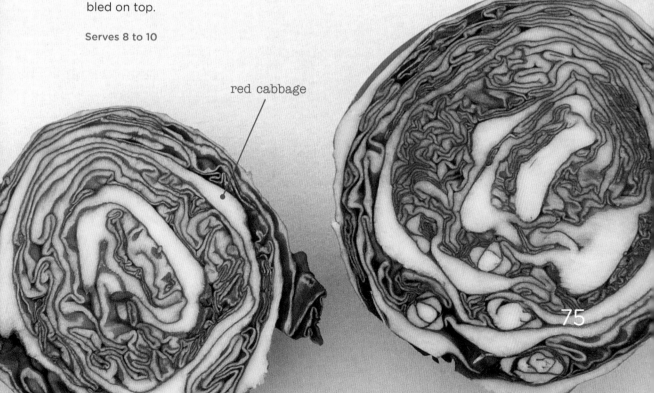

red cabbage

75

carrots

CARROTS ARE RELATED TO OTHER VEGETABLES and herbs with feathery tops such as parsnips, fennel, cumin, and dill. Orange is the most familiar color, but heirloom varieties produce carrots in white, yellow, red, and purple hues as well as diminutive, round **Parisienne** varieties. Purple carrots are thought to be the original variety cultivated thousands of years ago.

Raw carrot sticks or "baby" carrots with ranch dip or other dressings are a familiar kid-friendly dish. Shredded carrots make a great slaw (see Carrot-Raisin Slaw, below) and can be used in baked goods. One of the most kid-friendly preparations is Carrot-Orange Soufflé (page 135), which tastes almost like dessert.

GET COOKING!

Carrot-Raisin Slaw

This tasty slaw is served cold, so it makes a good lunchbox dish. The raisins and citrus dressing make it even more kid-friendly and a nice change from plain cooked carrots.

4 large carrots (about ¾ pound), shredded
½ cup shredded jicama, apple, or kohlrabi
1 cup raisins
1 tablespoon lemon juice
1 tablespoon orange juice
1 tablespoon white balsamic vinegar
3 tablespoons canola oil
2 tablespoons honey
Salt and freshly ground black pepper

1. Combine the carrots, jicama, and raisins in a medium bowl and toss to mix.

2. Whisk together the lemon juice, orange juice, vinegar, oil, and honey in a small bowl or cup, and season with salt and pepper. Pour over the slaw ingredients and stir to mix. Cover and refrigerate for a few hours to chill and allow the flavors to blend.

Serves 4 to 6

Good for Your Family Because . . .

CARROTS are rock stars when it comes to vitamin A as beta-carotene, offering almost seven times the recommended daily value in each one-cup serving. Beta-carotene consumption is associated with cardiovascular health, anticancer properties, and helping prevent age-related macular (eye) degeneration. Cooking carrots makes their beta-carotene more available. The antioxidant-rich vegetables also have vitamins K and C as well as B vitamins, and they are a good source of fiber.

Selection and Storage

LOOK FOR carrots at the farmers' market from summer through fall for most climates. Choose carrots with firm, deep-colored roots. Avoid those that are cracked or damaged. The root should not be rubbery or limp. If the greens are attached, these should be bright green and not wilted.

Like beets, the tops of the carrots should be removed before storing so they do not pull moisture away from the roots, causing them to wilt quickly. Store carrots in a bag in the coolest part of the refrigerator. They should keep for about two weeks. Be sure to store them away from apples or other produce that releases ethylene gas. This will cause the carrots to become bitter and not last as long.

Purple Haze carrots

cauliflower

CAULIFLOWER IS CLOSELY RELATED TO BROCCOLI but lacks the budded florets. Instead, the top part of the vegetable, called the curd, is smoother and dense with undeveloped flower buds. Most commonly cauliflower is white, as its outer leaves prevent the center curd from being exposed to sunlight and developing chlorophyll. Other varieties of cauliflower can be found often at farmers' markets, with colors that include yellow-orange and a deep violet.

Because of its mild flavor, cauliflower plays well with spice, particularly curry. It can be roasted with spices or steamed and puréed to add to a mash of mixed root vegetables. It is good in soups and stews as well. Its flavor is best when it's not overcooked. Actually, it's not good at all when it's overcooked, which explains why some adults won't touch it. Try, try again. Really.

Good for Your Family Because . . .

CAULIFLOWER is a good source of vitamin C, folate, and dietary fiber in addition to the cancer-fighting phytonutrients common to cruciferous vegetables. Colored varieties may be higher in phytonutrients than the white variety, especially the purple cultivar, which contains the same anthocyanins found in red wine and red cabbage.

Selection and Storage

LIKE BROCCOLI, cauliflower is usually a spring crop. Look for heads with a dense, firm curd. Avoid heads that have spots or whose bud clusters are separated. Cauliflower can be stored in a bag in the refrigerator for up to a week.

Honey-Spice Roasted Cauliflower

When faced with more challenging vegetables, a bit of spice, a bit of sweet, and a whole lot of heat — that is, roasting — can make all the difference in winning over picky eaters. This recipe offers the benefits of both steaming and roasting. For larger heads of cauliflower, make a double batch of the spice rub and cut the head in half before roasting.

1. Preheat the oven to 400°F.

2. Whisk together the honey, oil, cumin, salt, black pepper, cayenne, lemon juice, and lemon zest in a small bowl. Rub the mixture over the head of the cauliflower.

3. Place the cauliflower in a baking dish. Pour the water into the dish.

4. Roast the cauliflower for 15 minutes, then turn it over and roast for 10 to 15 minutes longer, until it is golden brown.

5. Cut into florets or slices and serve.

Serves 4

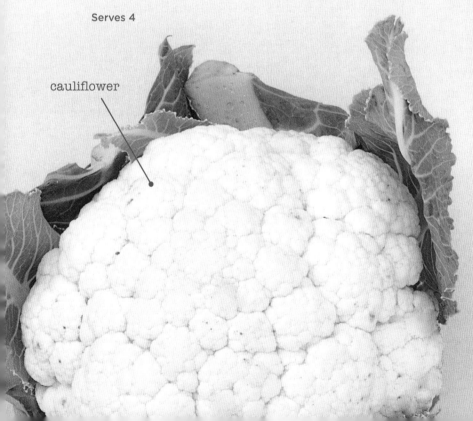

cauliflower

CAULIFLOWER

GET COOKING!

2 tablespoons honey
2 tablespoons extra-virgin olive oil
½ teaspoon ground cumin
½ teaspoon kosher salt
2 grinds black pepper
Pinch of cayenne pepper
Zest and juice of 1 lemon
1 small head cauliflower
¼ cup water

How to Zest a Lemon

There are several tools you can use to remove the zest. A traditional zester creates long thin strands of zest. A Microplane, like a cheese grater, creates shavings. You can also use a vegetable peeler, a knife, or the finest part of your cheese grater. However you do it, though, zest carefully. The zest layer is shallow, and beneath it lies the pith, the bitter white part of the peel. Even a little bit of the pith can lend a bitter undertone to your dish. One medium lemon generally creates a tablespoon of zest.

chard

CHARD, SOMETIMES KNOWN AS SWISS CHARD, is a leafy green with colorful stalks of green, white, red, yellow, or orange; pairing stalks of different colors gives the bunch the name "rainbow" chard. The flavor of chard is similar to that of spinach. Both the leaves and the tender parts of the stalk are edible.

Chard pairs well with pasta, cheese, and eggs, and it can be freely substituted for cooked spinach in recipes. These types of recipes are probably your best bet for introducing this green to kids and those occasional "vegephobic" adults as well — you know who they are.

Good for Your Family Because . . .

CHARD earns excellent marks for its concentrations of vitamin K, beta-carotene, vitamin C, magnesium, manganese, potassium, iron, vitamin E, and dietary fiber. Chard is also rich in phytonutrients like anthocyanins.

Selection and Storage

CHARD is typically in season during spring and early summer, with a brief second season possible in some climates that allow for a fall planting. The leaves and stalks should be crisp, not wilted, and should not have brown or yellow spots. Store chard in an airtight bag in the refrigerator crisper. It will keep for a few days.

Delicata-Chard "Side-or-Sauce"

CHARD

GET COOKING!

This recipe, a staple in Ali's house, pairs chard with delicata squash. Not only is the resulting salty-sweet combination delicious, it is also colorful and gorgeous. Other varieties of chard will taste just as good; the red variety will make the dish beautiful. Though you can use other varieties of squash, delicata is by far the simplest option because it does not need to be peeled, making preparation a snap. To convert this recipe to a main dish, toss with pasta and top with grated Parmesan cheese and toasted pine nuts.

1 large (12-ounce) bunch red chard
2 tablespoons extra-virgin olive oil
1 small delicata squash, seeded and chopped into ½-inch cubes
2 garlic cloves, chopped
½ cup chicken broth
1 tablespoon balsamic vinegar
  Kosher or sea salt and freshly ground black pepper

1. Separate the stems from the leaves of the chard. Chop the stems. Cut the leaves into chiffonade by rolling each into a cigar shape and cutting it horizontally into long strips.

2. Heat the oil in a large skillet over medium-high heat, then add the squash in a single layer. Cook, tossing occasionally, until the squash begins to soften, about 5 minutes.

3. Add the garlic and the chard stems. Sauté for 2 minutes, then add the broth and vinegar. Simmer until the squash is tender, about 4 minutes longer. Add the chard leaves and sauté just until they begin to wilt, about 2 minutes. Season with salt and pepper.

Serves 6

red chard

cucumber

CUCUMBERS BELONG TO THE SAME FAMILY as summer squash, zucchini, and watermelon. Most grocery stores carry only two kinds: the wax-coated variety with shiny, dark green skin and large seeds, and the long, seedless English variety, shrink-wrapped in plastic. If you hit the farmers' market, though, you'll find lots of other kinds. Among these lesser-known cucumbers are the variegated crispy **Armenian** cucumber, the small bumpy **Kirby** cucumber, and the surprising **lemon** cucumber, which looks like a lemon and is sweeter and more flavorful than other cucumbers.

Cucumber sticks with a touch of salt are a perennial kid favorite. Cucumbers also work beautifully in gazpachos, in salads, and with dips. For a refreshing spin on hydration, take a tip from the world's finest spas: add some sliced cucumbers to iced water. We've even tasted cucumber lemonade: puréed cucumber (seeds removed), lemon, sugar, and water. Now that's refreshment!

Some recipes require you to remove some of the water from cucumbers. To do this, simply slice the cucumbers, place in a colander, sprinkle with salt, and let sit for 30 minutes. Then rinse with cold water.

Good for Your Family Because . . .

CUCUMBERS are about 90 percent water, making them a great way to get some extra fluids into your family during the hot summer months. Cucumbers are also a decent source of vitamin A, vitamin C, pantothenic acid, magnesium, phosphorous, vitamin K, and potassium.

Selection and Storage

CUCUMBERS are in season in the summer months, when their cool, refreshing flavor is quite welcome. Select firm cucumbers that do not have blemishes or soft spots. Smaller cucumbers generally have fewer seeds than their larger brethren. Supermarket cucumbers are often covered with a wax coating to protect them during shipping; in this case, you'll want to peel the cucumber before serving. If you're buying organic cucumbers directly from the farm, it's fine to leave the skins on; just wash the cucumbers before using.

GET COOKING!

Basil-Mint Cucumbers

This recipe is incredibly refreshing on a warm day, and the herbs and red pepper flakes give it a nice twist.

1. Combine the vinegar and sugar in a small bowl, and stir until the sugar is dissolved.

2. Place the cucumber strips in a medium bowl. Pour the vinegar mixture over the cucumbers, and sprinkle with the mint, basil, and red pepper flakes, if desired. Cover and refrigerate for at least 2 hours, until well chilled.

Serves 4

½ cup white wine vinegar
2 tablespoons sugar
1 large cucumber, peeled, seeded, and sliced into ½- by 3-inch strips
1 tablespoon chopped fresh mint
1 tablespoon chopped fresh basil
¼ teaspoon crushed red pepper flakes (optional)

lemon cucumber

eggplant

EGGPLANTS ARE A MEMBER OF THE NIGHTSHADE FAMILY, like sweet peppers, tomatoes, and potatoes. The most familiar eggplant is the deep purple, elongated, large pear-shaped variety. However, eggplants can be found in other colors and shapes, such as green eggplants, egg-shaped white eggplants, long and thin **Japanese eggplants**, mini **Italian eggplants**, and even small, round, white and green mottled **Thai eggplants**. **White eggplants** are generally less bitter than the deep purple variety.

Eggplant flesh is spongelike and will quickly absorb cooking oil as well as the other flavors in a dish. For kids, the best introduction is often eggplant parmesan (see page 234), with its crisp bread crumb coating, cheese topping, and tomato sauce. Another kid-friendly approach is to sauté diced eggplant and zucchini and add these as a layer of vegetables in a lasagna. Asian varieties go well in a curry, and the vegetable is a main ingredient in the now-famous French dish ratatouille (see page 86).

To reduce the bitterness of some eggplant varieties, you may want to salt it. To do this, peel the eggplant and cut to the desired size. Place in a colander and lightly salt the eggplant. Leave it to drain for about

> " Eaters . . . must understand that eating takes place inescapably in the world, that it is inescapably an agricultural act, and that how we eat determines, to a considerable extent, how the world is used. "
>
> Wendell Berry, "The Pleasures of Eating," from The Art of the Commonplace

30 minutes, then rinse off the salt and pat dry. It should be less bitter and absorb less oil in cooking after this step.

Good for Your Family Because . . .

EGGPLANTS, particularly the dark purple varieties, contain phytonutrients that function as antioxidants, including phenolic compounds and flavonoids. They contain the phytochemical monoterpene, which may be helpful in preventing the growth of cancer cells. Eggplants are a good source of dietary fiber, potassium, manganese, copper, calcium, phosphorous, and thiamin (vitamin B_1).

Selection and Storage

EGGPLANTS are in season during the summer months through September, alongside tomatoes, peppers, and summer squash — which all pair beautifully with it in dishes. Choose eggplants that have vivid color and smooth skin that is free of blemishes and bruises. They should be firm and heavy for their size, with a bright green stem. Be sure to discard the stem and leaves; they are toxic.

You can store whole eggplants in a bag in the vegetable crisper of the refrigerator for several days.

Japanese

fairy tale

85

1 pound eggplant, diced into ½-inch cubes

½ teaspoon kosher salt

2 tablespoons olive oil

1 large onion, chopped

3 garlic cloves, chopped

1 red bell pepper, sliced julienne

1 green bell pepper, sliced julienne

½ pound baby okra, tops cut off and halved lengthwise (optional)

2½ pounds deep-red-fleshed heirloom tomatoes, such as Beefsteak or Cherokee Purple, or a mix of different colors for great flavor, quartered

½ pound zucchini, diced into ½-inch cubes

½ pound yellow squash, diced into ½-inch cubes

2 tablespoons red wine vinegar

1 tablespoon sugar

⅛ teaspoon red pepper flakes or hot sauce (optional)

Salt and freshly ground black pepper

Roasted Ratatouille

This dish is great served with roasted chicken and sourdough bread, but it makes a meal of its own without any meat. It can even be served cold the next morning with a fried egg on top and a dash of hot sauce for an amazing breakfast. There's nothing like getting in a serving of veggies before your day gets busy. Okra is not a traditional ingredient, but it gives the dish a Cajun twist; there's also a bit of heat from the red pepper flakes. For more heat, offer Louisiana Hot Sauce on the side.

1. Preheat the oven to 400°F.

2. Sprinkle the eggplant with salt and set aside in a colander to drain for at least 30 minutes. Rinse, drain, and pat dry.

3. Meanwhile, heat the oil over medium heat in a large Dutch oven or ovenproof skillet. Sweat the onion and garlic about 5 minutes (sweating uses lower heat than sautéing; you only want to release flavor here, not brown the aromatics). Add the bell pepper and continue to sweat the vegetables for another 5 minutes. Add the okra, if desired, and sweat for 10 minutes longer, stirring occasionally.

4. Add the tomatoes and smash a bit with the spoon. Stir in the diced eggplant, zucchini, yellow squash, vinegar, sugar, and red pepper flakes, if desired. Set the pot, uncovered, in the oven and bake for 30 to 40 minutes, stirring halfway through the cooking time, until the vegetables are browned just a bit on the edges. Season with salt and pepper.

Serves 8 to 10

WHILE NOT OFFICIALLY VEGETABLES, herbs can be used in place of, or in addition to, salad greens, as in a Caprese salad pairing basil with mozzarella and tomatoes. Few ingredients so escalate a dish from ordinary to extraordinary like fresh herbs.

Herbs are easy to grow in containers on a windowsill, making them perfect for a kitchen garden. They also can form the basis of a starter garden to get kids interested in growing food. In our personal experience, herbs fall into the "hard to kill" plant category — a good quality for young gardeners and those adults cursed with a "black thumb."

Good for Your Family Because . . .

WHILE NOT GENERALLY recognized as "health foods," herbs are worth exploring for their interesting history in medicinal uses as well as for the flavor they add to everyday meals. Basil offers flavonoids and has antibacterial properties. Rosemary's anti-inflammatory compounds were historically thought to improve circulation and memory. Sage is a proven mood-booster, and thyme has been shown to have some antimicrobial properties.

Selection and Storage

HERBS can be available all year round, depending on where and how they're grown. Many can be dried for use in the winter months. The least expensive option for fresh herbs is to keep a small garden. If you're purchasing herbs, select those that appear fresh, not wilted, and that have no dark spots or yellowing.

Most herbs store best when wrapped in a damp paper towel and stored in a bag in the vegetable crisper of the refrigerator. Use within a few days. Dried varieties should be kept in sealed glass containers away from light.

87

HERBS

GET COOKING!

1 shallot, peeled and thinly sliced
1 tablespoon tarragon vinegar or white balsamic vinegar
2 cups red grapes, sliced lengthwise
⅓ cup fresh tarragon leaves
3 ounces ricotta salata cheese
2 tablespoons extra-virgin olive oil
   Freshly ground black pepper

Tarragon, Red Grape, and Ricotta Salata Salad

This is a unique salad that uses herbs instead of salad greens. It has gotten a few skeptical looks, but once tasted, it becomes a favorite for guests. Ricotta salata is a pressed, salted version of ricotta that can be shaved or grated.

1. Combine the shallot with the vinegar in a small bowl, leaving it to marinate for about 20 minutes while you prepare the other ingredients.

2. Combine the grapes with the tarragon in a medium bowl. Shave the cheese over the salad (you can use a vegetable peeler to do this). Add the olive oil and the vinegar mixture and toss gently to coat. Season with pepper.

Serves 4

dill

thyme

tarragon

rosemary

88

kale

FORGET WHAT YOU MAY HAVE HEARD about kale; Ali's daughter confidently declares kale her "favorite vegetable ever." And it's no wonder: Kale is versatile and tasty, lending itself to both healthy soups and tasty snacks.

Kale is a member of the cabbage family, like collards and Brussels sprouts. This leafy green has a firm texture, so it is best cooked. Its strong flavor pairs well with garlic and sweet flavors such as winter squashes.

The leafy greens (cabbage, chard, collards, kale, spinach, and so on) are the vegetables most kids are missing in their diets, so you'll want to introduce a few servings into your family menu on a regular basis. Salt and Vinegar Kale Chips (page 241) is a good way to start children's relationship with leafy greens. They are enough like chips that kids can get past the green color . . . as well as their sneaking suspicion that you are trying to torture them with dinner.

Good for Your Family Because . . .

THE CABBAGE family is a nutritional powerhouse. Kale is very high in beta-carotene, vitamin A, vitamin K, and vitamin C, and it is rich in fiber and absorbable calcium. It also contains folic acid, vitamin B_6, manganese, and potassium.

purple kale

As if that weren't enough, kale also offers sulfur-containing phytonutrients, which are associated with a lower risk of cancer, including breast and ovarian cancers. Want more? Kale is great for growing healthy bones, boosting vision, keeping the immune system strong, and keeping lungs, joints, and hearts healthy.

Selection and Storage

KALE is in season from late winter through early spring, with a second late-fall crop available where weather permits. Look for firm leaves without any wilting or brown or yellow spots. Younger kale, with smaller leaves, will have a milder flavor.

For the best storage, wrap kale in a damp paper towel, seal in a plastic bag, and store in the refrigerator's vegetable crisper. Kale will keep for a few days.

Garlicky White Beans and Kale

3 tablespoons extra-virgin olive oil

2 garlic cloves, minced

⅛ teaspoon crushed red pepper flakes (optional)

1 bunch kale (about 12 ounces, or 6 stems), washed, stems removed

3 cups cooked cannellini or other white beans, including cooking liquid, or 2 (15-ounce) cans

1 tablespoon chopped fresh flat-leaf parsley (optional)

Sea salt and freshly ground black pepper

This easy dish pairs the sharp flavor of kale with the creaminess of cannellini beans. It works well on its own as a vegetarian main course or side dish, or you can add chicken sausage for a one-dish meal.

1. Heat the oil in a large skillet over medium heat. Add the garlic and red pepper, if desired, and sauté until the garlic begins to turn golden, about 3 minutes. Increase the heat to medium-high. Add the kale, turning to coat it with the oil, and sauté just until the kale begins to wilt, about 3 minutes. Transfer the kale to a bowl.

2. Add the beans and their liquid to the skillet and bring to a vigorous simmer. Return the kale to the pan and heat thoroughly, mixing it with the beans. Sprinkle on the parsley, if desired. Season with salt and pepper.

Serves 6 as a side dish or 4 as a main course

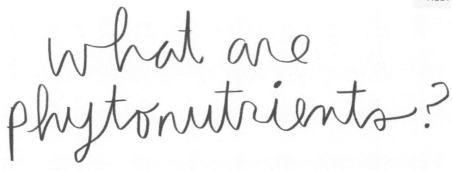

what are phytonutrients?

Phytonutrients are organic components found in plants that are thought to promote great health. They help the plant fight disease and stay healthy in an array of conditions; when you eat the plant, those healthy benefits are transferred to you. Phytonutrients support the immune system, have anti-cancer and antiaging properties, repair DNA damage, and enhance cell-to-cell communication.

Types of phytochemicals include carotenoids and flavonoids. Carotenoids include beta-carotene, lutein, and lycopene, which are thought to protect against certain cancers, heart disease, and age-related macular degeneration. Carotenoids are found in red and orange vegetables and fruits like citrus, tomatoes, watermelon, carrots, sweet potatoes, and winter squash, as well as in leafy greens.

Flavonoids include anthocyanins and isoflavones. Anthocyanins are the powerful antioxidants that give grapes and red cabbage their color and are also found in tea. Anthocyanins are currently being studied for their health effects against cancer, aging, diabetes, and inflammation. Isoflavones, a class of phytoestrogens, are found mainly in the legume family. Isoflavones are under study for their potential link to decreased risk of prostate cancer. They also have a limited impact on lowering bad (LDL) cholesterol.

> "To date, researchers have discovered more than ten thousand phytochemicals. No supplement can contain a sufficient amount. Thankfully, you can get all these nutrients today by eating a wide variety of plant-based foods."
>
> Joel Furman, MD, Eat to Live: The Revolutionary Formula for Fast and Sustained Weight Loss, Little Brown and Company, 2005.

91

lettuces

LETTUCE CAN BE FOUND in amazing variety, from crispy romaine to head lettuces like iceberg and leaf lettuces like butter. Lettuces are most often used when preparing salads, but many types of greens used in salads are not true lettuces (and some aren't even green). These include things like mâche, arugula, watercress, radicchio, endive, and frisée. Even herbs can be used as salad greens.

When preparing salads, using a mix of greens offers the best flavor and variety, creating an interesting salad. To woo kids, try topping salads with dried or fresh fruits, croutons, and cheeses. Sometimes it may take more toppings than greens, but give it time. The right dressing can make a big difference, too (see page 95).

Good for Your Family Because . . .

THE NUTRITIONAL content of lettuces varies according to type. Iceberg lettuce offers the least nutritional value, while romaine lettuce is a good source of vitamins A and C and folate. In general, the darker and leafier the lettuce, the more nutrition it offers.

Selection and Storage

LETTUCE is in season from spring through early summer, and then often again in the fall. Look for crisp leaves with no brown spots — with the exception of the speckled romaine variety — or any type of slimy coating. Cut lettuces should not have brown ends on the stems.

Don't trust that just because lettuce is bagged, it is ready to eat; it's always a good idea to wash lettuce before eating. A recent study showed that even "triple-washed" lettuce can contain surprising amounts of bacteria. To wash, immerse the lettuce leaves in a bowl of fresh water, and swish around to loosen any dirt. Rinse two or three

LETTUCES

mâche

Boston lettuce

watercress

red-leaf lettuce

93

arugula

times. Then dry in a salad spinner or by folding it into a towel. To store, set in a bag with a paper towel to absorb the excess moisture, removing the extra air from the bag before sealing, and then store in the refrigerator, where it will keep for a few days.

Fat-Free Dressings?

Why shouldn't you use fat-free dressings? Because a number of vitamins — A, D, E, and K — are fat soluble, meaning that they are absorbed by the digestive sytem only with the help of the lipids found in fat.

The same is true for micronutrients. A study published in the *American Journal of Clinical Nutrition* measured the absorption of lycopene, alpha-carotene, and beta-carotene after eating identical salad meals with no-fat, reduced-fat, and full-fat dressings. Despite the rich amount of the nutrients in the salads, the subjects who ate the fat-free dressings absorbed no beta-carotene whatsoever and had significantly less absorption of the other nutrients.

Besides, a little fat goes a long way toward making you feel full longer. Without sufficient fat, you'll find your stomach rumbling just a short time after you eat.

Cantaloupe and Honey Salad

4 cups mixed torn lettuces or arugula
1 small cantaloupe (1⅓ cups), diced in ¾ inch cubes
1 cup pecan halves
½ cup extra-virgin olive oil
¼ cup honey
¼ cup white balsamic vinegar
  Salt and freshly ground black pepper
  Blue cheese crumbles (optional)

Beth's daughter mixed this dressing — a great task for kids learning to cook. After turning away for a moment, Beth discovered that her helper had the bowl up and was drinking out of it. The dressing is pretty good.

1. Arrange the greens on a platter, and top with the cantaloupe and pecans.

2. Whisk together the oil, honey, and vinegar in a small bowl or cup, and season with salt and pepper. Dress the salad with as much of the dressing as you prefer. There may be some extra, which you can store in the refrigerator to use on your next salad. This salad is fantastic with a sprinkle of blue cheese, if desired.

94

Serves 8

Make-Your-Own Salad Dressings: Tastier, More Healthful, Less Expensive

One of the easiest ways to eliminate processed foods is to skip the prepared salad dressings in stores and make your own instead. It's more healthful, less expensive, and plenty easy. The basic formula for a vinaigrette doesn't change: It's two parts oil (usually olive or canola) to one part acid (like vinegar or citrus juice). Beyond that, other ingredients add flavor and seasoning.

Basic Mix for 1 Cup Dressing

⅔ cup oil, such as olive, canola, walnut, sesame, or flaxseed
⅓ cup acid, such as red wine vinegar, balsamic vinegar, white wine vinegar, or citrus juice
  Seasoning to taste, such as salt, pepper, fresh or dried herbs, or fresh or dried spices
1 teaspoon to 1 tablespoon of flavoring, such as alliums, mustards, wasabi, honey, or preserves

Whisk together your chosen ingredients. Store any leftovers in the refrigerator.

Following are some examples of how this formula can be varied.

Fig Balsamic Vinaigrette

⅔ cup extra-virgin olive oil
⅓ cup balsamic vinegar
1 tablespoon fig jam (or blueberry, blackberry, or raspberry)
  Salt and freshly ground black pepper

Blackberry Balsamic Vinaigrette

⅔ cup extra-virgin olive oil
⅓ cup balsamic vinegar
1 tablespoon blackberry preserves
  Salt and freshly ground black pepper

Stone-Ground Mustard Vinaigrette

⅔ cup extra-virgin olive oil (for a tangier blend, use a bit less)
⅓ cup red wine vinegar
1 tablespoon stone-ground mustard
  Salt and freshly ground black pepper

95

peppers

BELL PEPPERS come from the same botanical genus as hot peppers but have a recessive gene that eliminates capsaicin, the compound that creates hot peppers' heat. Red, yellow, orange, and green are the most familiar colors, but bell peppers can also be purple, chocolate brown, and even a deep, gothic black.

Many kids consider pepper strips with fun dips a great snack. Because of their sweet flavor, peppers (especially red peppers) are generally kid-friendly.

Good for Your Family Because . . .

THE NUTRITIONAL content of bell peppers will vary depending on the color of the pepper. Green peppers are a good source of folate and vitamin K. Red peppers top the charts for vitamin C content, with more than 100 percent of the daily value in a cup. Red peppers are also rich in lycopene and beta-carotene.

Selection and Storage

BELL PEPPERS are in season at the height of summer's heat, from late July through September. Peppers should have a deep color and smooth skin that's free of wrinkles, blemishes, and soft spots. They should be firm to the touch, with fresh-looking stems.

Store peppers in the vegetable crisper of the refrigerator. They will keep for up to a week, with green peppers generally keeping slightly longer than yellow or red ones.

96

Roasted Summer Vegetables

This medley of summer's best and sweetest vegetables tastes great with or without the sun-dried tomato pesto. It makes a fantastic side for serving a crowd. Or you can add cooked pasta or tortellini to make it a full meal.

1. Preheat the oven to 475°F.

2. Coat two baking sheets with cooking spray. Place the tomatoes and artichoke hearts on one baking sheet. Place the peppers, shallots, and mushrooms on the other baking sheet.

3. Whisk the vinegar and olive oil together in a small bowl. Pour half the oil and vinegar mixture over each of the two vegetable mixtures and toss to coat.

4. Place both baking sheets in the oven. Roast the tomatoes and artichoke hearts for 10 minutes. Remove from the oven. Turn the vegetables on the tray with the peppers and mushrooms and roast for 10 minutes longer.

5. Mix the vegetables together in a large bowl. Add the pesto, if desired, and toss to coat. Season to taste with salt and pepper. Garnish with the Parmesan before serving.

Serves 8

1 pound cherry tomatoes, halved lengthwise and seeded, or larger tomatoes, cored, seeded, and diced

1 (15-ounce) can artichoke hearts, drained

3 large red, yellow, or orange bell peppers

4 shallots, peeled and halved

2 large portobello mushroom caps, cut into ½-inch pieces

½ cup balsamic vinegar

2 tablespoons extra-virgin olive oil

Salt and freshly ground black pepper

½ batch Sun-Dried Tomato Pesto (optional; see recipe below)

¼ cup grated Parmesan cheese

Sun-Dried Tomato Pesto

Store leftover pesto, with a bit of olive oil on top, in an airtight container in the refrigerator for up to a week.

Toss the basil, sun-dried tomatoes, Parmesan, pine nuts, goat cheese, garlic, and salt and pepper to taste into a food processor and pulse until chopped, but not total mush. This works well with Roasted Summer Vegetables and also as a topping for bruschetta or pastas like cheese tortellini.

Makes about 1½ cups

1 cup packed fresh basil leaves

½ cup sun-dried tomatoes packed in oil (shake excess oil off, but do not rinse)

¼ cup grated Parmesan cheese

2 tablespoons pine nuts

1 tablespoon goat cheese

1 garlic clove

Salt and freshly ground black pepper

potatoes

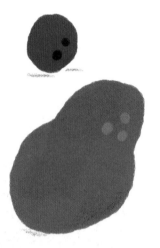

OKAY, SO POTATOES ARE THE ONE VEGETABLE that kids are actually eating *too* much of — mostly in the form of French fries. But when removed from their deep-fried, served-with-a-side-of-ketchup context, potatoes are versatile, tasty, and surprisingly nutritious.

There are about 5,000 varieties of potatoes, from the blushing **Rose Fin Apple** fingerling to the jewel-toned **Purple Viking**. Traditional potatoes tend to fall into two categories: boiling and baking. Boiling potatoes, like red potatoes and fingerlings, tend to have more moisture and waxier skins, with less starch. These potatoes hold their shape better for casseroles and salads but don't mash particularly well. Baking potatoes, like russets, have more starch and drier skins and give you lighter, fluffier mashed and baked potatoes. New potatoes can be any variety; they are simply younger and more tender than mature potatoes. As such, they often are good for baking whole. See an unusual-looking variety of potato at the farmers' market? Ask the farmer how it's best prepared.

Good for Your Family Because . . .

BECAUSE OF their high carbohydrate count, potatoes have been dismissed as unhealthful. Yet potatoes are good sources of vitamin C, vitamin B_6, selenium, potassium, manganese, and fiber. Potatoes also contain several phytochemicals that work as antioxidants, including carotenoids, flavonoids, and caffeic acid. In fact, researchers have found 60 different kinds of phytochemicals and vitamins in the skins and flesh of 100 wild and commercially grown potatoes. Among these are kukoamines, which can help lower blood pressure and which otherwise have been discovered only in a medicinal plant from China.

new potato

banana
fingerling

white potato

red potato

red fingerling

99

Selection and Storage

YOU CAN find potatoes in season at farmers' markets in early summer, as well as fall in some climates. Look for potatoes that are firm, without withered skin, sprouts, or green flesh. If there is dirt on the potatoes, leave it during storage; this dirt actually forms a protective "coat" for the potato. Store potatoes in a dark, cool location away from onions. A paper bag with holes, or a burlap bag, works well for holding them. Do not keep potatoes in the refrigerator, however, as the temperature will be too cold and their starches will turn to sugars. New potatoes keep only for a week, while regular potatoes, if stored properly, can keep for up to two or three months. Before using, scrub well and remove any sprouts or green flesh.

Golden Roasted Potatoes

1½ pounds new potatoes, skin on, scrubbed, and cut into ¾-inch cubes

1 garlic clove, minced

3 tablespoons extra-virgin olive oil

1 tablespoon lemon juice

1 tablespoon fresh rosemary, or 1 teaspoon dried

1 teaspoon coarse salt

1 tablespoon finely chopped fresh flat-leaf parsley or chives (optional)

Roasted potatoes are a tried-and-true kid favorite. They're more healthful than fries, and they present an opportunity to introduce new flavors, like this garlic, lemon, and rosemary combination. Over time, you can begin replacing some of the potatoes in this recipe with other root vegetables, like carrots, beets, and parsnips.

1. Preheat the oven to 425°F.

2. Place the potatoes and garlic in a large bowl. Whisk together the oil and lemon juice in a small cup.

3. Pour the oil-lemon mixture over the potatoes and stir to coat them. Spread them in a 9- by 13-inch baking pan. Sprinkle with the rosemary and salt. Cover with foil, and bake for 20 minutes.

4. After 20 minutes, remove the foil, stir, and continue to roast for 15 minutes longer, until the exterior of the potatoes looks brown and crispy and the insides are tender. Remove from the oven and garnish with the parsley, if desired.

Serves 6 to 8

root vegetables

ROOT VEGETABLES are the edible fleshy plant parts that grow underground. They include true roots as well as tubers, rhizomes, and bulbs. While beets, carrots, garlic, onions, potatoes, and sweet potatoes get main-stage status in this book, we couldn't bear to overlook a few of the other great root vegetables.

Parsnips look like thick, pale carrots. They have a strong flavor and are terrific roasted and in stews. **Daikon radishes** resemble giant white carrots and have a spicy flavor. These can be used like other radishes and are great in slaws and relishes. **Turnips** are generally available as white and purple spheres and are terrific in early spring, when they are small and packed with flavor. Turnip tops can be eaten like mustard greens. **Rutabagas** are a cross between turnips and cabbages, with a yellower flesh and an earthy, mellow sweetness. **Celeriac** is a gnarly, globular root; while it might not win any beauty contests, its flavor is delicious, like celery with a touch of parsley. It is terrific mashed, roasted, grilled, or in soups and salads. Other common root vegetables include ginger, fennel, sunchokes, horseradish, jicama, and salsify.

Good for Your Family Because . . .

ROOT VEGETABLES drink in the nutrients from the soil, storing vitamins, minerals, and phytonutrients for the plant. As such, they are filled with health-boosting nutrients; depending on the vegetable, these might include vitamins C and A, folic acid, and fiber. Because they adapt well to home storage, they are a terrific, reliable source of winter nutrition.

101

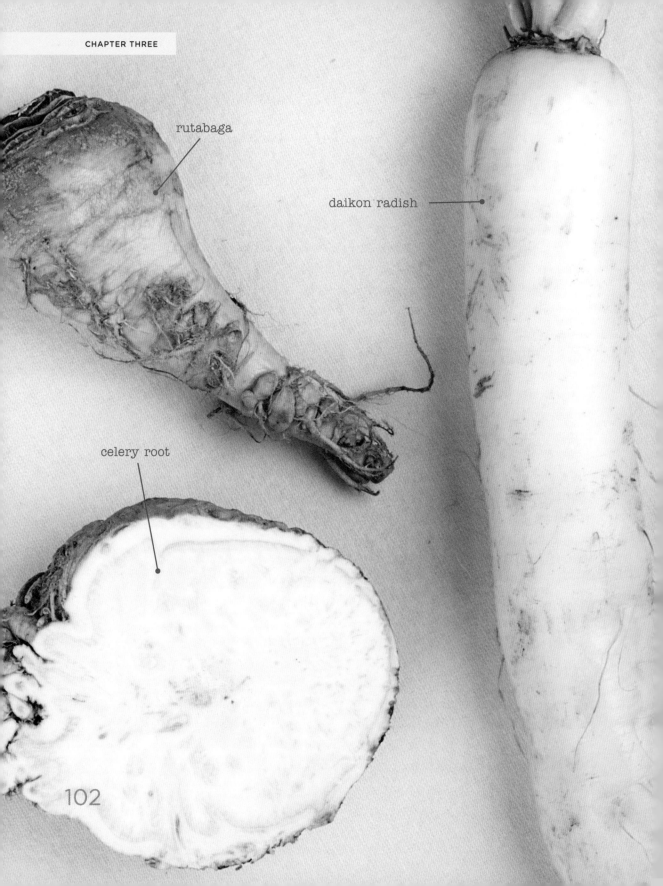

rutabaga

daikon radish

celery root

Selection and Storage

ROOT VEGETABLES are generally available in the fall. Some, like radishes and baby turnips, can be found in the spring months as well. Look for root vegetables that are free of cracks or bruises; firm, crisp vegetables are best. Most root vegetables store well in cool, dry locations. Be sure to remove any rot before storing to prevent them all from spoiling. Turnips are the one exception; they don't store that well after being harvested.

Honey-Glazed Turnips with Shallots

To prepare the turnips, you will want to remove the greens. (You can save the greens and cook with them as well.) Look for turnips that do not have purple areas, because the purple color means that the turnips are more mature and tougher in texture. If they have some purple, you will want to peel them for better texture and flavor; you don't need to peel the small, tender white ones.

1. Preheat the oven to 400°F.

2. Toss the turnips, shallots, rosemary, thyme, honey, oil, and salt and pepper to taste in a large bowl. Spread the mixture evenly on a baking sheet. Roast for about 20 minutes, turning once during cooking to evenly brown the turnips.

Serves 8

6 medium turnips, peeled and cut into ½-inch cubes

3 large shallots, quartered
   Leaves from 1 sprig fresh rosemary, or 1 tablespoon dried leaves
   Leaves from 3 sprigs fresh thyme, or 1½ teaspoons dried

¼ cup honey

2 tablespoons extra-virgin olive oil
   Kosher salt and freshly ground black pepper

103

green and yellow beans

snap beans

SNAP BEANS, of which the common green bean is the standard example, are one of the easier vegetables to sell to kids, especially if you use fresh beans (not canned or frozen) and don't overcook them, so that they retain their crisp texture and sweet taste. Although snap beans belong to the same family as shell beans, like kidney beans and black beans, they are one of the few types of beans in which the whole pod is edible.

Varieties of snap beans include **green**, **Roma**, **wax**, **yellow**, and even **purple** beans, as well as the delicate French beans **haricots verts**. Also look for **Asian long beans**, a unique snap bean that is about 10 inches in length and has a delicate flavor.

Roasted beans are a great kid-friendly way to enjoy this vegetable. You can also blanch the beans in boiling water for two minutes and then shock them in an ice bath to stop cooking and preserve their crisp texture and flavor. Beans prepared this way are great on salads or with a vegetable dip like hummus.

Good for Your Family Because . . .

SNAP BEANS are a good source of vitamins K and C. The quantities of these vitamins aren't quite as off the charts as in your cruciferous veggies, but they are high enough to make beans a strong contender. They are also a source of vitamin A as well as beta-carotene, folate, iron, and fiber.

Selection and Storage

SKIP THE CAN. Fresh beans, in season from summer through early fall, are the way to go. Look for beans that are dark green, without brown or black spots. The beans should snap when you break off the stem ends.

Store snap beans in a bag in the vegetable crisper of the refrigerator. They should keep for several days.

105

Green Beans Sautéed with Roasted Tomatoes and Shallot

1 pound green beans, washed, ends trimmed

¼ cup slivered almonds or pine nuts

2 tablespoons extra-virgin olive oil

1 large shallot, minced, or ¼ cup minced onion and ½ garlic clove, minced

⅓ cup Roasted Tomatoes (recipe follows) or chopped sun-dried tomatoes

Salt and freshly ground black pepper

Green beans and tomatoes are in season at the same time. This recipe is a great way to enjoy both of these vegetables at their peak.

1. Steam the green beans for 8 to 10 minutes, until tender crisp. You can do this in an electric steamer. Alternatively, fill a large pot with a couple inches of water, set a steaming basket in it, and bring to a boil. Set the beans in the basket, cover, and let steam.

2. Meanwhile, heat a large skillet over low heat. Add the almonds or pine nuts to the dry skillet and toast, shaking the skillet constantly, just until they show a bit of brown color. Remove the almonds from the skillet and set aside to cool.

3. Heat the oil in the skillet. (If you're using sun-dried tomatoes that were packed in oil, use oil from the jar for enhanced flavor.) Add the shallot and sauté for 2 minutes. Add the steamed green beans and sauté for a couple minutes to brown slightly and flavor with the oil. Add the tomatoes and sauté until heated through. Remove from the heat. Sprinkle on the almonds and season with salt and pepper.

Serves 6

1½ pounds cherry tomatoes (about 4 cups), halved

¼ cup extra-virgin olive oil

5 garlic cloves, coarsely chopped

1¼ teaspoons crushed red pepper flakes

1 tablespoon chopped fresh marjoram, or 1½ teaspoons dried

Kosher salt and freshly ground black pepper

1 tablespoon chopped fresh basil

Roasted Tomatoes

These also make a delicious and easy meal when tossed with cooked pasta and a bit of grated Parmesan.

1. Preheat the oven to 450°F.

2. Toss the tomatoes, oil, garlic, crushed red pepper, and marjoram in a large bowl. Place the tomatoes in a single layer on baking sheets. Sprinkle generously with salt and pepper.

3. Roast until the tomatoes are blistered, about 20–25 minutes. Top with the chopped basil.

Makes about 3 cups

spinach

JUST ONE SERVING OF BOILED SPINACH is enough to turn you off this healthy green for life. Do yourself a favor and try it again with a fresher, lighter approach. From salad to sauté, this versatile green can be used in so many ways that there's sure to be one you and your kids love.

Spinach is best purchased fresh, either as large leaves or as young, "baby" leaves. Asian varieties such as **water spinach** are worth exploring as well. Spinach will lose up to 75 percent of its volume when cooked; keep this in mind when purchasing raw spinach for cooking in recipes.

Good for Your Family Because . . .

LIKE OTHER greens, spinach is rich in vitamins A, C and K. It is also loaded with flavonoid compounds that function as antioxidants and as anticancer agents. It is a great source of folate, magnesium, calcium, lutein, and — as Popeye taught us — iron. Lutein has been shown to help prevent degeneration of eyesight with aging.

Selection and Storage

SPINACH does best in cool weather, so it is typically a spring and fall crop. Choose spinach leaves that are dark green in color and firm, not wilted. Avoid any yellowing. Even bagged spinach should be washed well before eating. Baby spinach leaves are more tender than their full-grown brethren, so they make terrific salads.

Wash spinach thoroughly to remove sand (see instructions for washing lettuce on page 92.) Spinach leaves will keep, loosely bagged, in the refrigerator crisper for a few days.

107

Spinach Sautéed in Butter and Parmesan

1 tablespoon butter
2 garlic cloves, finely chopped
2 bunches spinach, chopped
⅓ cup grated Parmesan cheese
  Salt and freshly ground
    black pepper

This recipe is lighter in calories and saturated fat than the beloved "creamed spinach" version. Since childhood, Beth avoided spinach, associating it only with the chopped, frozen spinach she'd eaten in childhood. She first tried this version in an Italian restaurant and fell in love with cooked spinach again. It may seem like a lot of spinach, but expect to lose most of the volume during cooking.

Heat the butter in a large skillet and sauté the garlic until just turning golden, 1 to 2 minutes. Add the spinach and sauté until just wilted. Turn off the heat, add the Parmesan, and toss until it melts into the greens. Season with salt and pepper.

Serves 6

spinach

108

Summer Squash

LIKELY THE MOST ABUNDANT OF THE SUMMER CROPS, summer squashes — **zucchini**, **yellow squash**, **pattypans**, **scalloped squash**, and their cousins — can be used in a wide variety of recipes. They can even be used in quick breads and other baked goods, good news for those desperate to use up the steady supply. Some squashes, like **zucchini**, even have edible blossoms, which can be eaten raw, stuffed with ricotta and fried, or used in a quesadilla with queso fresco.

Summer squash is terrific on the grill for a simple, quick dish. Its mild flavor isn't challenging for kids, and it works especially well with tomatoes. To introduce this vegetable to kids, try using squash in a vegetable lasagna or on pizza, or bake it in bread or muffins.

Summer squash is also terrific when roasted; Ali's daughter declared zucchini roasted with a touch of garlic "the best zucchini ever." In a hurry? Simply slice your summer squash, and then microwave it until softened (there's no need to add water).

If you find yourself in possession of an enormous zucchini — the kind that looks like it might effectively thwack a baseball — slice it in half, lengthwise, scoop out the seeds, and briefly parboil it, just enough to soften (a few minutes in the microwave also does the trick). Fill with a mixture of cheese, herbs, and butter, and bake in a preheated 350°F oven until browned on top.

Good for Your Family Because . . .

SUMMER SQUASH is a good source of vitamins C and A; a one-cup serving has about 16 percent and 10 percent of the daily recommended values, respectively. It provides essential minerals like manganese and magnesium, potassium, copper, folate, and phosphorus. In addition, summer squash is a good source of omega-3 fatty acids and fiber.

Selection and Storage

SQUASHES dominate farmers' markets in the summer months through September. These vegetables are among the best buys, as they are so abundant. Look for smooth, unblemished skins and a heavy weight for the size. Choose the "medium" sizes for best flavor and texture. If you can find them, "baby" squashes are a sweet treat. Squash will keep in a bag in the refrigerator crisper for up to a week.

Zucchini-Bacon Fritters

6 slices thick-cut bacon, or 10 to 12 slices of thinner bacon
½ cup cornmeal
½ teaspoon baking powder
½ teaspoon salt
Freshly ground black pepper
1 medium zucchini, grated
2 scallions, chopped, including 1 inch of the green parts
1 egg, lightly beaten
1½ tablespoons pure maple syrup

The maple syrup complements the bacon and takes the slight bitter edge off the cornmeal (all the best cornbread has a bit of sweet to it as well). Though it has plentiful bacon, this is not a greasy dish. After Beth chowed down four fritters, her daughter insisted on a trip to the park. Running a mile while full of bacon fritters, chasing a kid on a tricycle, is enough jostling to dislodge anything remotely greasy. No worries here.

1. Cook the bacon until crisp. You can do this in a skillet on the stove top. Alternatively, lay it on a baking sheet and bake in the oven at 350°F for about 15 minutes, until browned and crisp. Alternatively again, you can sandwich the strips between paper towels on a plate and microwave for about 5 minutes.

2. Combine the cornmeal, baking powder, salt, and a generous grind of black pepper in a bowl, and mix well. Crumble the bacon into the bowl, then stir in the zucchini, scallions, egg, and maple syrup. Mix to combine. The mixture might not seem like it will hold together, but it will.

3. Spray a large skillet with cooking spray, and heat over medium heat. Spoon the batter into the skillet about 1 tablespoon at a time. Flatten each spoonful of batter slightly with the back of the spoon. Cook for about 2 minutes per side, until golden and cooked through.

Serves 6 (makes 10 to 12 small fritters)

110

squash blossom

Zephyr straightneck

green pattypan

yellow pattypan

111

sweet potatoes

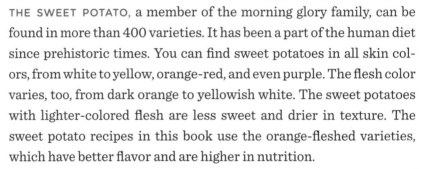

THE SWEET POTATO, a member of the morning glory family, can be found in more than 400 varieties. It has been a part of the human diet since prehistoric times. You can find sweet potatoes in all skin colors, from white to yellow, orange-red, and even purple. The flesh color varies, too, from dark orange to yellowish white. The sweet potatoes with lighter-colored flesh are less sweet and drier in texture. The sweet potato recipes in this book use the orange-fleshed varieties, which have better flavor and are higher in nutrition.

Orange vegetables like sweet potatoes rank among the sweetest of the vegetables and are often the easiest to get kids to like. Unless your child decides one day — for no fathomable reason — to refuse orange foods. Should this emergency arise, the Sweet Potato Parmesan "Fries" recipe is the one to turn to. After experimenting with nearly 50 different orange-food recipes and hundreds of tries, you can trust us on this. Postcrisis, you can introduce the other 49 recipes again.

Good for Your Family Because . . .

JUST ONE SWEET POTATO offers more than 250 percent of the daily value of vitamin A as beta-carotene. With both beta-carotene and vitamin C, sweet potatoes have antioxidant and anti-inflammatory benefits. Sweet potatoes also provide dietary fiber, vitamin B_6, and minerals such as manganese, potassium, and iron.

For diabetics and anyone concerned with blood glucose levels, sweet potatoes, despite their rich flavor, have a lower glycemic index than white potatoes.

Selection and Storage

SWEET POTATOES are in season from early fall through November in most climates. Select sweet potatoes that have smooth skins that are free of cracks, bruises, blemishes, or soft spots. Store them loose at room temperature in a cool, dark spot that is well ventilated.

Sweet potatoes that have been washed will keep for around ten days. Sweet potatoes that have been well cured and still have dirt on them will keep, unwashed, in a cool, 60°F basement for significantly longer. Which is good information just in case you happen to buy yours 40 pounds at a time at the end of the season.

Sweet Potato–Parmesan "Fries"

You can vary this recipe a bit to better pair it with a main course. For example, skip the Parmesan and use a sprinkle of cumin on the sweet potatoes with a more southwestern menu. Or use a spice blend like a curry or garam masala, adding 1 tablespoon of honey to the olive oil that gets tossed on the fries, if your menu is leaning more toward Indian food. For crisper fries, cut the sweet potato sticks ⅛ inch thick and use a light coat of nonstick cooking spray instead of the olive oil. Reduce the baking time to 10 minutes per side.

1½ pounds sweet potatoes (3 medium)
3 tablespoons extra-virgin olive oil
  Coarse salt and freshly ground black pepper
¼ cup grated Parmesan cheese

1. Preheat the oven to 350°F. Coat a baking sheet with cooking spray.

2. Peel the sweet potatoes and julienne them (cut into sticks about ¼ inch by 3 inches). Toss in a large bowl with the olive oil, and season with salt and pepper to taste. Place in a single layer on the prepared baking sheet.

3. Bake for 15 minutes, then flip the fries and bake for 10–12 minutes longer until golden.

4. Remove from oven and set the oven to a low broil, 400°F. Sprinkle the fries with the Parmesan, and broil for about 2 minutes to turn the cheese golden and crisp the fries a bit.

Serves 4

tomatoes

THE TOMATOES YOU FIND IN THE GROCERY STORE are generally cultivated for a perfect shape, a uniform red color, and the ability to survive shipping. They are picked while still green, washed, then gas-ripened off the vine. The end result is a tasteless, mealy tomato.

It's no surprise, then, that people who love tomatoes are often sticklers for the garden-fresh real thing. If you still haven't yet met a tomato you like, try some heirloom varieties before you say "never." Heirlooms come in all shapes, sizes, colors, and flavors, from the deep red-fleshed **Cherokee Purple** to the light, creamy **Garden Peach** and the tangy **Green Zebra**. For kids, **Sun Gold** cherry tomatoes are an ideal "gateway" vegetable; their bright orange color and sweet taste often make these tomatoes irresistible to young skeptics.

Tomatoes are probably among the most common vegetables that kids eat without realizing it. Disguised as pizza sauce and spaghetti sauce, tomatoes are the basis of many of kids' favorite dishes. That said, ketchup does not count as a vegetable serving.

Good for Your Family Because . . .

TOMATOES ARE a great source of vitamin C, as well as A and K. Red tomatoes also provide lycopene, a powerful antioxidant recognized for its cardiovascular and anticancer benefits. Raw tomatoes will offer the most vitamin C, because this nutrient is easily lost in cooking. Cooked tomatoes will provide up to eight times more lycopene than raw. Lycopene is more readily absorbed with a bit of fat, so olive oil and tomato sauce make a natural and healthy combination.

Selection and Storage

NOTHING BEATS an in-season, vine-ripened tomato from the garden or farmers' market. Tomatoes are in season from July to September for most climates. Look for ripe tomatoes that yield just a bit to pressure, with a deep color, and no soft spots or bruises. Heirlooms are sometimes called "ugly" because some have irregular shapes with bulges and ridges. In our opinion, the explosion of stripes and deep pinks, greens, yellows, purples, and other colors is anything but ugly.

Do not store tomatoes in the refrigerator; the cool temperature causes a loss in flavor. Store tomatoes on the counter, away from the sun (unless you're trying to ripen an immature tomato). They will keep for several days.

▬ What Is an Heirloom Vegetable?

Who knew that there were once 400 varieties of sweet potatoes alone? Or well over 600 different tomatoes? Where did all this variety go?

Most of the produce available in grocery stores is grown in vast, monocultural plots. Only a few varieties of each type of crop are grown, and these are selected for their consistency, productivity, tolerance of drought and frost, ability to survive pesticides, and most of all, their ability to withstand the very long trip to supermarkets. Flavor, nutrition, variety, and biodiversity are compromised. As a result, thousands of different and unique vegetable cultivars have become rare and unfamiliar. Many of these are heirloom varieties.

Research has shown that emphasizing yield and fast growth over diversity can result in vegetables that have less nutrition than heirloom varieties.

To qualify as an "heirloom" variety of vegetable, the type of seed must be at least 50 years old, predating the industrialized agriculture boom after World War II. The varieties must also be open-pollinated. These old varieties of seed are the kinds of things you don't see on store shelves. Heirloom tomatoes are probably the most familiar: sexy, tasty, ugly tomatoes full of flavor and character and, apparently, more nutrition. But unique varieties exist for all vegetables and even legumes.

If you've only done your vegetable shopping in the megamart produce section, try expanding your horizons. By seeking heirloom vegetables from your farmers' market or farm stand, you'll be rewarded with great nutrition, flavor, and variety. There's a lot to gain.

2 cups bread cubes, about
1 inch size (from a firm,
rustic loaf)

⅔–1 cup extra-virgin olive oil,
plus 2 tablespoons

½ pound bacon

1 large shallot, chopped

½ cup red wine vinegar

3 pounds tomatoes, cored,
seeded, and chopped into
¾-inch pieces

2 avocados, peeled and
chopped to ½-inch cubes

1 medium cucumber, peeled,
seeded, and diced into
½-inch pieces

Salt and freshly ground
black pepper

Green Zebra

Panzanella

Ali's daughter would tell you emphatically that she dislikes both tomatoes and bread. And yet she adores this salad, which is largely composed of tomatoes and bread. Perhaps the trick lies in using good, fresh-from-the-farmers'-market tomatoes, or perhaps it is the flavor infused by the bacon. Either way, it's become a favorite summer dish.

1. Preheat the oven to 350°F.

2. Arrange the bread cubes on a baking sheet. Drizzle 2 tablespoons of the olive oil over the bread. Bake for 10 to 15 minutes, until dry. (If you don't do this, you get really soggy bread. Crisp is good.)

3. Meanwhile, cook the bacon until crisp. You can do this in a skillet on the stove top. Alternatively, lay on a baking sheet and bake in the oven with the bread cubes for about 15 minutes, or until browned and crisp. Alternatively again, you can sandwich the strips between paper towels on a plate and microwave for about 5 minutes.

4. Combine the shallot with the vinegar in a small bowl and set aside to marinate while you prepare the rest of the salad.

5. Combine the tomatoes, avocados, and cucumber in a large bowl. Crumble the bacon into the bowl. Add the bread cubes and toss to combine. Add ⅔ cup of the remaining olive oil to the vinegar and shallot mixture and whisk to emulsify. Taste and add oil if desired. Pour over the salad, using as much dressing as you like. (Save any leftovers for another salad.) Season with salt and pepper. Gently toss all the ingredients to coat.

Serves 8

Garden Peach

Jubilee

Plum

Sun Gold

Cherokee Purple

117

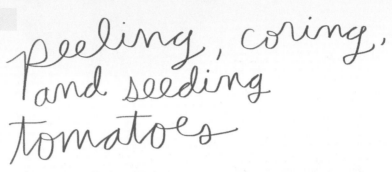

peeling, coring, and seeding tomatoes

When cooking, you'll get the most out of your tomatoes if you can master the basics of peeling, coring, and seeding.

Peeling

Many recipes, for example tomato sauce, require you to peel the tomatoes. The easy way to do this is to cut a ½-inch by ½-inch X in the bottom of each tomato. Bring a large pot of water to a boil, and set a larger bowl of ice water nearby. Drop the tomatoes into the boiling water (tongs are handy; there's no need to add burns to other kitchen battle scars). Return the water to a boil, then remove the tomatoes (tongs, please) and put them immediately into the ice water. Let them sit for at least 1 minute. The peel will pull away easily from the flesh.

Coring

Coring removes the hard whitish center from the tomato. Because the core has no flavor and a hard texture, most recipes in this book require coring the tomato. Using a tomato knife (or other knife with a small serrated blade), cut out a cone shape from around the stem, about 1 inch deep for a medium tomato. Lift out the core.

Seeding

Seeding eliminates excess moisture and seeds from the tomato flesh. Left in the tomato, this "goo" will add excess liquid to a recipe, and the seeds will lend a bitter taste. That's why seeding is a common step for preparing tomatoes in many recipes, such as Panzanella (page 116) and Roasted Summer Vegetable (page 97). You can seed a tomato by cutting it in half and either scooping out the seeds and gel or giving it a gentle squeeze. It will splatter and can stain; be warned.

winter squashes

IF YOU'VE EVER WONDERED how the original American locavores (that is, Native Americans and the early European settlers) survived the winter months without a supermarket nearby, the answer, in part, is winter squash. These hard-rinded gourds ripen in late fall, and some varieties can be stored for up to six months with no refrigeration required.

Winter squashes come in a huge variety (and some came in a plain huge size), from the tiny "single-serving" **acorn squash** and delicious **delicata** to the **butternut**, **Hubbard**, and **Cushaw**. More unusual varieties include the odd-looking **Turk's Turban**, the wrinkled **Black Futsu**, and the 60-plus-pound **Big Max**. The thick skins can be practically any color, depending on the variety.

Pumpkins are a type of winter squash, though you'll want to be sure to get eating pumpkins (sometimes called sugar pumpkins) rather than decorative pumpkins (for Halloween carving). And explore some of the exciting heirloom varieties, particularly French ones such as **Musque de Provence** (Fairy Tale) and the deep auburn beauty **Rouge Vif d'Etampes** (Cinderella).

Farmers' markets are a great source for unusual winter squash. When in doubt, ask the farmer whether the squash is for decoration or eating.

Winter squashes are beloved in pies, but these versatile vegetables can be eaten in both savory and sweet recipes and used in all kinds of dishes from soups, sides, and stews to, yes, your Thanksgiving dessert.

Good for Your Family Because . . .

A 1-CUP SERVING of winter squash provides nearly 150 percent of the daily value for vitamin A as beta-carotene, as well as one-third of the daily value for vitamin C. Foods rich in these carotenoids may also help regulate blood glucose levels.

Winter squash also provides 14 percent of the daily value for folate, which is a key nutrient to prevent birth defects for pregnant women. Folate also helps break down homocysteine, a metabolic byproduct, which can damage blood vessel walls. Winter squash is also a good source of potassium, fiber, and manganese.

Selection and Storage

LOOK FOR WINTER SQUASH to be in season in the fall, at about the same time that Halloween costumes start hitting the store shelves. When selecting a winter squash to cook, be sure it is an "eating" pumpkin or squash and not a decorative one. Eating squashes are generally heavy for their size and have thick, deep orange flesh. Carving pumpkins tend to have thin rinds and pale, bitter flesh. Ask the farmer at the market, the produce manager, or consult a vegetable seed guide for the more unusual varieties. Don't be afraid of the "unique" ones, which are often great for cooking. Gourds are usually decorative and make poor choices for eating.

Choose squash with firm flesh and no bruises or cracks. To store, keep in a cool, dark place. Depending on the variety, winter squash will store well for up to six months. The heavier the rind, generally, the longer the squash will keep.

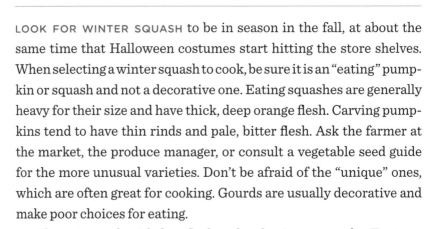

Black Beans and Winter Squash

Pairing winter squash with a southwestern flavor? You bet. Pumpkin shows up in many traditional Mexican recipes. The sweet flavor goes well with a bit of spice from the ancho chile. For a bit more flavor of the Southwest, top this dish with crumbled *queso blanco*.

1. Heat the oil in a large pot over medium-high heat. Add the onion and garlic and sauté until just golden, about 3 minutes. Add the chile powder, cumin, squash, and stock. Bring to a boil, then reduce the heat and simmer until the squash is tender, about 10 minutes.

2. Add the black beans. Return to a simmer, and simmer for a few minutes, until heated through. Season with salt and pepper. Stir in the cilantro just before removing the pot from the heat.

Serves 6 to 8

1 tablespoon extra-virgin olive oil
½ onion, diced
1 garlic clove, minced
1 teaspoon ancho chile powder, or any mild pure chili powder
½ teaspoon ground cumin
1½ pounds winter squash, peeled, seeded, and cut into ½-inch cubes
1 cup organic chicken stock
2 (15-ounce) cans black beans, rinsed and drained
  Salt and freshly ground black pepper
1 bunch fresh cilantro (about ½ cup), chopped

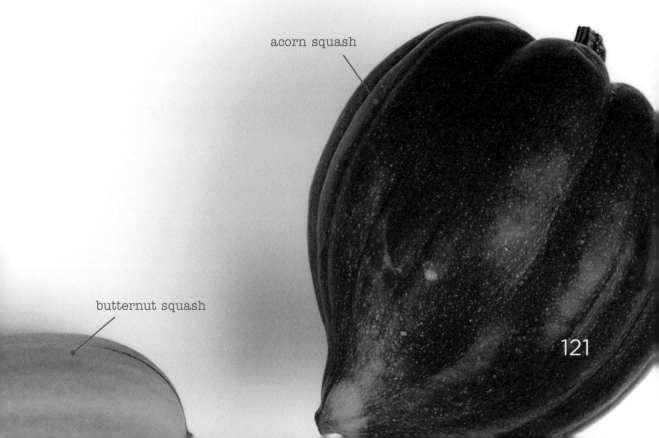

acorn squash

butternut squash

121

the "un-vegetables"

MANY OF THE ITEMS WE THINK OF AS VEGETABLES are actually not vegetables at all, and they aren't even fruits. Technically anything that is produced by a plant for the purpose of reproduction is a fruit, while the stems, leaves, flowers, and roots are vegetables. Which makes tomatoes a fruit. And cucumbers.

But then there are the "un-vegetables": **corn** (grain), **green peas** and **soybeans** (legumes), and **mushrooms** (fungi). Though they are neither vegetable nor fruit, all deserve power-food status for their versatility, nutrition profile, and just plain tastiness!

Corn

NOTHING SAYS SUMMER quite like farm-fresh corn on the cob. Corn, a grain, has taken some heat lately thanks to heavily subsidized industrial corn, which is used as cheap animal feed and forms the basis of high-fructose corn syrup and other cheap food additives. Yet fresh-picked corn on the cob remains the apex of finger-food pleasure for kids aged 2 to 92. It's also a good source of vitamin C, thiamin, folate, fiber, and pantothenic acid, a B vitamin that is necessary for metabolism of carbohydrates, proteins, and lipids.

Heat rapidly transfers corn's sugars to starch, so the best corn will be picked fresh, stored in the shade or refrigerated, then eaten immediately — preferably on the day it is picked. If buying from a farmers' market or farm stand, select corn that has been kept in the shade. Look for firm, green husks that haven't wilted. Peel back a tiny bit of the husk and look for corn silk that is soft, free from decay, and a glossy golden color. If permitted, press your fingernail on a kernel; the freshest corn will release a good amount of milky white juice — this liquid is packed with flavor, so the more, the better. If you can't peel the husk back, simply feel the kernels through the husk; they should feel full from top to bottom.

Boiling or steaming corn on the cob remains the most popular approach to cooking it. Corn on the cob can also be grilled, either in its husk or husked and wrapped in foil. In a hurry? Perhaps the fastest way to prepare corn is to microwave it (see below).

To remove the kernels for salads or other recipes, simply run a thin sharp knife down the cob from tip to base. The kernels will fall right off.

easy, microwaved CORN ON THE COB

For summers on the go — after camp, days in the garden, and afternoons by the pool — you may find yourself wishing for a rapid, no-fuss way to serve up fresh corn, ideally with minimal cleanup. In this situation, microwaving corn on the cob can be a great approach. An added bonus is that there's no pot of boiling water to overheat your kitchen on a hot day.

Leave the husks and corn silk on. You'll probably find the corn silk is easier to remove from microwaved corn than from uncooked corn. Place the corn in the microwave. For a single ear, cook on HIGH for 3 minutes. For each additional ear, add 2 minutes.

Remove from the microwave and let sit for a few minutes. Removing the husks immediately after microwaving can release a dangerous amount of steam. Serve with a touch of butter and a sprinkle of salt.

123

Edamame (Soybeans)

THE TASTY BEANS hiding inside the fresh, green, fuzzy pods are a favorite green food for us and an easy, addictive snack our children love. It's a pretty amazing feat — passing plant foods off as snack food.

The flavor of soybeans is nutty and buttery, somewhere between popcorn and a fresh green bean. The easiest preparation is to just blanch the pods in boiling salted water and serve, letting kids enjoy "popping" the beans from the pods into their mouths. The beans are also good in stir-fries and even puréed in dips.

Soybeans offer all nine essential amino acids, and they are the only legume that offers a complete protein — 57 percent of the daily adult value for protein in just one cup, without saturated fat. Soy protein contains a compound called lunasin. This compound is thought to be the reason why whole soy foods help lower "bad" LDL cholesterol and raise "good" HDL cholesterol levels.

Soybeans are a good source of iron and omega-3 fatty acids, as well as fiber and vitamin B_{12}. One caveat: Soy is one of the more common food allergens.

For dried soybeans, look for beans that are not cracked and that contain no moisture. These will need to be sorted, rinsed, soaked, and prepared like other dried beans.

You can usually find green soybeans in the freezer section marked as edamame, either in the shells or shelled. In some markets, fresh green soybeans can also be found in late summer, when they're in season. Look for firm, green pods, free of bad spots. Fresh edamame should be eaten within a couple of days. Store in the vegetable crisper of the refrigerator. Frozen soybeans will keep for a few months.

is fresh better than frozen?

It's a common assumption that fresh produce packs more nutritional benefits than frozen. Is that true?

It depends. If you're purchasing in-season produce that was harvested recently, at peak ripeness, fresh is best. This is the produce you're likely to find at the farmers' market, at farm stands, or at the finest supermarkets that source locally grown produce.

However, plenty of fresh produce is harvested long before peak ripeness so that it can withstand a cross-country or even an international journey to your plate. While it may ripen during the journey, it probably won't reach peak nutritive value, as it would if it had ripened on the plant. In addition, the longer the time between harvesting and eating, the more nutrients get lost. Add to that the exposure to light and heat that often happens as produce is shipped from farm to supermarket, and you end up with a vegetable that's not as nutritious as it could be.

Frozen produce, on the other hand, is typically harvested at peak ripeness, which means it starts off with robust nutrition. Some of that nutrition is lost during the blanching process, but what remains is often kept during the flash-freezing process. This makes frozen produce a pretty good bet for nutrition.

Bottom line? If you're looking for peak nutrition, buy fresh foods when they're in season, ideally from as local a source as possible. But if it's the middle of winter, look carefully at the fresh produce you're buying. If the broccoli is yellowed, the green beans shriveled, or the berries white, you may well be better off buying frozen instead.

125

Peas

GREEN PEAS ARE LEGUMES. Avoid canned peas and you'll have better luck getting your kids to try this one. A fresh, raw pea straight from the pod is a sweet taste revelation, especially as a salad topping. Also try serving stir-fry-friendly varieties like sugar snaps and snow peas.

Peas are an excellent source of folate and vitamins C, K, B_1, B_2, B_3, B_6, plus fiber and even zinc. If you can find fresh early spring peas in the pod, keep them refrigerated. Heat will rapidly change their sugars to starch, causing them to lose that sweet taste. The pods should be velvety in texture and firm. Snow peas are best and sweetest when smaller in size. Peas can be stored in a bag in the refrigerator for a few days.

Mushrooms

EDIBLE MUSHROOMS come in an amazing variety, from the common button and cremini mushrooms to such exotics as the lion's mane, the bluefoot, the highly prized morels, and something called a puffball. Mushrooms are not a vegetable at all but rather a fungus. Which doesn't sound nearly as good as mushrooms taste!

Mushrooms are high in antioxidants and trace minerals that support the function of enzymes in the body. They are also good sources of selenium, iron, zinc, and vitamins B_2 and B_3. A few species are being researched for their anticancer properties.

Mushrooms are cultivated year-round, but wild ones are foraged in the spring. (And if you're buying foraged wild mushrooms, be sure to use only a reliable source.) Choose mushrooms that are firm, not soggy. They should appear plump and clean. Gently wash mushrooms with as little water as possible, or use a mushroom brush to clean off the grit before cooking. Store them in a loosely closed paper bag in the refrigerator for up to a week.

126

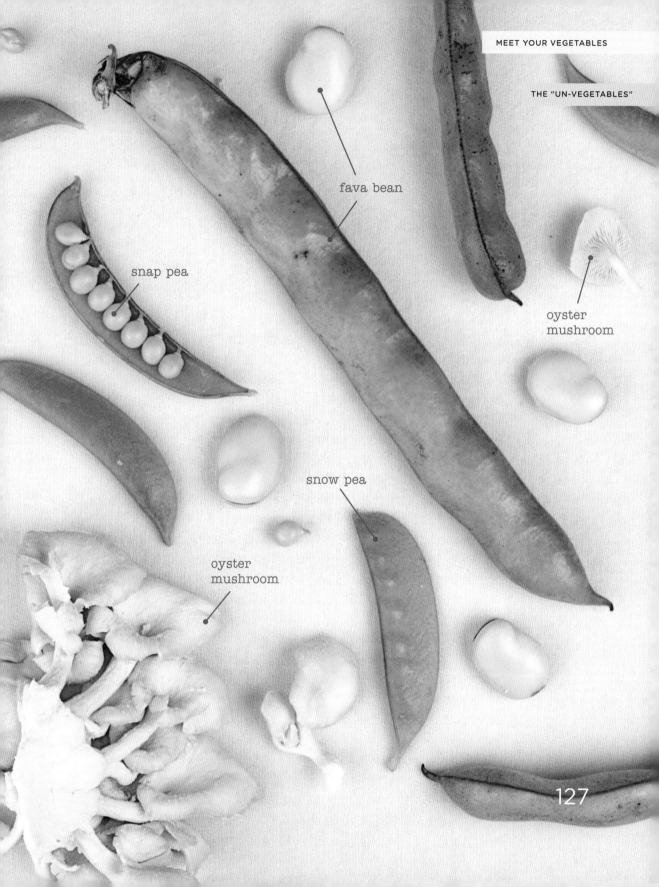

fava bean

snap pea

oyster mushroom

snow pea

oyster mushroom

127

ORGANIC VS. CONVENTIONAL:
where we stand

The debate about organic produce kicked into high gear with the planting of an organic garden on the White House lawn. Whether organic produce is healthier than conventionally grown produce remains the subject of some controversy, and this is sure to be hotly debated for some time to come.

Here's what we can say confidently about organic produce: By definition, it is grown without chemical pesticides, which we think is good for both our children's health and for the planet they will inherit. It isn't fertilized with sewage sludge or irradiated, and it contains no genetically modified organisms. We like organic produce for these reasons.

However, there's no denying that organic produce has a higher out-of-pocket cost than conventional produce. This cost is probably closer to the "true" cost of the food — and although less expensive, conventional produce can create external costs, like damage to the environment and the health impacts of a higher chemical exposure. But the fact remains that if you can't afford these added out-of-pocket costs — and some people can't — then you can't afford it. We get that.

What's *most* important is eating more fresh produce. Period. Fruits and vegetables contain the nutrients and micronutrients you need to prevent disease, fight cell damage, boost energy, lower blood pressure, stay mentally alert, and keep your appetite in check. Eating more fresh produce can also help boost local economies (see the sidebar on page 130) and preserve farmland.

Americans get more calories from soft drinks than they do from fruits and vegetables. Shift that balance. Eat more leafy greens, more broccoli, more plums and blueberries and grapefruit — of any kind. You'll be better off.

the DIRTY DOZEN vs. THE CLEAN FIFTEEN

The Environmental Working Group (EWG) compiled data from nearly 96,000 tests for pesticide residues in produce between 2000 and 2008 and collected by the USDA and the FDA. Based on this, they developed rankings of the "Dirty Dozen," the fruits and vegetables most likely to contain pesticides when grown conventionally, and the "Clean Fifteen," those that carry the least pesticide load.

Though the lists change slightly every year, the lists below can make it easier to decide when it's important to buy organic.

▬ The Dirty Dozen
Always buy organic

1. Celery (worst)
2. Peaches
3. Strawberries
4. Apples
5. Blueberries
6. Nectarines
7. Sweet bell peppers
8. Spinach
9. Cherries
10. Kale & Collards
11. Potatoes
12. Grapes (imported)

▬ The Clean Fifteen
Conventionally grown with low pesticide content

1. Onions (best)
2. Avocados
3. Sweet corn
4. Pineapples
5. Mangos
6. Sweet peas
7. Asparagus
8. Kiwifruit
9. Cabbages
10. Eggplants
11. Cantaloupe
12. Watermelons
13. Grapefruit
14. Sweet potatoes
15. Honeydew melon

more vegetable-rich SIDE DISHES

HUNGRY FOR MORE? These recipes offer some unique ways to combine and prepare your favorite vegetables. It's always easier to succeed at that "repeated exposure" when there are several options and not the "same old, same old." Besides, you want to eat your vegetables, too. You might as well enjoy it.

FACT: Research suggests that if the U.S. population fully adopted the USDA Dietary Guidelines for Americans, it could be a boon to local economies. Researchers at Michigan State University examined what would happen if residents of their state increased their consumption of fresh produce to meet USDA guidelines (approximately double current consumption levels) and bought this produce from existing local growers who now sell their produce largely to national processors. This market shift would increase farmer net income by up to $164 million. And farmers with that much more money to spend would stimulate an additional 1,900 new jobs in Michigan's economy.

Honey-Lemon Spring Vegetable Sauté

If you don't like leafy greens, there's a good chance you have been eating them overcooked. Only a light sauté is required to bring out their flavor. Too much cooking and the greens can become bitter and mushy. For a main dish, serve this light sauté over rice.

1. Steam the asparagus tips for 7 minutes. You can do this in an electric steamer. Alternatively, put a couple of inches of water into a large pot, set a steaming basket in it, and bring to a boil. Set the asparagus tips in the basket, cover, and let steam.

2. Meanwhile, heat the oil in a large Dutch oven or skillet over medium-high heat. Add the garlic and scallions and sauté until just golden, about 2 minutes. Stir in the lemon zest, lemon juice, honey, salt, and red pepper flakes. Add the bok choy, chard, and kale, and toss until heated through and just starting to wilt, about 3 minutes.

3. Season with black pepper. Add the hot asparagus tips, and toss with the greens to mix. Serve immediately.

Serves 6 to 8

1 cup asparagus tips

2 tablespoons extra-virgin olive oil

1 garlic clove, minced

2 large scallions, thinly sliced (about ⅓ cup)

Zest of 1 lemon, plus 1 tablespoon lemon juice

1½ tablespoons honey

1½ teaspoons coarse salt

¼ teaspoon crushed red pepper flakes

3 small heads bok choy, sliced (about 2½ cups)

1 small bunch chard, tough stems removed, chopped (about 1 cup packed)

1 small bunch kale, chopped (about 1 cup packed)

Freshly ground black pepper

FACT: It turns out fruits and vegetables are a healthy bone must-have. A 2004 study demonstrated that girls who consumed the most produce have the strongest bones. Another study found that boys who consumed the most fruits and vegetables over seven years had the strongest bones, even though nearly all boys had adequate intake of dairy products.

Source: Tylavsky et al. "Fruit and vegetable intakes are an independent predictor of bone size in early pubertal children." *American Journal of Clinical Nutrition*, Vol. 79, No. 2, 311–317.

Roasted Beets
with Mixed Herbs and Shallots

This is a simple recipe that is also a great "starter" to introduce beets to young eaters. Leftovers make a good topping for salad.

3 bunches mixed golden and red beets (about 12 medium beets), peeled, cut into ¾-inch cubes

5 large shallots, quartered

2 tablespoons extra-virgin olive oil

1 tablespoon balsamic vinegar

2 tablespoons fresh thyme, or 1 tablespoon dried

2 tablespoons fresh rosemary leaves, or 1 tablespoon dried

   Coarse salt and freshly ground black pepper

4 ounces goat cheese, crumbled

1. Preheat the oven to 400°F.

2. Combine the beets, shallots, olive oil, balsamic vinegar, thyme, and rosemary in a large shallow baking dish. Season with salt and pepper and mix well. Roast for 1 hour, until the beets are tender when pierced with a fork.

3. Top with the goat cheese and serve warm.

Serves 8

Baby Kale and Garlic-Mustard Dressing

This recipe uses tender baby kale, which can be found early in the season. The younger leaves are less bitter, requiring only a quick sauté before the dish is ready to go. If you cannot find baby kale, you can use the soft Tuscan or dinosaur kale and sauté it a couple minutes longer.

½ cup plus 1 tablespoon extra-virgin olive oil

⅓ cup balsamic vinegar

2 garlic cloves, chopped

2 tablespoons stone-ground mustard

   Salt and freshly ground black pepper

1 bunch baby kale leaves (about ½ pound)

1. Whisk together ½ cup of the oil with the vinegar, garlic, and mustard in a small bowl, and season with salt and pepper.

2. Heat the remaining 1 tablespoon oil in a large skillet over medium-high heat. Add the kale and sauté just until it begins to wilt, about 2 minutes. (It's too good to overcook!) Toss with the dressing and serve.

Serves 4

Marinated Broccoli

Sometimes kids won't eat the more strongly flavored and crunchy raw broccoli, nor will they eat soft, overcooked florets. The broccoli in this recipe is lightly steamed to tender crispness, hitting the mark for the best texture.

1 large head broccoli
1 tablespoon sesame oil
1 garlic clove, chopped
1 tablespoon soy sauce
2 tablespoons honey
1 tablespoon rice wine vinegar
1 teaspoon lemon juice
1 teaspoon grated lemon zest
1 tablespoon chopped fresh cilantro
   Pinch of crushed red pepper flakes
1 teaspoon sesame seeds

1. Trim the broccoli of all but about 1 inch of its stem. Cut into florets.

2. Steam the broccoli for about 5 minutes. You can do this in an electric steamer. Alternatively, put a couple of inches of water into a large pot, set a steaming basket in it, and bring to a boil. Set the broccoli in the basket, cover, and let steam. Immediately place the steamed broccoli in a bowl of ice water to stop the cooking. Drain and set aside in a large bowl.

3. Heat the oil in a small saucepan over medium-high heat. Add the garlic and sauté for 2 minutes. Stir in the soy sauce, honey, vinegar, lemon juice, and lemon zest, then remove from the heat. Pour the sauce over the broccoli, and toss to combine. Cover and refrigerate for at least 2 hours, and up to 4 hours.

4. Garnish with the cilantro, red pepper flakes, and sesame seeds.

Serves 4 to 6

" Back to basics — that's how we begin, and it doesn't take too much wit to learn . . . so it goes, a step or two at a time, and pretty soon they'll call you an accomplished cook."

Julia Child, in her introduction to Julia and Jacques, Cooking at Home.

Red Cabbage Slaw
with Dried Fruit and Savory Praline

⅓ cup walnut oil

¼ cup balsamic vinegar

1 tablespoon honey

1 tablespoon orange
   marmalade

   Salt and freshly ground
   black pepper

1 head red cabbage, cored
   and thinly sliced

1 cup dried fruit (blueberries,
   cherries, cranberries,
   currants, raisins, currants,
   or a blend)

1 cup pecans

½ teaspoon kosher salt

   Dash of cayenne pepper

⅓ cup sugar

This sweet and savory slaw is a good way to introduce a colorful side dish into your family's diet.

1. To make the dressing, whisk together the walnut oil, vinegar, honey, and marmalade in a small bowl or cup, and season with salt and pepper.

2. Place the cabbage and dried fruit in a large bowl, pour the dressing over, and toss to coat. Cover and refrigerate for at least a few hours, and for as long as overnight.

3. To make the praline pecans, toss the pecans with the kosher salt and cayenne; set aside. Coat a baking sheet with cooking spray. Heat the sugar in a small saucepan over medium-low heat, without stirring. Just as the sugar turns golden brown, add the pecans and mix well. Remove from the heat. Spread the nuts on the prepared baking sheet and let cool. Break into pieces carefully (the pieces can have sharp edges).

4. Toss the slaw with the pralines just before serving.

Serves 8 to 10

Sautéed Red Chard
with Clementines, Feta, and Balsamic Reduction

Citrus pairs well with greens, and it also gives kids a familiar favorite flavor in the dish to help them want to try it. This dish blends four flavor types: sweet orange, salty feta, tangy balsamic vinegar, and "green" chard.

1. Heat the olive oil in a large sauté pan over medium-high heat. Add the chard and sauté just until it starts to wilt, about 2 minutes. Remove from the heat and season with salt and pepper to taste. Allow to cool until just warm.

2. Toss the greens with the orange sections in a bowl.

3. Reduce the balsamic vinegar in a small saucepan over medium heat by two-thirds, or until it is of a syrupy consistency and will coat the back of a spoon.

4. Drizzle the greens and oranges with the balsamic reduction. Top with the cheese. Serve warm.

Serves 4 to 6

2 tablespoons extra-virgin olive oil

1 (12-ounce) bunch red chard, stemmed and sliced into chiffonade

Salt and freshly ground black pepper

2 clementines, oranges, or tangerines, peeled and sectioned

⅓ cup balsamic vinegar

2 ounces feta cheese, crumbled (about ¼ cup)

Carrot-Orange Soufflé

Lighter in calories and fat than Indian-style carrot pudding, this dish definitely blurs the line between a vegetable side and a dessert. It is not a true soufflé, since you don't whisk the egg whites, but it has a lovely, light texture. It's even better served cold the next day.

1. Steam the carrots until very soft, about 30 minutes. You can do this in an electric steamer. Alternatively, put a couple of inches of water into a large pot, set a steaming basket in it, and bring to a boil. Set the carrots in the basket, cover, and let steam. Let cool completely.

2. Preheat the oven to 350°F.

3. Pulse the carrots until puréed in a food processor or blender. Add the remaining ingredients separately in order, from the sugar through the extracts, pulsing as you go. Process until all the ingredients are well mixed.

4. Spray a soufflé dish with cooking spray. Pour in the soufflé batter. Bake for about 50 minutes, until the sides are puffed up and just golden on the edges and the center is set.

Serves 8 to 10

2½ pounds carrots, about 12 medium, peeled and chopped into 1-inch pieces

⅔ cup sugar

¼ cup unbleached all-purpose flour

3 tablespoons plain low-fat yogurt

3 eggs

2 tablespoons butter, melted

1 teaspoon baking powder

½ teaspoon salt

¼ teaspoon ground mace or nutmeg

½ teaspoon vanilla extract

½ teaspoon orange extract

Caramelized Onions and Chard Sauté

1 (12-ounce) bunch chard
1 tablespoon balsamic vinegar
1 tablespoon extra-virgin olive oil
2 teaspoons brown sugar
½ teaspoon kosher salt
1 onion, thinly sliced
¼ teaspoon paprika (preferably smoked)
¼ cup raisins
   Freshly ground black pepper
2 tablespoons chopped walnuts

This easy dish has a lovely, complex flavor and surprising touch of sweetness from the brown sugar and raisins, which ups the kid-friendly factor. Dumping sugar on everything may make it sound more like a box of "Frosted Fruity-O-Sugar-Bombs" than a vegetable dish, but if a scant two teaspoons can help win kids over to healthy greens, it's not such a bad approach. Moderation with sugars and fats is the key. If you have leftovers the next day, place them on a hunk of crusty bread and melt blue cheese over the top.

1. Separate the chard stems from the leaves. Chop the stems and leaves, keeping them separated.

2. Combine the vinegar, oil, sugar, and salt in a large skillet with a lid over medium-high heat. Heat, stirring, until the sugar is dissolved.

3. Add the onion and chard stems and sauté until the onion is translucent, 2 to 3 minutes. Reduce the heat to low, cover, and cook for 10 minutes longer, stirring occasionally.

4. Remove the cover. Add the paprika and raisins, and sauté for 1 minute. Add the chard leaves and sauté, turning with tongs, just until they start to wilt, 2 to 3 minutes. Remove from the heat. Season with black pepper, and stir in the walnuts. Serve warm.

Serves 4 to 6

it's a bird, it's a plane, it's leafy and green!

Leafy greens are the superheroes of the natural world. They offer a bumper crop of vitamins, including vitamins A, C, K, E, and an array of B vitamins. They're chock-full of minerals, like manganese, iron, niacin, zinc, copper, and potassium. Looking for cancer-fighting antioxidants? Omega-3 fatty acids? Amino acids? Fiber? Leafy greens have all of these things in spades.

Leafy greens can fight cancer, lower your blood pressure, keep your mind sharp, improve your eyes, boost your immune system, prevent diabetes, lower your stroke risk, strengthen your teeth and bones, make your skin look better, and even keep reproductive functions healthy. If that's not the nutritional equivalent of leaping tall buildings in a single bound, we don't know what is.

Alas, as a group we aren't eating enough of these vegetables. USDA data from 2005 reveals that among adults, leafy green consumption is less than a quarter of what it should be. Our children are faring even worse. The Feeding Infants and Toddlers Study (FITS) showed that fewer than 10 percent of babies and toddlers are consuming leafy greens and vegetables, leading to a host of nutritional deficiencies. Seventy percent of American teens eat fewer than two servings of any vegetables per day — and a good chunk of the veggies they do eat are potatoes.

It's too bad. Not only do these folks lose out on the health benefits of these nutritional marvels, but they also miss some fantastic flavors. Leafy greens are both versatile and genuinely delicious. Most can be prepared quickly, with just a few ingredients.

Note that leafy greens are one of the Environmental Working Group's "dirty dozen" for pesticide residue (see page 129). Buy organic, or buy direct from a farm that uses sustainable practices or organic methods.

Tangy Kohlrabi Slaw

1 bulb kohlrabi, peeled and grated

3 medium carrots, shredded

1 head Savoy cabbage, chopped

½ red onion, sliced

¼ cup canola mayonnaise

¼ cup apple cider vinegar

¼ cup honey

2 teaspoons Dijon mustard

½ teaspoon kosher salt

½ teaspoon freshly ground black pepper

If you've ever gotten a CSA package containing a strange-looking green or purple orb with leaves growing out of the sides, that vegetable is likely a kohlrabi. The flavor is somewhere between radish and jicama, with a crunchy texture. Kohlrabi tops the list of "Now, what do I cook with *this*?" questions. Here's the answer. This spicy, tangy slaw goes well with a smoky, sweet barbecue dish like brisket or pork ribs, or even a barbecued tofu or sweet chili tofu for vegetarians.

1. Combine the kohlrabi, carrots, cabbage, and onion in a large bowl and toss to blend.

2. Whisk together the mayonnaise, vinegar, honey, mustard, salt, and pepper in a small bowl. Pour the dressing over the vegetables and toss to mix. Cover and refrigerate for at least 2 hours before serving.

Serves 12

Asian Slaw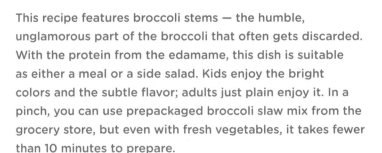

1 (1-pound) bag shelled edamame

2 carrots

½ small head red cabbage, cored

4 broccoli stalks, peeled

1½ tablespoons tamari sauce or soy sauce

2 tablespoons rice vinegar

¼ teaspoon ground ginger

Pinch of crushed red pepper flakes

1 teaspoon toasted sesame oil

2 teaspoons honey or maple syrup

Juice of ½ lime

3 scallions, chopped

This recipe features broccoli stems — the humble, unglamorous part of the broccoli that often gets discarded. With the protein from the edamame, this dish is suitable as either a meal or a side salad. Kids enjoy the bright colors and the subtle flavor; adults just plain enjoy it. In a pinch, you can use prepackaged broccoli slaw mix from the grocery store, but even with fresh vegetables, it takes fewer than 10 minutes to prepare.

1. Bring a pot of water to a boil, and cook the edamame in the boiling water for 5 minutes. (Alternatively, combine the edamame with 3 teaspoons water in a bowl and microwave on HIGH for 3 minutes.) Drain, then rinse with cold water to cool.

2. Shred the carrots, cabbage, and broccoli stalks in a food processor. Place in a serving bowl and add the edamame.

3. Whisk together the tamari, vinegar, ginger, red pepper flakes, sesame oil, honey, and lime juice in a small bowl. Drizzle over the vegetables and toss. Sprinkle the scallions over the top.

Serves 8

Thai Summer Salad

Long beans are a tasty variety, but if you can't find them, fresh green beans will work just as well in this light summer salad. You can control the level of heat in the dressing through the type of pepper you use, from jalapeño for just a bit of heat all the way up to the tiny Thai chiles or a habanero if you and the kids like a good burn.

1. Bring a large pot of water to a boil. Add the beans and boil for 2 minutes to blanch. Immediately place the beans in a bowl of ice water to set the color and stop the cooking. When they're cooled, chop them into 1½-inch pieces.

2. Whisk together the lime juice, oil, hot pepper, garlic, brown sugar, and ginger in a small bowl. Add the peanut butter and whisk again to incorporate. Season with salt.

3. Combine the cucumbers, long beans, bell pepper, scallions, ½ cup of the peanuts, and the cilantro, basil, and mint in a large bowl, and toss to combine. Pour the dressing over the mixture, and toss to coat evenly.

4. Arrange the spinach on a serving platter. Spread the dressed vegetables over the greens. Top with the remaining 2 tablespoons peanuts.

Serves 10

1 (1-pound) bunch long beans
Juice of 4 limes
1 tablespoon canola oil
1 hot pepper (cayenne, jalapeño, or 1 small Thai chile), diced
1 large garlic clove, minced
2 tablespoons brown sugar
1 teaspoon minced fresh ginger
¼ cup peanut butter
Salt
2 medium cucumbers, peeled, seeded, and cut into strips
1 red bell pepper, cored, seeded, and cut into strips
1 bunch scallions, white and dark green parts, chopped
½ cup plus 2 tablespoons crushed peanuts
½ bunch fresh cilantro, chopped (about ¼ cup)
¼ cup packed chopped fresh basil
1 tablespoon chopped fresh mint
1 (12-ounce) bunch water spinach or regular spinach

Greens Gratin

The creamy cheese sauce is a nice complement to the sharp greens. Feta and walnuts add a bit of a twist to this classic.

2 pounds leafy greens (beet greens, turnip greens, collard greens, chard, kale, or a mix), chopped, tough stems removed

1 tablespoon butter

2 scallions, whites and 1 inch of the greens, chopped

2 tablespoons unbleached all-purpose flour

¾ cup whole milk

¼ teaspoon ground nutmeg

½ teaspoon salt

Freshly ground black pepper

½ cup grated Parmesan cheese

2 ounces feta cheese, crumbled (about ½ cup)

¼ cup walnuts

1. Preheat the oven to 350°F.

2. Steam the greens for about 5 minutes, until they just begin to wilt. You can do this in an electric steamer. Alternatively, put a couple of inches of water into a large pot, set a steaming basket in it, and bring to a boil. Set the greens in the basket, cover, and let steam. Place the steamed greens in a 9-inch square baking dish.

3. Heat the butter in a small saucepan. Add the scallions and sauté just until translucent. Add the flour and stir until the mixture turns golden brown. Slowly add the milk, stirring with a whisk to make it smooth.

4. Add the nutmeg, salt, and pepper to taste. Add the Parmesan. Stir until smooth, then taste and adjust the seasonings as desired. Pour the sauce over the greens evenly. You will have a lot more greens than sauce. Sprinkle the top with the feta and walnuts.

5. Bake for 20 minutes, until the greens are tender but not mushy and the feta just gets golden in places. Serve warm.

Serves 8

Variation:
Broccoli or Cauliflower Gratin

You can exchange broccoli or cauliflower florets for the greens, or use a mix of both. Use one large head of either (about 1½ pounds), removing the large stalks and using the florets and more tender stems. Steam the broccoli and/or cauliflower just as you would the greens.

Summer-Squash Fritters

Fritters look enough like a pancake to have some appeal and novelty for kids. These have a nice mix of sweet-and-spice heat that makes them taste great, too. No need to tell the kids that they are loaded with vitamins. You can make these ahead and reheat them in the oven. The warm fritters go well with a bit of sour cream on top.

1. Place the grated squash in a colander. Position the colander over a bowl. Sprinkle the squash with ½ teaspoon of the salt. Set aside for 30 minutes to drain the excess moisture. It's important not to skip this step, or the fritters will get soggy.

2. Heat the oil in a skillet over medium-high heat. Add the scallions and bell pepper and sauté until the scallions are translucent and peppers are softened, about 4 minutes. Add the corn and sauté a bit longer, until the vegetables get some golden color. This adds a nice caramelized flavor. Place the vegetables in a mixing bowl to cool.

3. When the vegetables have cooled, stir in the diced chiles and cilantro. Squeeze the grated squash to get all the moisture out and add to the bowl. Mix well.

4. In another bowl, prepare the batter by stirring together the cornmeal, cumin, remaining ¼ teaspoon of salt, chile powder, and baking powder. Then add the milk, honey, egg, and sugar, and mix well. Season with black pepper. Pour the batter into the vegetable mixture and fold together gently. Add the cheese and fold in.

5. Spray a skillet (you can wipe out the used one to save a pan) or a griddle with cooking spray and heat over medium heat. Drop a heaping tablespoonful of the mixture into the skillet for each fritter. Flatten slightly to help the fritters cook evenly. Turn over when dark golden brown. Repeat with the remaining batter.

Serves 12 (makes about 24 fritters)

1 medium summer squash, grated
¾ teaspoon kosher salt
1 teaspoon extra-virgin olive oil
2 scallions, white part and 2 inches of the green, chopped
½ red bell pepper, diced
1 cup corn kernels (fresh or frozen)
1 (4-ounce) can diced green chiles, drained
⅓ cup chopped fresh cilantro

FOR THE BATTER
2 cups cornmeal
½ teaspoon ground cumin
½ teaspoon ancho chile powder (or any mild pure chile powder)
½ teaspoon baking powder
½ cup milk
¼ cup honey
1 egg
¼ cup sugar
Freshly ground black pepper
2 ounces Monterey Jack cheese, grated (about ½ cup)

cooking at its simplest

When your meals rely on fresh, seasonal ingredients, there is
a certain amount of unpredictability. You may find out there
was a late freeze and the tender spring greens you'd counted
on are not at the market. Or your CSA box arrives with more
beets than carrots. Even on a trip to the grocery store, the
produce you may have planned on is too expensive that day
or just plain doesn't look good. That's why it's important to
master a few skills that will allow you to quickly and easily
prepare just about any vegetable without using a recipe. Two
of these skills, roasting and sautéing, allow you to prepare
delicious vegetables with just a touch of oil and seasoning.

▬ Roasting

Plants store simple carbohydrates to use as energy. As these
sugars cook, they caramelize, creating the browning in color
and enhanced sweetness. This process yields the flavor we
most often associate with "cooked," such as the crust on bread
or the browning on meats.

Sugars will caramelize only at temperatures above 338°F.
This explains why vegetables will not "brown" when steamed
or boiled; water cannot be heated above 212°F — it turns to
steam and evaporates. Only dry-heat methods such as baking,
roasting, and grilling will brown foods. This browning leaves
you with an intense, almost sweet flavor that is difficult to
match.

Most vegetables can be roasted, but the method works
especially well for starchy vegetables like potatoes and root
vegetables. A small number of more delicate vegetables, like
collards and spinach, don't lend themselves to roasting, as
they will dry out and burn too quickly.

To roast, simply trim or chop your vegetable to a uniform
size, coat with a bit of canola or olive oil and salt and pepper,

spread in a single layer on a baking sheet or in a baking pan, and bake at 350°F or more (many cooks recommend 400°F). Baking time will vary based on the size of the vegetable pieces and firmness of the vegetable.

Generally speaking, if it is pleasingly browned and soft enough to be pierced with a fork, it is done. If you are roasting vegetables of different densities — say, zucchini and potatoes — you'll want to roast them in separate pans and for different lengths of time. Generally, vegetables harvested during the same season can be roasted together well.

Certain herbs lend themselves to roasting; rosemary and thyme are terrific complements to roasted vegetables. A sprinkle of balsamic vinegar or lemon juice, tossed with the oil, also enhances the flavor of roasted vegetables.

> "Once you have mastered a technique, you barely have to look at a recipe again."
>
> Julia Child, Julia's Kitchen Wisdom: Essential Techniques and Recipes from a Lifetime of Cooking.

Sautéing

Sautéing and other methods that use oil (like deep-frying, panfrying, and stir-frying) are, like roasting, considered "dry" cooking methods, because they use oil instead of water, which can be heated to a higher temperature and so will brown foods. This method is a quick-cook method, and it is less suited to starchy vegetables, which take longer cooking times or may require steaming first before being added to a sauté for browning.

To sauté with good results, use just enough oil to cover the bottom of the pan, and heat the skillet over medium-high heat before adding the item to be sautéed. For the best results, use a large enough pan to allow the food to be in a single layer. Toss or stir only as needed to get the best browning and texture in the finished result. If you are using more than one type of vegetable in your sauté, follow this simple order. First, add aromatics like onion or garlic. Then, add more dense vegetables, finely chopped, such as carrots, followed by softer vegetables such as asparagus, peppers, or mushrooms. Last, add delicate vegetables like greens or herbs, which require less time.

143

1 large, long zucchini
    (unpeeled)
½ pound spaghetti
⅓ cup Basil Pesto (page 145)
1 cup Roasted Tomatoes
    (page 106)
¼ cup grated Parmesan cheese

Squaghetti

Is it a noodle or squash? Now, let's see 'em pick the green vegetable out of that dish! Actually, they won't bother. The strands mix so well with the other flavors that they are likely to love it.

1. Prepare the zucchini strands by using a lemon zester and pulling it lengthwise along the zucchini. Place the strands in a metal colander that will fit into the pasta pot.

2. Bring a large pot of water to a boil for the pasta. Before you place the spaghetti in the water, put the colander in and blanch the squash for 1 to 2 minutes. Remove from the water, and set aside to cool. Cook the pasta according to the package directions.

3. Drain the pasta, and combine the hot pasta and pesto in a large bowl. Gently fold in the squash strands, as they will be more delicate. Top with the tomatoes and the Parmesan.

Serves 6

Soyccatash

good for lunch!

2 cups frozen edamame
    (green soybeans)
1 cup frozen corn
¼ cup water
1½ teaspoons butter
1 cube low-sodium, organic
    vegetable bouillon
1 red bell pepper, cored,
    seeded, and diced
½ large red onion, chopped
    Salt and freshly ground
    black pepper
2 tablespoons chopped fresh
    basil

This can be served hot, at room temperature, or even cold. Because the recipe uses frozen vegetables, it's versatile for both winter and "between seasons." It goes great in lunch boxes and as a nice colorful side on a chilly spring day.

1. Bring a large saucepan of salted water to a boil. Add the edamame and boil for 4 minutes. Add the corn to the boiling water and boil for 2 minutes longer. Drain and set aside.

2. Add the water, butter, and bouillon cube to the hot saucepan. Return the pan to the stove and turn the heat to medium. Stir to dissolve the bouillon. Add the red pepper and onion to the saucepan and cook until the onion is fragrant and translucent, about 2 minutes. Add the edamame and corn to the saucepan and toss to combine well.

3. Remove from the heat, and season with salt and pepper. Stir in the chopped basil.

Serves 4

Lemony Couscous Salad

good for lunch!

This light salad is a perfect welcome to early summer. With the mint, feta, and cucumber, the flavors are a bit like that old standby, Americanized "Greek salad." But better. Kids can help stir the dressing, crumble the cheese, and toss all the ingredients together. Best of all? It can be created in a few minutes flat.

1. Whisk together the lemon juice, lemon zest, honey, vinegar, and oil in a small bowl or cup, and season with salt and pepper.

2. Combine the tomatoes, cucumber, scallions, arugula, basil, mint, couscous, and feta in a large bowl, and toss to combine. Pour the dressing over the salad, and toss lightly. Cover and set in the refrigerator to chill for at least 2 hours before serving.

Serves 8 to 10

FOR THE DRESSING
- Juice of 2 large lemons
- Zest of 1 large lemon
- 2 tablespoons honey
- 1 tablespoon white balsamic vinegar
- ⅔ cup extra-virgin olive oil
- Salt and freshly ground black pepper

FOR THE SALAD
- 1 pound grape or cherry tomatoes
- 1 large cucumber, seeded and diced
- 2 scallions, white parts and 1 inch of green parts, sliced
- 2 cups packed arugula leaves
- ¼ cup chopped fresh basil
- 1 tablespoon chopped fresh mint
- 2 cups cooked couscous, prepared according to package directions
- 4 ounces feta cheese, crumbled (about ⅓ cup)

Basil Pesto

This basic recipe works well in a variety of dishes, from vegetables to pasta to chicken. Freeze extra in small portions (½ cup sauce per pound of pasta).

1. Combine basil, Parmesan, pine nuts, and garlic in a food processor.

2. Pulse to combine while slowly adding olive oil. Add salt and pepper to taste and pulse.

Makes about 2 cups

- ⅔ cup basil
- ½ cup grated Parmesan cheese
- ¼ cup pine nuts
- 1 clove garlic
- ¼ cup olive oil
- Salt and freshly ground black pepper

145

Orange-Basil Sweet Potatoes

2½ pounds sweet potatoes, peeled and cut into 1-inch cubes
½ cup orange juice
1 tablespoon finely chopped fresh basil, or 1½ teaspoons dried
Kosher salt

If you want more orange flavor, you can add ½ teaspoon of orange extract or orange zest to bump up the citrus. You can also serve it garnished with mandarin orange slices to help entice a young child.

1. Steam the sweet potatoes for 20 to 30 minutes, until fork-tender. You can do this in an electric steamer. Alternatively, put a couple of inches of water into a large pot, set a steaming basket in it, and bring to a boil. Set the sweet potatoes in the basket, cover, and let steam.

2. Mash the sweet potatoes in a large bowl. Mix in the orange juice, basil, and salt to taste.

Serves 8

Honey-Chipotle Mashed Sweet Potatoes

3 pounds sweet potatoes, peeled and cut into 2-inch cubes
1 tablespoon extra-virgin olive oil
1 tablespoon honey
1 tablespoon brown sugar
Sea salt
¼ cup half-and-half
2 tablespoons butter
1 chipotle pepper in adobo sauce, chopped
1 tablespoon adobo sauce

Because the sweet potatoes in this dish are roasted, the texture will be coarser than mashed potatoes, but the flavor is worth it. You can find chipotle chile peppers in adobo sauce in cans in many supermarkets. Use orange, rather than pale, sweet potatoes for this recipe.

1. Preheat the oven to 400°F.

2. Toss the potatoes with the oil, honey, brown sugar, and salt in a large bowl. Transfer to a large baking dish or a baking sheet and roast for about 40 minutes, until fork-tender.

3. Mash the potatoes with the half-and-half and the butter. Add the chopped chipotle and the adobo sauce and mix well.

Serves 10

146

Everything you ever wanted to know about fats... and then some!

Your body needs fats to absorb nutrients, so to understand healthy eating of any variety, you need to know a little something about fats. Most nutrition experts divide fats into four main categories: polyunsaturated fats, monounsaturated fats, saturated fats, and trans fats. The term *saturation* refers to the carbon-hydrogen makeup of the oil; the more hydrogen in the fat, the greater the degree of saturation and the greater the solidity of the oil. Different kinds of fats have dramatically different effects on the human body.

Unsaturated Fats

Both **polyunsaturated** and **monounsaturated fats** are generally considered in the "good for you" category. Monounsaturated fats, like olive oil, are generally liquid at room temperature but solidify when refrigerated. These are especially good for you because they raise blood levels of HDL (the good cholesterol) while also lowering blood levels of LDL (the bad cholesterol). Polyunsaturated fats, like soybean and safflower oil, lower the levels of LDL but also lower the levels of HDL. Polyunsaturated oils rarely solidify, even when refrigerated. *When stored and used properly, unsaturated fats have positive health benefits.*

Saturated Fats

Saturated fats come from animals — think butter, lard, and bacon grease. They also come from some plants; coconut oils, palm kernel oils, and palm oils are all saturated fats. These fats are solid at room temperature. *Because saturated fats raise LDL (bad cholesterol) levels, most experts recommend eating them in limited quantity.*

Trans Fats

Trans fats, or trans-fatty acids, are the byproduct of partial hydrogenation. These are the fats that you should never consume if you can avoid it. Research has clearly demonstrated that trans fats increase your risk of heart disease and death, and researchers are currently investigating the role of trans fats in type 2 diabetes and Alzheimer's. *Cut trans fats out of your diet completely.*

Sounds simple, right? Hold on, because there are a few other things you should know about fats.

147

Omega-3 Essential Fatty Acids

Omega-3s are types of polyunsaturated fats. They are essential to human health yet cannot be manufactured by the body. Omega-3s reduce the risk of heart disease and stroke and reduce symptoms of hypertension, depression, joint pain, certain skin ailments, and even ADHD. Research suggests that omega-3s can reduce your risk of diabetes, minimize insulin resistance in diabetics, boost bone density, strengthen immunity, inhibit the growth of certain cancer cells, and protect against Alzheimer's. Omega-3s are wonder fats. Think of them as A-list celebrities, the beloved darlings that everyone wants at their party.

Sources of Omega-3s
The best sources of omega-3s are:

- Coldwater fish such as salmon, mackerel, halibut, sardines, and herring
- Flaxseeds, including flaxseed oil
- Canola (rapeseed), including canola oil
- Soybeans, including soybean oil
- Pumpkin seeds, including pumpkin seed oil
- Some leafy greens, like purslane
- Perilla seeds, including perilla seed oil
- Walnuts, including walnut oil
- Krill and algae (often available as supplements)

Omega-6 Essential Fatty Acids

Omega-6 fatty acids are present in such foods as vegetable oils, meats, eggs and dairy products, grains and cereals. Like omega-3s, omega-6 EFAs do some very good things: support skin health, lower cholesterol, and encourage proper blood clotting. However, they also increase inflammation in the body, and they can cause damage if they aren't balanced with sufficient amounts of omega-3s. The typical American diet tends to contain 14 to 25 times more omega-6 fatty acids than omega-3 fatty acids. Researchers think that this imbalance is a major factor in the rising rate of an array of health disorders in the United States. Although no one is entirely sure what the ideal ratio is, virtually all researchers agree we need to replace some of our most-commonly eaten foods with foods that are rich in omega-3s.

Hydrogenation

If omega-3s are the darlings of the party circuit, consider hydrogenated oil the irascible drunk who no one wants around: nasty, hurtful, and always unpleasant. And, by the way, if you let him hang around long enough, he might even try to kill you. Hydrogenated oils and partially hydrogenated oils are oils that have been treated with hydrogen and heavy metal. Hydrogenation creates trans fats. *Avoid foods that contain hydrogenated or partially hydrogenated oils.*

Tips for the Healthful Use of Oils

Got the basics of oils down? Here are just a few more tips:

■ **Forget everything you just learned.** Well, maybe not *everything*. Trans fats really are that bad. But for saturated and unsaturated fats, the above information makes a good guiding principle, while the full picture is a little more complex than we can explain here. For example, if an animal was pasture raised, its meat has more omega-3s than that of its grain-fed counterparts. Farmed fish often have lower levels of omega-3s than their wild cousins. As with everything food related, the *quality* of the oils and fats plays an important role in the nutrition profile.

■ **Don't fear the fat!** The truth is, food stops tasting good if it doesn't contain enough fat. Besides, the fats are filling, ultimately helping people eat less. Andrew Weil, MD, suggests that most people can enjoy optimum health on a diet of up to 30 percent fat, or even more, as long as they're the right *kinds* of fats.

■ **Never let oil smoke.** When oils are heated to the point of smoking (see chart that follows), they begin to decompose. This decomposition releases free radicals, which increase health risks, including cancer.

■ **Be sure to store oils properly.** Any oil can turn rancid. Keep oils in a cool, dark place, and ideally in a tinted or opaque container. Keep more delicate oils, like nut oils, in the refrigerator.

■ **Beware oxidation.** When oxygen reacts with unsaturated fatty acids, the oils begin to smell and taste bad. They go rancid. This is not merely unpleasant, it's also bad for your health. Oxidation generates free radicals, highly reactive molecules that promote arterial damage, inflammation, premature aging of cells, and cancer. The oils that are most at risk of oxidation are those that are primarily polyunsaturated, and the higher the percentage of omega-3s, the greater the risk. Never consume any oils (or oil-rich foods, like nuts, cookies, or chips) that taste or smell off.

149

■ **Never reuse oils.** Reusing oils creates oxidative stress in the body, which has been implicated in an array of diseases and negatively affects the body's aging process.

■ **Consume omega-3 oils fresh, not cooked.** The oils that are richest in omega-3s should generally not be used for cooking. Unless the oil has been refined to withstand high heat (like canola oil), heat turns these good fats into harmful ones. You can drizzle these oils on warm food just before serving, or use them in cold dishes that will not require lengthy storage.

Flaxseed oil

Contains 50–60 percent omega-3 fatty acids in the form of alpha-linolenic acid (ALA). Nutty flavor. The nutrients that give flaxseed its nutrition also give it a short shelf life. Keep refrigerated or it will turn rancid.

smoke point: 225°F ●
primary oil type: Polyunsaturated
uses: Used primarily as a health supplement, it can also be drizzled over salads or steamed vegetables.

Pumpkinseed oil

Robust, nutty, fragrant oil that is rich with omega-3s. Rare in the United States, but a treat if you find it.

smoke point: 225°F ●
primary oil type: Polyunsaturated
uses: Drizzle over salads, steamed vegetables, yogurt, or ice cream.

Butter

Butter is one of the most prized fats because of its rich taste and terrific mouthfeel. For a treat, try cultured butter, which is made from sour cream.

smoke point: 350°F ● ●
primary oil type: Saturated
uses: Used widely as a spread and baking ingredient. Due to its low smoking point, it shouldn't be used for frying (use ghee instead).

●
low heat

● ●
medium heat

● ● ●
medium-high heat

● ● ● ●
high heat

Note: Most fats contain a mix of saturated, polyunsaturated, and monounsaturated fats. Unless otherwise specified, the type of fat listed here is the primary type of fat.

Walnut oil

Delicate in flavor and color. Do not use for pan-frying, as it goes rancid when heated. Because walnut oil can be expensive, it is generally used as a specialty oil.

smoke point: 320–400°F ● ● / ● ● ●
primary oil type: Polyunsaturated
uses: Used in cold dishes and dressings.

Sesame oil

Comes either plain or toasted. Highly concentrated; a little of the sesame flavor goes a long way. Contains 43 percent polyunsaturated, 42 percent monounsaturated.

smoke point: 350–450°F depending on how refined ● ● / ● ● ●
primary oil type: Polyunsaturated/monounsaturated
uses: Commonly used in Asian dishes.

Lard

Rendered hog fat. Long maligned by nutrition experts, lard is making a comeback. Lard contains 47 percent monounsaturated fats and just 41 percent saturated fats.

smoke point: 370–400°F ● ● ●
primary oil type: Saturated/monounsaturated
uses: Good for frying and baking; adds a flakiness and golden brown color to pie crusts.

Extra-virgin olive oil

Golden-green oil with a strong flavor that has many uses. If you keep just one oil on hand, make this the one. Highest monounsaturated content of any of the edible oils. There is great variation in flavor, color, and fragrance depending on how it's harvested.

smoke point: 400°F ● ● ●
primary oil type: Monounsaturated
uses: Great for dressings and medium-heat roasting and sautéing. Can even be a partial fat substitute for baking in many recipes.

Cottonseed oil

All-purpose cooking oil often used by food manufacturers. Cotton grown for oil is one of four most common genetically modified crops.

smoke point: 420°F ● ● ●
primary oil type: Polyunsaturated
uses: Used to create commercial salad dressings, mayonnaise, shortening, and similar products.

Almond oil

Fragrant, with a lovely almond taste. Many people use almond oil as a body oil.

smoke point: 425°F ● ● ●
primary oil type: Monounsaturated
uses: Drizzle over vegetables, use as substitute for olive oil, toss with pasta, or use as accent in baked goods.

Hazelnut oil

Highly fragrant oil, with a nutty, creamy flavor similar to the hazelnut itself. Often expensive. Can mix with a lighter-flavored oil to cut the taste or to stretch this delicacy.

smoke point: 430°F ● ● ●

primary oil type: Monounsaturated

uses: Great for salad dressings and baking delicacies.

Sunflower oil

Light in appearance and taste. High-oleic sunflower oils have monounsaturated levels of 80 percent and above.

smoke point: 440°F ● ● ●

primary oil type: Polyunsaturated

uses: Common cooking oil; flavor generally too mild for dressings.

Peanut oil

All-purpose cooking oil made from steam-pressing peanuts. Flavor ranges from mild to strong.

smoke point: 440°F ● ● ●

primary oil type: Monounsaturated

uses: Good for frying/sautéing, especially spicy/Asian foods, and salads.

Corn oil

Mild oil pressed from corn kernels. Usually highly refined and made from genetically modified corn. Not recommended.

smoke point: 450°F ● ● ●

primary oil type: Polyunsaturated

uses: Common cooking oil. Flavor too mild for dressing.

Palm oil

Made from the flesh of palm fruit. Contains 51 percent saturated fat, 39 percent monounsaturated fat. Not recommended.

smoke point: 450°F ● ● ●

primary oil type: Monounsaturated/saturated

uses: Increasingly used by food manufacturers as an alternative to trans fats.

Safflower oil

Colorless, flavorless all-purpose vegetable oil. Nutritionally similar to sunflower oil.

smoke point: 450°F ● ● ●

primary oil type: Polyunsaturated

uses: Used as a cooking oil and in salad dressings.

Canola oil

Produced from rapeseed, which belongs to the mustard family. Name comes from "Canadian oil, low acid." Although unrefined canola oil is high in omega-3s, most canola oil is highly refined.

smoke point: 460°F ● ● ● ●

primary oil type: Monounsaturated

uses: All-purpose oil used in cooking, baking, salads.

Soybean oil

All-purpose inexpensive vegetable oil. Most oils sold as "vegetable oil" are soybean oil. Most are genetically modified; look for organic types.

smoke point: 495°F ● ● ● ●
primary oil type: Polyunsaturated
uses: Used to make mayonnaise, margarines, and commercial dressings. Fine for cooking.

Ghee (clarified butter)

Butter that has been rendered to separate the milk solids and water from butterfat. Clarified butter has a higher smoke point and longer shelf life than fresh butter.

smoke point: 485°F ● ● ● ●
primary oil type: Saturated
uses: Can be used like butter; contains much of butter's flavor but can be cooked at higher temperatures.

Avocado oil

Mild flavor, loaded with antioxidants, including vitamins D and E. Beautiful green color makes it lovely for salads.

smoke point: 520°F ● ● ● ●
primary oil type: Monounsaturated
uses: Good for sautéing, stir-frying, and salads.

Margarine

Margarine is a general term used for many different varieties of butter substitutes. The manufacturing process varies, so the health profile of each margarine brand is different. Some brands are decidedly unhealthful, and all are made by large-scale manufacturers. Unless you do research beyond the health claims on the packaging, use only with caution.

smoke point: Do not use.
primary oil type: Polyunsaturated
uses: Do not use.

Palm kernel oil

Made from the pit of the palm fruit. Usually solid at room temperature. Not recommended.

smoke point: Do not use.
primary oil type: Saturated
uses: Used primarily by food manufacturers. Do not use.

FACT: Did you know that olive oil can be used to replace butter or margarine when baking cookies, breads, brownies, muffins, and other baked goods? According to Lisa Sheldon, author of *Olive Oil Baking* (Cumberland House Publishing, 2007), if a recipe calls for more than a half a cup of butter, start by replacing half of the butter with olive oil. Not only is the flavor still good, but the olive oil also actually enhances the flavors of certain types of baked goods, like fruit bars.

Most packed lunches need more nutrition. A study of preschool children who brought packed lunches to school revealed that just 29 percent of the packed lunches contained adequate fruits and vegetables, and only 20 percent of children had a milk serving at lunch. About 11 percent didn't get enough whole grains.

Source: Sweitzer, S., Briley, M., Robert-Gray, C. M. "Do Sack Lunches Provided by Parents Meet the Nutritional Needs of Young Children Who Attend Child Care?" *Journal of American Dietetic Association* Volume 109, Issue 1, Pages 141-144 (January 2009)

CHAPTER FOUR

MEAL-TIME

recipes to make it work

We'll go ahead and say it: feeding kids is a never-ending task...

It doesn't matter if you fed them three hours ago, or even half an hour ago. There they are, asking to eat again. It doesn't matter that you have prepared dinner every single night for the past 3,209 nights: the only one that seems to matter is the one that they haven't eaten yet.

Sometimes it might feel like your life is playing a continuous loop of instructions: prepare, serve, clear, wash, repeat. Some find pleasure in it — the routine, the way the family comes together in the kitchen, then at the table. Others do it because they know that teaching kids about quality food is just like teaching them to look both ways before crossing the street or not to swish their hands in the toilet bowl; it's part of keeping them safe and healthy.

Still, there are times when even the most committed of us feel the lure of convenience foods, the siren call of something fast, inexpensive, and guaranteed to please. The less cooking is part of our routine, the louder that call. That's why it's helpful to have some strategies in our pockets. Recipes are great, especially if you can memorize a handful of favorites. Knowing basic techniques helps — like how to mix a quick salad dressing, how to roast or sauté vegetables, how to prepare a big pot of lentils on the fly. But something else helps, too: planning and organization. That part gets better with practice.

This chapter is filled with easy, delicious recipes as well as tips and tricks to help you get a handle on that whole planning and organizing thing. Many of the recipes take less time to prepare than a wait in the drive-through lane. Others will help you learn how to cook just once and get everything you need for several easy weeknight meals at the same time.

"Whys," a parable from Beth's kitchen

"BE CAREFUL, KIDDO, you're going to fall."

"Why?"

"Because you are leaning off the couch."

"Why?"

"Uh, gravity . . . you see . . . uh . . . oh. Because I said so," I say, running over.

[Thump.]

I try to navigate all the whys at least until I run out of answers the kiddo can grasp. I can usually go six rounds before I give up and latch on to the "said so" standby, even when the why is as obvious as the floor beneath us. I persevere because I respect "why." I get it. It's one of the most important questions that can and should be asked.

Asking why is what pushed Ali and me down the path of making our own recipes. Of questioning the food supply and where our food comes from, of how food is produced, and of understanding how a few of our own cooking attempts have gone horribly awry and felt kind of like that thump.

Once you know the why, you can look in the CSA bag or at the farmers' market that day and cook with whatever is fresh. You can look into the pantry and know how to pull together a decent meal with whatever you have on hand. This knowledge frees you from the process of finding a recipe, then going to the megamart to get the listed ingredients, regardless of season. Learning the techniques for yourself will let you cook a meal without needing a recipe, make your own recipes, make better use of your leftovers, and be able to modify recipes to allow for things like food allergies and personal preferences. It really is as simple as just asking "Why?" and it sure does save a lot of headaches.

breakfast

IT TURNS OUT YOUR GRANDMOTHER WAS RIGHT: Breakfast is the most important meal of the day. A wide range of research, dating all the way back to the 1950s, demonstrates clearly that children (and adults) who eat a healthy breakfast think more clearly, crave less junk, perform better on a wide range of tasks, have better memory and attention, and have more energy.

A study of 4,000 elementary school students compared how students did on a battery of attention tests — like memorizing a series of digits, or naming all the animals they could think of in 60 seconds — after eating breakfast or skipping it. Across the board, breakfast eaters did better than breakfast skippers.

It makes sense. The brain's basic fuel is glucose, or blood sugar. Essentially, while kids are sleeping, their bodies are fasting. When they awake, they need a fresh supply of glucose to kick-start those brains again. But all glucose is not the same. Glucose can come from simple sugars and simple carbohydrates, which are likely to create a rush of blood sugar, only to leave kids empty and hungry a short time later. Glucose can also come from complex carbohydrates — like fruits and whole grains — that will keep them going longer.

Of course, breakfast comes at the very worst time for making a rational decision. Most of us are bleary-eyed and scrambling to get everyone out the door on time. Speaking personally, we have found we've had better luck serving a healthful breakfast if we plan the night before — setting places, taking peanut butter and bread from the cabinet, soaking steel-cut oats so that they'll cook quickly, or even hard-boiling eggs in advance.

Some people don't have an appetite in the morning. After fasting all night, metabolism slows down, which leads some people to feel a lack of hunger. Even these folks, though, can benefit from a healthful breakfast.

159

Experts recommend that most breakfast foods contain a mix of whole grains, proteins, and fresh produce. There's no reason, of course, that breakfast must look traditional. Last night's leftovers often taste even better the next day, and we have served our kids everything from cooked beans to miso soup in the morning.

quick and easy breakfast options

- **Fruit salad** with **cottage cheese** and a sprinkling of **nuts** or **flaxseed**
- **Yogurt parfait** made with layers of not-too-sugary **granola** and **fruit**
- A **fruit smoothie** made with **yogurt** or tofu
- **Whole-grain toast** or waffle with **peanut** or **almond butter** and a side of **fruit**
- **Whole-grain waffle** topped with **fresh fruit** and plain **yogurt**
- A **hard-boiled egg**, **toast**, and **fruit**
- Baked **apples** with **nuts**, topped with **yogurt** or **cream**
- Steel-cut **oats** with **dried fruit** and milk
- **Couscous** prepared with milk instead of water, topped with **raisins** or dried **cranberries** and served with **honey** or maple syrup
- Breakfast wrap with **eggs** or **tofu**, **vegetables**, and **melted cheese**
- **Pita** stuffed with **eggs** and **salsa**
- Breakfast sandwich made with a whole-grain **English muffin**, **turkey sausage** or sautéed tofu slices, and **melted cheese**
- Breakfast pizza: an English muffin topped with **tomato slices** and covered with **melted cheese**; add a sliced hard-boiled egg for extra protein
- **Healthful muffin** (not the cakelike kind) made with whole grain and copious amounts of **shredded zucchini** or **fruit**
- **Whole-grain bread** with a little **almond butter**, **sliced banana**, **raisins** on top, and a sprinkling of **cinnamon**

Slow-Cooker Oatmeal

Steel-cut oats are one of the best hot cereals but often get overlooked for a "quicker" breakfast. Making these in a slow cooker the night before makes this healthful, delicious hot breakfast ready when you are. No slow cooker? Soaking the oats before bed cuts the cooking time in half. Store the leftovers in the refrigerator and reheat in the microwave. For extra nutty flavor, toast the steel-cut oats in a 350°F oven for about 10 minutes before you put it in the slow cooker.

1 cup steel-cut oats
⅓ cup chopped dates
⅔ cup raisins
⅓ cup chopped dried figs
½ teaspoon ground cinnamon
⅓ cup chopped almonds or walnuts
4 cups water
½ cup half-and-half

1. Mix all of the ingredients together in a slow cooker before you head to bed. Set to LOW and cook for 8 to 9 hours.

2. Stir to combine.

Serves 10

Variation:

You can also use 2 cups total dried blueberries, cranberries, and cherries instead of the other dried fruits here. Skip the cinnamon and use ½ teaspoon vanilla extract instead for this version.

FACT: Oatmeal beats sugar cereal when it comes to boosting brain power. Researchers from Tufts University gave breakfast to children and then gave them academic tasks like memorizing the names of countries on a map. One week, the kids ate oatmeal. Another week, they ate a popular brand of sugar cereal. After eating oatmeal, the kids performed better on a variety of tasks, including spatial memory, short-term memory, and listening.

Source: Mahoney C. R., Taylor H. A., Kanarek R. B., Samuel P. "Effect of breakfast composition on cognitive processes in elementary school children." *Physiol Behav.* 2005 Aug 7; 85(5):635-45.

buying eggs

Eggs not marked otherwise are generally factory-farmed (this goes for most of the chickens we buy at the grocery store too). While less expensive, chickens raised in conventional commercial "cage and floor operations" have some of the most depressing living conditions of any livestock being produced on a large scale. Crowded into cages, many are "force molted" — starved for up to 14 days — to encourage egg production. Many of us strive to consume eggs from chickens raised in a more humane environment. But it can be hard to decipher the terms producers use to describe their operations. Cage-free, free-range, pastured, vegetarian-fed, high in omega-3s . . . egg producers are making all kinds of claims these days. What does it all mean?

Free-Range Is Not Always Free

Supporting producers who raise "free-range" chicken and eggs can encourage humane production techniques. But buyer beware: A chicken that technically has "access" to the outdoors can be called free-range or cage-free, but this chicken may only have limited access to the outdoors and still live in a pen — a larger enclosure instead of a smaller cage. The chickens' diet may be the same commercial feed as that of a caged, factory-farm chicken. While supporting genuine free-range production techniques may be a more humane choice, it might not increase the nutrition content of the egg, since the nutrition content is most impacted by what the chickens eat.

"Vegetarian-Fed"

Chickens are not vegetarians by nature. If given an option, they eat bugs, grubs, and other protein sources in addition to grasses and their feed. But many industrial farms supplement commercial chicken feed with animal by-products, like bone, feathers, blood, manure, and animal parts. These "animal by-products" are often from beef. This is the same ingredient that has been banned from commercial feed for beef cattle because of concerns about Mad Cow disease. Ironically, the "meat by-product" now used for the protein source in commercial cattle feed is chicken by-products and feather meal.

The label "vegetarian-fed" simply means that the chickens are not fed animal by-products. It says nothing about the chickens' living conditions, or whether they have access to their natural diet.

Omega-3s, Pastured Eggs, and Egg Nutrition

The nutritional value of an egg is determined primarily by the chicken's diet. A chicken that has access to pasture and a natural diet of bugs and grass in addition to grain produces eggs that are higher in omega-3 essential fatty acids and other nutrients.

Factory-farmed eggs can be made higher in omega-3s and some nutrients by supplementing the chickens' diet with products rich in omega-3s, like flaxseed. These eggs are more nutritious than conventional eggs, but not as complete as eggs produced from pastured chickens' natural diet.

A good clue to the nutritional content of an egg is the color of the yolk. Pastured chickens' eggs often have a deep orange color resulting from yellow and orange plant pigments, called xanthophylls. If a chicken's diet is low in these pigments, the yolk will be milder in color.

The yolk holds the egg's vitamin content including six B vitamins, as well as vitamins A, D, and E. The yolk also contains the antioxidants lutein and zeaxanthin and trace amounts of carotene, phosphorus, iron, and magnesium.

So, What Kind of Eggs Are Best?

The eggs that are best for our health, for the chicken, and for the environment tend to come from a chicken that has unlimited access to pasture and a natural diet of grasses and bugs, as well as grain that has not been supplemented with antibiotics or animal by-products. You can't find these eggs in most grocery stores. For the moment, you probably have to find the farmer or a grocery store that sources quality local eggs. Don't hesitate to ask your supermarket, though; the more people who ask, the more likely grocers are to stock local, pastured eggs.

163

8 eggs
4 ounces goat cheese, crumbled
¼ cup packed chopped chives
½ teaspoon salt
  Freshly ground black pepper
1 tablespoon butter
1 pound asparagus, cut into ½-inch pieces
1 cup packed spinach leaves
1 ounce Parmesan cheese, grated (enough to lightly dust the top of the frittata)

Asparagus and Spinach Frittata

This easy breakfast works just as well for a quick and delicious dinner, paired with a green salad on a busy weeknight.

1. Preheat the oven to broil.

2. Whisk the eggs, then stir in the goat cheese and chives and season with salt and pepper.

3. Melt the butter over medium heat in an ovenproof skillet. Add the asparagus and sauté for about 5 minutes, until just a bit golden. Add the spinach leaves, turning until wilted, about 2–3 minutes. Add the egg and cheese mixture, and mix well. Allow the frittata to cook until set.

4. Remove the skillet from the stove. Sprinkle on the cheese, and broil for about 5 minutes, until puffed and golden brown on top.

Serves 6 to 8

Hash Brown, Chard, Tomato, and Ham Frittata

This frittata works as a "one-dish" meal for any time of day, incorporating vegetables with the eggs and potatoes.

1. Put oven rack in middle position and preheat the oven to 375°F.

2. Combine the cheeses. Whisk together eggs, milk, pepper, and salt in a large bowl until combined, then whisk in ¾ cup of the cheeses. Save the remaining ¼ cup of cheese for the top.

3. Heat the oil in a 10-inch cast-iron skillet over medium-high heat. Sauté the shallot until just golden, about 3 minutes. Add the hash browns and cook, stirring occasionally, until golden. Remove from the heat and mix in the ham, tomatoes, and chard. Pour in the egg mixture.

4. Sprinkle the top with the remaining cheese. Bake about 25 minutes, until set 2 inches from the edge but still slightly wobbly in the center and the cheese on top is golden.

Serves 6 to 8

¾ cup grated Gouda cheese
¼ cup grated Parmesan cheese
6 large eggs
1 cup whole milk
   Black pepper
½ teaspoon salt
3 tablespoons extra-virgin olive oil
1 large shallot, chopped
1 (1 pound) bag frozen hash browns, thawed
¼ pound ham, diced small (in ¼-inch cubes)
1 cup roasted tomatoes (page 106)
1 (12-ounce) bunch chard, chopped

FACT: Skipping breakfast makes the brain more responsive to high-calorie, fatty foods. Using functional magnetic resource imaging, researchers at the Imperial College of London showed that when healthy people skip breakfast, the brain's "reward center" — the part of the brain that responds to pleasure — is markedly more active when shown photos of unhealthful foods like pizza, cake, and chocolate. The same individuals showed no such response after eating a healthful breakfast.

Source: The Endocrine Society's 91st Annual Meeting, Washington, D.C., June 10–13, 2009. News release, The Endocrine Society.

Shirred Eggs

This classic dish is an easy way to make many servings of eggs at once without a lot of time at the stove, making it a great brunch entrée. The individual serving cups are elegant and effortless.

4 very thin slices Canadian bacon, ham, or prosciutto
4 eggs
2 tablespoons cream
2 tablespoons grated Gruyère or other cheese

1. Preheat the oven to 350°F.

2. Spray four ramekins or muffin pan cups with cooking spray. Line each with a slice of ham, pushing it into the cup to make a pocket. Crack an egg into each ramekin on top of the ham.

3. Place the ramekins or muffin pan on a baking sheet and bake for about 9 minutes, just until the eggs are set. Remove from the oven and top each egg with 1½ teaspoons of cream and 1½ teaspoons of cheese. Return to the oven and bake for 5 to 7 minutes longer.

   To get the tops brown and bubbly, broil for just a minute at the end.

Serves 4

Variation:
Shirred Eggs with Spinach

Heat a medium skillet over medium heat. Add a bunch of spinach to the skillet while the leaves are still damp from washing. Heat, turning the leaves, until they begin to wilt, about 3 minutes. Divide the cooked spinach among the ramekins, placing it on top of the ham.

Breakfast Panini

This is one complete breakfast you can eat on the go. Just be sure you turn the stove off before you race out the door.

1. Whisk the eggs with the milk in a medium bowl. Spray a skillet with nonstick spray. Place over medium heat and add the eggs. Scramble the eggs and remove from the skillet.

2. Add 1½ teaspoons butter to the skillet. Lay 2 slices of the bread in the skillet. Lay half of the cheese, sun-dried tomatoes, and roasted peppers evenly on 1 slice. Add half of the arugula and basil to 1 slice and 1 slice of ham, if desired, to the other. Add half of the scrambled eggs to 1 slice.

3. When the bread is golden brown on the bottom, carefully flip one fully loaded slice on top of the other. Using the spatula (because who really needs that expensive panini press?) or a grill press, press down on the sandwich to flatten it a bit. Turn the sandwich over and press again. Remove to a plate.

4. Repeat with the other 2 pieces of bread and the remaining half of the filling ingredients. Cut each sandwich in half.

Serves 2 to 4

4 eggs

1 tablespoon 2 percent milk, or half-and-half

1 tablespoon butter

4 large slices rustic bread

4 ounces semisoft cheese, such as fontina, Gouda, or provolone, shredded (about 1 cup)

4 sun-dried tomatoes packed in oil, chopped

2 roasted red peppers, chopped

½ cup torn arugula leaves

1 tablespoon chopped fresh basil leaves

2 slices ham (optional)

FACT: If parents eat breakfast, kids are more likely to eat breakfast. A recent review of 24 studies on the subject, focusing on both children and adolescents, showed that adolescents are most likely to eat breakfast if their parents do the same.

Source: Pearson N., Biddle S. J., Gorely T., "Family correlates of breakfast consumption among children and adolescents." A systematic review. Appetite. 2009 Feb; 52(1):1–7.

Ginger-Banana-Oatmeal Pancakes

3 small, ripe bananas, mashed
2 tablespoons melted butter
1 tablespoon lemon juice
1 tablespoon brown sugar
1 tablespoon crystallized ginger
2 eggs
⅔ cup whole-wheat flour
⅔ cup old-fashioned oatmeal
1 teaspoon Ceylon or regular ground cinnamon
½ teaspoon baking soda
½ teaspoon kosher salt
¼ teaspoon ground mace or nutmeg
  Natural peanut butter for topping
  Honey for topping

Topping these with peanut butter makes these hearty pancakes into a complete meal. You won't need anything else to stay full.

1. Mix the bananas, butter, lemon juice, brown sugar, ginger, and eggs in a large bowl. Mix the flour, oatmeal, cinnamon, baking soda, salt, and mace in another bowl. Add the dry ingredients to the banana mixture and stir until just blended.

2. Preheat a griddle over medium heat. Drop batter onto the griddle by the ¼ cup and cook until bubbles appear, about 3 minutes. Flip and cook on other side until golden.

3. Serve topped with peanut butter and honey.

Makes about 6 pancakes

Banana–Peanut Butter Smoothie

1 (12-ounce) block silken tofu
1 cup milk or soy milk
2 ripe bananas
⅓ cup natural peanut butter
1 tablespoon flaxseed oil (optional, but adds to omega-3 content)
1 tablespoon honey

Tofu is an unlikely ingredient here, adding body, protein, and substance to this easy breakfast alternative.

Put all of the ingredients into a large blender for a spin until well blended. Chill and serve cold, reblending if needed.

Serves 4

Health Rounds

As easy to grab as a power bar, these make-ahead, no-cook rounds make a solid breakfast on those mornings you don't have time to sit down.

1. Crush the whole-grain cereal flakes by putting them in a large plastic bag and running a rolling pin over them. Mix the crushed cereal with the peanut butter, dry milk, honey, and vanilla in a large bowl. (Depending on the moisture content of your nut butter, you may need to add a sprinkle of water.)

2. Shape into 1-inch rounds, roll in coconut flakes or cocoa, if desired, and refrigerate; they will harden when chilled, making them easy to handle.

Makes about 16 rounds

2 cups whole-grain cereal flakes

½ cup peanut or almond butter

¼ cup nonfat dry milk

3 tablespoons honey or maple syrup

¼ teaspoon vanilla extract

3 tablespoons coconut flakes, or cocoa powder (optional)

FACT: A recent Consumer Reports nutritional analysis of 27 popular children's breakfast cereals found that only four of them could be rated "very good" for kids. The number one problem? Sugar content. Two of the cereals were 50 percent sugar, and another nine cereals had at least 40 percent sugar. Ten of the cereals contained as much sugar as a glazed doughnut. Heaping sucrose on fructose, the magazine also found that, on average, youngsters filled their bowls with 50 to 65 percent more than the suggested serving size.

Source: Consumer Reports. "Better cereal choices for kids?" Available at: www.consumerreports.org/health/healthy-living/diet-nutrition/healthy-foods/breakfast-cereals/overview/breakfast-cereals-ov.htm.

lunch

THERE'S A REVOLUTION HAPPENING in your child's school right now. Nope, it is not the final overthrow of geometry, or even the contentious evolution debate. The battle lines have been drawn in the lunchroom. The skirmishes are over everything from banning soda machines and branded junk food options in the cafeteria to reauthorizing all of the legislation that governs the school nutrition program as a whole.

The most forward-thinking districts are bringing farm-to-school programs to their kids' tables; the USDA has even begun a program to support this effort. Other schools are beginning to reconsider Tater Tots and mac and cheese — menus that look more like a drive-through lane than an actual meal. School gardens and salad bars are springing up. For any parent interested in making sure their kids eat actual food, there is a lot of positive change ahead.

Since we still have a long way to go before every school has an edible schoolyard, you can help shape that healthier lunchroom. Until the kale chip completely replaces the potato chip, however, you might want to remember that the majority of school lunches, even though they meet USDA standards, are not healthy. This section will offer some tips for packing both you and your child a healthy lunch made with real food.

lunch-box strategies

YOU CAN KEEP PACKED LUNCHES SIMPLE, satisfying, and safe with these easy tips.

▪▪▪ **The right container matters.** Get the right containers, and packing lunches will be easier. Consider investing in a bento-style lunch box, with many small containers that fit together neatly. Sending hot lunches? Be sure to use microwave-safe containers or a good stainless-steel Thermos.

■ **Make sure you have leftovers.** Sometimes, a healthful lunch is as easy as setting aside a small amount of the previous night's dinner. Make sure you set some aside before you sit down to the dinner table, so that it doesn't all disappear.

■ **Think small.** Kids, especially younger children, love bite-size foods. Minimuffins, tiny sandwiches . . . often children will eat these, when they might turn up their nose at the adult-size portion. And they may be more likely to eat fruits and vegetables if they're presliced.

■ **It's all in the presentation.** For young children, consider making healthful sandwiches, and then using a cookie cutter to turn them into stars, hearts, or other favorite shapes. Or include a toothpick to make eating grapes and cheese and meat cubes more fun.

■ **Keep it colorful.** Not only are children more attracted to fruits and vegetables of many colors, this colorful variety also ensures a wide range of healthful foods.

■ **Let them pack it.** Children are more likely to eat foods that they packed themselves. Offer a range of healthful choices, and then let them pack it themselves, providing helpful suggestions as they go.

■ **Keep it safe.** By the time your child eats lunch, it will have sat around for several hours. Keep hot foods hot with a Thermos, and cold foods cold with ice packs.

■ **Be realistic.** You'll be packing lunches daily for at least 200 days of the year. If you're too ambitious, you'll quickly burn out. It doesn't have to be gourmet; simple and healthful is fine.

Look for this brown-bag icon on recipes throughout this book. These recipes are a great addition to your kid's lunch bag.

171

easy lunch-box favorites

MANY OF THE RECIPES in this chapter make fantastic leftovers, which can be easily packed in a lunch box. No leftovers? Consider these fast, easy lunch-box options, which can be made from pantry staples:

- **Peanut butter** or **almond butter** on whole-grain crackers

- **Mini sandwiches** with cheese and nitrate-free meats

- **Hard-boiled egg**, cheese stick, sliced fruit, and Crispy Rice and Almond Square (page 263)

- Pita bread stuffed with **hummus** and **vegetables**

- **Stuffed apple:** Core an apple; fill with peanut butter. Sprinkle raisins on top. Slice the apple three-quarters of the way through. Child can pull the slices off and eat them.

- **Sliced apple:** Soak the slices in apple juice ahead of time, and they can sit in a lunch box all morning without turning brown.

- **Cottage cheese** topped with toasted nuts or seeds

- **Bite-size raw vegetables** with a sesame dipping sauce, ranch dressing, or bean dip

- Sandwich toppings on a tortilla, rolled up into a spiral, and cut into rounds

- **Bean roll-up:** Fat-free refried beans on a whole-wheat tortilla wrap.

- Quick **bean salad:** Drizzle kidney beans with olive oil and balsamic vinegar; add salt, basil, and oregano.

- **Mini frittatas**, cooked in muffin tins. Frittatas freeze well, and if you take them out in the morning, they should be thawed just in time for lunch.

- **Lentil/yogurt salad:** Mix cooked lentils with a splash each of olive oil, plain yogurt, and red wine vinegar. Add a pinch of salt, dill, and/or other herbs.

- Homemade **guacamole** with whole-grain crackers (sprinkle lemon juice on the top and cover tightly to keep it from turning brown)

- Make-your-own **trail mix:** Roasted nuts, dried fruits, shelled sunflower or pumpkin seeds, and roasted garbanzo beans. Ingredients can be varied depending on whether your child wants a berry theme, a tropical theme, and so on.

- Food on a stick: **chicken kabobs** or **fruit kabobs**

- **Breakfast for lunch:** A slice of bacon, a sliced hard-boiled egg, and a single pancake, smeared with nut butter and a touch of maple syrup, all rolled up together for easy handling

- **Mini meatballs,** served with a toothpick

- Homemade **macaroni and cheese**, in a shallow Thermos

- Leftover **soups and stews** in a microwavable container or a Thermos

- Simple **pasta salad** with vegetables, olive oil, and a touch of vinegar

- **Cold rice balls:** Use short-grained rice; when it's still warm, press a child's favorite vegetable inside a small portion and then roll into a ball and cover with sesame seeds.

great lunch-box recipes

SOME OF THE SLAWS, SALADS, AND OTHER RECIPES from this book travel well and don't need any reheating, making them excellent lunch-box choices. They include:

Lunch Sides

Broccoli and Cauliflower Salad (page 71)

Carrot-Raisin Slaw (page 76)

Marinated Broccoli (page 133)

Red Cabbage Slaw with Dried Fruit and
    Savory Praline (page 134)

Asian Slaw (page 138)

Soyccatash (page 144)

Lunch Entrées

Fall Vegetable Soup (page 181)

Chicken Salad with Red Grapes, Blueberries,
    and Almonds (page 194)

Golden-Crisp Chicken Nuggets (page 199)

Lamburgers in Pita (page 213)

Lunch Dips and Extras

Lima Bean Hummus (page 239)

White Bean–Pesto Dip (page 240)

Apple Cider Applesauce (page 253)

Chocolate-Walnut Zucchini Bread (page 257)

Crispy Rice and Almond Squares (page 263)

173

Dinner

CHANCES ARE, YOU'VE SEEN THE HEADLINES about the benefits of family dinners. Research shows that children who eat with their families are less likely to drink, smoke, or use drugs. They also do better in school, develop better verbal skills, and have a lower risk of eating disorders and depression.

But does the dinner itself protect kids? Or is it simply that families most likely to sit down to dinner are the ones most likely to demonstrate the traits that benefit children? That depends. In some cases, it's the routine that is important. In other cases, it appears that family dinners are generally associated with well-functioning families — and it's the "well-functioning" part that matters most.

We've had our share of family dinners that left us feeling more frustrated than functional. We've also had plenty of nights when we didn't even attempt a family meal, choosing instead to hurl food at our children like they were hungry lions. Still, on better days, we recognize that there are benefits to eating together. Family meals are a chance to come together at the end of a harried day. They can help instill values, like good manners, conversation, and shared tasks. They can establish eating routines — this is what dinner is, this is what a healthy meal looks like.

They aren't always easy, however. More parents are working, and they are working longer hours than ever. Children are dizzyingly busy with after-school activities and homework. There are plenty of households where by the time the parents arrive home from work, prepare a meal, and set the table, the children have already snacked themselves silly. Or perhaps they haven't eaten at all, and instead have just plain fallen apart. Neither of these scenarios makes for an ideal family dinner.

You know your family best. Will sitting down together nightly as a family help bring you together, or will it end in increased stress and frustration?

If a nightly meal is out of the question, you might consider setting aside just a few evenings a week — or even one — as Family Dinner Night. You might also consider making another meal the family meal (breakfast, anyone?). Or perhaps you'll find it's easier to feed the kids early, and then let them sit at the "grown-up" table and drink a glass of milk while you eat a little later. The key is finding your own family's routine.

Remember, too, that family dinners don't always look like you think they will. Family dinners may be civilizing for kids, but children rarely come to the table civilized. Plenty of aspects of family dinners — like sitting in a chair for an extended period of time, engaging in polite conversation, using utensils properly, and not smearing spaghetti's sauce on one's head — don't come all that naturally to kids. That's okay. That's real life. Like everything you do with your kids, it's a work in progress, not a finished product.

> "Sitting down to dinner, at any age, should be an invitation to the fabulous banquet that is life. The most important lesson we learn at the table is that great rewards await those who take chances. Do we really want to be telling our children, 'Just eat your nice chicken nuggets'? It would make so much more sense to say, 'Pull up a chair. Take a taste. Come join us. Life is so endlessly delicious.'"
>
> — Ruth Reichl, Teach Your Children Well, *Gourmet Magazine*, March 2007.

175

faster-than-drive-thru dinners

Some nights, cooking isn't simple. You're delayed at work, or the dance lesson runs late, or the errands take longer than you planned. For those instances, it's good to be armed with insta-recipes: foods that can be made from scratch in a matter of minutes. Here are some supper solutions that require less time than takeout.

- Mix a can of **garbanzo beans** with **olive oil**, **lemon juice** or **vinegar**, **chopped tomatoes**, and **parsley**. Serve with whole-grain **pita**.

- Sauté **chopped garlic** in ample olive oil. When it is soft, add some diced **tomatoes**, and let it cook over low heat while you boil **spaghetti**. Mix in the cooked spaghetti, along with a touch of balsamic vinegar. Toss together in the pan. Serve with grated **Parmesan**.

- **Poach or scramble eggs** in one pan, sauté some **greens** in another, and serve the eggs atop the greens.

- Slice **apples** and **cheddar cheese** and serve on **crusty bread** with **honey mustard**.

- Jazz up a **simple grilled cheese** by adding a touch of **pesto** and **tomatoes**. While the sandwich is in the pan, press down on it with a kettle filled with hot water for an insta-panini.

- Sauté **onions and garlic**. Add a can of **black beans** and half a can of **diced tomatoes**. Simmer for 5 minutes, then season with cumin, salt, and pepper. Serve over a microwaved **sweet potato**.

- Cook a pot of **rice**. Add a steamer basket filled with **vegetables** during the last 5 minutes. Serve the veggies over the rice and crumble **feta cheese** over the top.

- Place 2 cloves of **garlic** in a roasting pan. Cover with a thin fillet of **fish**, and then brush the top with **lemon juice** and **olive** oil. Cook at 450°F for about 10 minutes, until the fish flakes easily. Serve with **salad greens** or **chopped vegetables**.

- Soak ½ cup of **sun-dried tomatoes** in warm water for 5 minutes to soften them. Cut into strips, then combine with a can of **cannellini beans** and 2 chopped **tomatoes** in a saucepan. Cook until heated through. At the last minute, add some baby spinach and mix until just wilted.

- Make your own **burritos**, using refried **beans**, whole-wheat **tortilla wraps**, lots of **chopped vegetables**, and shredded **cheese**.

- **Wrap anything in a whole-grain tortilla** or flatbread: goat cheese and spinach. Leftover chicken and tomatoes. Shredded carrots, greens, and feta. Avocado and beans. Tomatoes and mozzarella. Hummus and lettuce. Whatever it is, heap on the vegetables, wrap, and serve.

177

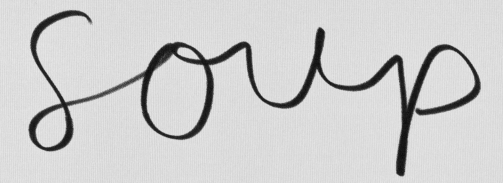

Soup

SOUPS ARE A GREAT WAY to use leftover vegetables and meats. Packed in a Thermos, soup adds a hearty touch to a lunch box. These easy soups also work great for a light weeknight dinner. Once you know the basic soup methods, you can create a soup easily from what you have on hand.

▬ Soup Definitions

Mirepoix

Say it: *meer-uh-PWAH*. It's fun. This is a mixture most commonly of two parts onion, one part carrot, and one part celery by weight. It's added to things like soup stock to give the stock more depth of flavor and aroma. Mirepoix is the first step in many soup recipes, with the vegetables being "sweated" in a bit of oil over low heat to get them to give up their moisture, but not brown. Some advise to add a bit of salt here to encourage the sweating, but nearly all commercial stocks have salt and plenty of it. Salting early and then adding these products will ruin the soup.

Roux

Say *roo*. If you are doing a cream- or cheese-based soup, the last step will be to make a roux in a separate saucepan by browning equal parts by weight of butter and flour. The roux is used to thicken the cream or stock to make a sauce. Cook until the mixture begins to smell nutty and is just starting to get frothy and bubbly but is not turning golden.

Béchamel

Béchamel, one of the five primary sauces of French cooking, is made simply by adding cream or milk to roux. It's used in many cream- or cheese-based soups.

Velouté

"Cream of" soups are sometimes made with velouté, which is prepared by adding stock to the roux instead of cream. The soup may be finished with cream just before serving to add a bit of richness.

▬ Basic Soup Techniques

Soup is a flexible dish to create, and a great way to use leftovers. Once you know the basic steps for each type of soup, you can create a pot of soup from the vegetables you have on hand just by understanding the "whys" and the basic quantities of liquid to garnish, meaning the vegetables and/or meats you use in the soup. Recipes follow that show each of the basic types and how to vary them.

Broth-Based Soup

1. Sweat the mirepoix.
2. Add the stock or broth, and bring to a simmer.
3. Add the seasonings.
4. Add the next ingredients, from longest cooking time (meats) to shortest cooking time (delicate vegetables), at the appropriate intervals.
5. Simmer until all the ingredients are cooked.

"Cream of" Soup

1. Follow the steps for a broth-based soup.
2. Using a stick blender, or processing in batches in a blender, purée the soup to the desired texture.
3. Prepare a velouté in a separate saucepan, then add to the purée.
4. Finish the soup with bit of cream, if desired.

Cheese-Based Soup

1. Follow the steps for a broth-based soup.
2. Using a stick blender, or processing in batches in a blender, purée the soup to the desired texture (usually chunky).
3. Prepare a roux in a separate saucepan.
4. Convert the roux to béchamel by adding warm milk or cream, whisking constantly. Simmer until thick.
5. Add the cheese to the béchamel, and whisk until it melts and is thoroughly combined.
6. Add the cheese sauce to the puréed soup.

Summer Vegetable Soup

2 tablespoons extra-virgin olive oil

1 large onion, chopped

⅔ cup chopped carrot (about 2 medium)

⅔ cup chopped celery (about 3 stalks)

2 garlic cloves, minced

10 cups vegetable or chicken stock

2 teaspoons dried savory

1 teaspoon dried thyme

1 bay leaf

1 pound fresh shelled purple hull peas or black-eyed peas

2 Parmesan rinds (optional), or use a bit of grated Parmesan for serving

2 cups cauliflower florets

1 cup chopped fresh green beans (1-inch pieces)

5 medium tomatoes, peeled, cored, seeded, and chopped

1 bunch flowering bok choy, stemmed and chopped (about 2 cups)

Salt and freshly ground black pepper

Broth-based soups are a great way to use in-season produce. Make vegetable substitutions based on what you have, what's in season, and what tastes good together.

1. Heat the oil over medium-low heat in a stockpot, and add the onion, carrot, and celery. Sweat the mirepoix until the onion is translucent, about 4 minutes. Add the garlic, turn up the heat to medium, and sauté for a couple of minutes.

2. Add the stock and the savory, thyme, and bay leaf. Bring to a boil, then reduce the heat to a simmer. Add the peas and Parmesan rinds, if desired, and simmer for 45 minutes.

3. Add the cauliflower, and simmer for 15 minutes longer. Add the green beans and tomatoes, and simmer for 10 minutes longer. Test the beans to make sure they are cooked to al dente texture. When they are, add the bok choy, and simmer for 5 minutes longer.

4. Remove the bay leaf and Parmesan rinds. Season with salt and pepper. Freeze some if you like for a cold, rainy or snowy day.

Serves 12 to 14

Variation:
Summer Vegetable Soup with Dried or Canned Beans

Though fresh beans are incredible, you can also prepare this soup with dried or canned black-eyed peas. If you're using dried beans, you'll need ½ cup, and they'll need to be soaked overnight, then rinsed and drained. Increase the cooking time for step 2 to at least 90 minutes, and add more stock or water to the pot as necessary, since dried beans absorb liquid as they cook.

If you're using canned beans, rinse and drain them well, and add them to the pot with the bok choy near the end of the cooking.

Fall Vegetable Soup

When the cooler months arrive, you can use the same technique as for Summer Vegetable Soup, but change the ingredients according to what is in season.

1. Heat the oil over medium-low heat, and add the onion, carrot, celery, and garlic. Sweat the mirepoix until the onion is translucent.

2. Add the stock and the savory, thyme, and bay leaf. Bring to a boil, then reduce the heat to a simmer. Add the sweet potato, squash, peas, and Parmesan rinds, if desired, and simmer for 60 minutes.

3. Test the peas to make sure they are cooked to al dente texture. When they are, add the greens, and simmer for 5 minutes more.

4. Remove the bay leaf and Parmesan rinds. Season with salt and pepper.

Serves 12 to 14

2 tablespoons extra-virgin olive oil
1 large onion, chopped
⅔ cup chopped carrot (about 2 medium)
⅔ cup chopped celery (about 3 stalks)
2 garlic cloves, minced
10 cups vegetable or chicken stock
1 tablespoon dried savory
2 teaspoons dried thyme
2 bay leaves
1 pound sweet potatoes, peeled and diced small (in ¼-inch cubes)
1 pound winter squash, peeled and diced small (in ¼-inch cubes)
1 pound fresh shelled purple hull peas or black-eyed peas
2 small Parmesan rinds (optional)
2 bunches (about 1½ pounds) kale or chard, stemmed and chopped
Salt and freshly ground black pepper

▬ Parmesan Rinds

These are the secret to a rich flavor in nearly any soup.

When you use up a wedge of Parmesan cheese, save the rind, wrap it well in plastic, and store it in the freezer. When added to a hot soup, the rind will melt a bit and tiny bits of the Parmesan incorporate into the soup, adding a layer of depth and richness. Incredible. Remove the large chunk of rind from the soup before serving.

Fennel, Potato, and Leek Soup

1 tablespoon extra-virgin olive oil
2 medium leeks, white and light green parts only, chopped
1 fennel bulb, chopped
2 large shallots, chopped (about ⅓ cup)
4 cups chicken stock
4 medium baking potatoes (russets), peeled and chopped
1 tablespoon chopped fennel fronds
2 tablespoons chopped fresh flat-leaf parsley
  Salt and freshly ground black pepper
  Grated Gruyère cheese for serving

Fennel, leeks, and herbs add a nice depth to potato soup. By using the fronds and the bulb, the fennel serves a dual purpose: as both vegetable and herb.

1. Heat the olive oil over medium-low heat in a Dutch oven, or large stockpot.

2. Add the leeks, fennel, and shallot and and sweat the vegetables for about 10 minutes.

3. Add the stock and the potatoes. Bring to a boil, then reduce the heat to a simmer. Simmer until the potatoes are tender, about 30 minutes.

4. With a stick blender (or transfer to a food processor), carefully blend the soup until smooth. Hot liquids expand when blended, so work with small quantities at a time. Return to the pot over the heat if using the food processor method. Add the fennel fronds and parsley, and season with salt and pepper. Serve topped with a bit of Gruyère cheese.

Serves 8

Better-Than-Takeout Egg Drop Soup

1 tablespoon canola oil
2 scallions, chopped, white and green parts separated
4 cups chicken broth
½ teaspoon sherry
½ teaspoon soy sauce
¼ teaspoon salt
⅛ teaspoon ground ginger
⅛ teaspoon white pepper
1½ tablespoons cornstarch
3 drops sesame oil
2 eggs

Ali's daughter loves egg drop soup. By mastering this recipe, Ali ended the seemingly endless requests for Chinese takeout.

1. Heat the canola oil in a large saucepan over medium-low heat. Add the white parts of the scallions and sweat for five minutes.

2. Pour 3½ cups of broth into the pan, reserving ½ cup. Add the sherry, soy sauce, salt, ginger, and white pepper. Bring to a boil and let cook for 5 minutes.

3. Mix the cornstarch with the reserved broth in a small bowl, and add to the pan. Add the sesame oil. Turn the heat to low. In a separate bowl, beat the eggs, then add to the broth while stirring rapidly in a clockwise motion. Stir for 1 minute, until the eggs have cooked and look like shreds.

4. Sprinkle the soup with the scallion greens. Serve hot.

Serves 4

Hearty Kale-Potato Soup

Recently, Ali's daughter declared that if she could choose just one food to eat for the rest of her life, it would be a toss-up between ice cream and this soup. Using the immersion blender makes the texture more appealing to younger children.

1 tablespoon canola oil
¾ pound sweet Italian sausage, casings removed or chopped very small
2 garlic cloves, chopped
8 cups chicken broth
1 pound potatoes, chopped to ½- to ¾-inch pieces
1–2 Parmesan rinds, if available
12 oz (6 to 8 stems) kale, stemmed and chopped fine
Salt and freshly ground black pepper
½ lemon
¼ cup grated parmesan, optional

1. Warm the oil in a large stockpot over medium heat. Add the sausage and cook until browned, about 6 minutes. Mix in the garlic and sauté 1 minute. Set the mixture aside in a bowl.

2. In the same stockpot, add the broth and potatoes. Bring to a boil, then reduce the heat and simmer until the potatoes are tender, about 20 minutes. Using an immersion blender, or processing in a blender, purée until the texture is chunky-smooth. (If you think your kids will have issues with the kale, hold off on the purée. Add the kale and simmer for 12 to 15 minutes, then purée and add the sausage, Parmesan rinds, and seasonings.)

3. Add the Parmesan rinds, if using, kale, and the sausage mixture. Bring to a boil, reduce heat, and simmer for 12 to 15 minutes, until the kale is cooked but still retains its bright color.

4. Season to taste with salt and pepper. Remove the rinds.

5. Squeeze a bit of lemon juice over each bowl. Add about 1 teaspoon of grated parmesan, if using, on each serving, and serve hot.

Serves 8

183

Squash, Carrot, and Lentil Soup

1 (5-pound) Hubbard or other
   winter squash, halved and
   seeded
1 teaspoon extra-virgin olive
   oil
1 tablespoon butter
1 large onion, diced
2 garlic cloves, minced
1½ teaspoons chopped fresh or
   ¾ teaspoon dried thyme
1½ teaspoons chopped fresh or
   ¾ teaspoon dried sage
8 cups vegetable stock
1½ cups grated carrots (about
   6 medium)
1 cup green lentils, rinsed and
   drained
½ cup half-and-half
2 teaspoons sugar
   Salt and freshly ground
   black pepper

Puréed soups don't have to lack texture. Adding some of the ingredients after the soup is blended gives this soup texture, flavor, and nutrition. Cooking large items like the squash or pumpkin in halves in the oven makes using those ingredients much easier, with less chopping.

1. Preheat the oven to 400°F.

2. Rub the squash halves with the olive oil. Place them cut side down on a baking sheet sprayed with nonstick cooking spray. Roast in the oven for about 40 minutes, or until the flesh is fork-tender. Remove from the oven and allow to cool. Scoop out the flesh into a bowl.

3. Heat the butter in a Dutch oven. Sweat the onions and garlic until translucent. Add the thyme, sage, and 4 cups of the stock. Add half of the grated carrots and all of the squash. Bring to a boil, then reduce the heat to a simmer and cook for about 30 minutes.

4. Meanwhile, in a smaller saucepan, add the lentils and 2 cups of the broth. Bring to a boil, then reduce the heat to a simmer and cook until the lentils are cooked to al dente texture, about 30 minutes.

5. Carefully blend the soup until it is smooth with a stick blender (or transfer to a blender or food processor). Add the remaining 2 cups of broth and the rest of the carrots. Simmer until the carrots are tender, about 20 minutes. Add the lentils and any remaining liquid and bring back to a simmer.

6. Before serving, stir in the half-and-half and sugar. Season with salt and pepper.

Serves 12 to 14

Pumpkin–White Cheddar Soup

Pumpkin works well in this soup, but you can substitute mashed sweet potatoes, or even use canned pumpkin if desired. If you like, serve with a dollop of sour cream or crème fraîche, or even a bit more of the shredded white cheddar.

1. Set an oven rack in the lowest position and preheat the oven to 350°F.

2. To prepare the pumpkin, cut it in half and scrape out the seeds and pulp. Lightly oil the skin and place on a baking sheet, cut side down. Bake for about 1 hour, until the sides of the pumpkin give easily when pressed.

3. Remove from the oven and allow to cool a bit. Scrape the flesh from the skin into measuring cup (you need 5 cups). Purée in a food processor until smooth. (Any extra pumpkin purée can be frozen for future use. Store in 1-cup or 15-ounce portions to be equal to a can of pumpkin purée.)

4. Heat the remaining 2 tablespoons olive oil in a large stockpot over medium-low heat. Add the onion, carrot, sage, and thyme. Sweat the vegetables for about 10 minutes.

5. Add the flour and stir to coat the veggies and cook the flour for a couple minutes. Add the stock and the cider and bring to a boil. Reduce the heat to a simmer. Simmer, stirring occasionally to let the soup thicken a bit, for 10 minutes. Add the pumpkin and stir, bringing back to a simmer. Add the milk, bringing the soup back just to a simmer.

   Last, add the cheese in small handfuls, stirring as you go to melt it in completely. Taste and season with salt and pepper as needed.

Serves 8

1 (10-pound) pumpkin (to make 5 cups of purée)
2 tablespoons extra-virgin olive oil, plus more for brushing pumpkin skin
1 large onion, chopped
1 cup carrot diced small (in ¼-inch cubes)
2 tablespoons chopped fresh or 1 tablespoon dried sage
1 teaspoon chopped fresh or ½ teaspoon dried thyme
¼ cup unbleached all-purpose flour
4 cups chicken or vegetable stock
1 cup apple cider
3½ cups milk
12 ounces white cheddar cheese, grated (about 3 cups)
Salt and freshly ground black pepper

185

Bread and Tomato Soup

3 pounds tomatoes

2 tablespoons olive oil

1 onion, chopped

2 garlic cloves, coarsely chopped

2 tablespoons chopped fresh rosemary

½ loaf rustic bread, crust removed and bread cut into 2-inch cubes (about 3 cups)

1½ cups chicken broth

Salt and freshly ground black pepper

Grated Parmesan or sliced fresh mozzarella cheese

The little one around Beth's house will eat two helpings of this recipe. She calls it "pizza soup," since her favorite pizza is Margherita with fresh tomatoes and basil. Served with good crusty bread, and a slice of fresh mozzarella on top, this is about as close to pizza soup as you can get.

1. Preheat the oven to 450°F.

2. Core the tomatoes and cut them into wedges. Heat the olive oil in a large ovenproof pot over medium-high heat. Place the tomatoes and onion in the pot. Cook until the peels begin to brown and wrinkle, 5 to 7 minutes. Stir in the garlic and rosemary.

3. Place the pot, uncovered, in the oven and roast for about 15 minutes. Remove from the oven and place back on medium heat on the stove. Mix in the bread cubes and chicken broth. Cook until the juices and broth are absorbed and the texture of the soup looks smooth and creamy, about 10 minutes longer. Season with salt and pepper. Remove from the heat.

4. Pulse the soup with a stick blender or in the food processor until it is a bit smooth, but not totally puréed. The soup is best if it can chill for an hour so that the flavors blend. You can serve it cold, or reheat it gently. Serve with grated Parmesan or sliced mozzarella on top.

Serves 8

Cauliflower-Cheese Soup

with Carrots and Greens

You can make this soup with broccoli or cauliflower. The creamy texture and cheese make these traditionally disliked vegetables a lot more kid-friendly.

1. Heat the oil in a large stockpot over medium heat. Add the celery, carrot, and onion, and sweat the mirepoix for about 10 minutes.

2. Add the stock, bay leaf, and thyme. Bring to a boil, then reduce the heat to a simmer. Add the cauliflower and cheese rinds and simmer until the cauliflower is tender, about 20 minutes.

3. Meanwhile, in a separate saucepan, prepare a roux by melting the butter. Whisk in the flour and cook, whisking constantly, for a couple minutes, until the mixture smells nutty. Add the warm milk. Bring to a simmer, then add the Parmesan and whisk to melt evenly into the sauce.

4. Remove the bay leaf and cheese rinds from the soup. Carefully purée about half the vegetables in the soup with a stick blender or in the food processor or blender, bringing it to a chunky-smooth texture.

5. Stir in the cheese sauce. Bring to a boil, then reduce the heat and simmer for 10 minutes.

6. Add the greens and simmer until the greens are tender, 5 to 10 minutes longer. Season with salt and pepper. Serve garnished with more grated Parmesan if desired.

Serves 8

2 tablespoons extra-virgin olive oil
1 cup chopped celery
½ cup chopped carrot
½ cup chopped onion
4 cups chicken stock
1 bay leaf
2 teaspoons dried thyme
4 cups cauliflower florets (from 2 small heads of cauliflower)
2 Parmesan cheese rinds (see page 181)
1 tablespoon butter
2 tablespoons unbleached all-purpose flour
1 cup whole milk, warmed
8 ounces grated Parmesan cheese (about 2 cups), plus more for garnish (optional)
1½ cups chopped greens, such as baby bok choy
Salt and freshly ground black pepper

187

poultry

IT'S IMPORTANT TO USE SAFE HANDLING with all poultry, even "natural" chickens. In a 2007 Consumer Reports test, the largest sampling yet, 83 percent of the chickens tested — including both factory-farmed and organic brands — tested positive for campylobacter or salmonella. Always cook poultry, with the exception of duck, until a thermometer reads 170°F when placed in the meat of the thigh, away from the bone. (The inside of the thigh is usually the last part of the bird that cooks.) Other signs of doneness include clear juices running from the cavity and the thigh and leg joints moving easily in their sockets.

■ Do 30-Minute Meals Really Exist?

While we like the concept of quick and tasty meals, let's talk about this a bit.

Have you ever read the timing on a recipe (20 minutes active time, 30 minutes cook time) and based a dinner on that? Two hours late, the components are getting done one at a time, at the wrong time, and your dinner becomes a late-night snack. To use a child's endless refrain for everything, "Why?"

Simply this: Those 30-minute meals are 30 minutes only if the ingredients are all prepped and ready to go. Prep times in recipes are also based on an experienced cook who possesses a chef's knife and the ability to "mise en place" (page 192). Master these, and you will be on your way to 30-minute meals that really are 30 minutes.

Pan-Seared Chicken
with Roasted Tomatoes, Pesto, and Goat Cheese

The preparation of this dish is similar to that of the Chicken Scallopini (see page 191), but it has a more familiar "tomato and cheese" bent that kids like.

1½ pounds boneless, skinless chicken breasts
½ cup unbleached all-purpose flour
  Salt and freshly ground black pepper
¼ cup canola oil
1 shallot, minced
1 cup chicken broth
2 cups Roasted Tomatoes (page 106)
4 ounces goat cheese
¼ cup Basil Pesto (page 145)

1. Place the chicken 1 piece at a time in a gallon-size ziplock bag. Set the bag on a sturdy cutting board. Using a kitchen mallet, pound the chicken to an even thickness of about ½ inch. Remove the chicken from the bag. Repeat for all the chicken pieces. (The plastic bag keeps the raw chicken off the board and from splattering in your kitchen.)

2. Mix the flour with generous pinches of salt and pepper in a shallow dish.

3. Preheat the oven to 350°F.

4. Heat half of the oil in a large ovenproof skillet (*not* a non-stick skillet). Dredge 1 chicken breast in the flour, and set it in the skillet. Repeat until about half of the chicken is in the skillet. Fry for 4 minutes on medium-high heat. (Do not disturb the chicken during this time or else it will not brown evenly.) Using tongs, flip the chicken; the bottom side should be golden brown. Fry until cooked through and golden brown on both sides, about 4 minutes longer. Set the cooked chicken in a dish and keep warm. Repeat with the remaining oil and chicken.

5. Sauté the shallot in the same skillet until golden brown. Pour in the broth and scrape up the *fond* (crispy chicken bits) from the bottom of the skillet. Simmer until the broth is reduced by one-half, 5 to 8 minutes. Remove from the heat.

6. Return the chicken to the skillet, and top with the tomatoes and goat cheese. Set in the oven to heat through for a few minutes. Serve each portion with a tablespoon of pesto.

Serves 6

tastes like chicken?

Ever wonder why any generic, bland, nearly flavorless white meat of dubious origin is jokingly described as "tastes like chicken"? Whether it's iguana or frog legs or mystery nuggets, we can assure you that it does *not* taste like chicken. In our opinion, factory-farmed chicken does not even taste like chicken.

The flavor of meat, as well as the texture and nutrition, come from what the animal eats and how it lives. So, what kind of chicken actually tastes like chicken? Pastured chicken, just like pastured eggs, is the healthiest, tastiest poultry option. Generally, you have to purchase this chicken direct from a responsible farmer.

As with egg producers, chicken producers offer up various claims about their chicken that can be hard to decipher. The website for Sustainable Table (see Resources) has some handy guides to meat labeling that are free for downloading and helpful to take shopping. Here are a few of the labels you might encounter on meat packaging and what they mean.

"Pastured." This label means the animal had access to pasture. With plentiful access to pasture, an animal has a more diverse diet than one kept confined and fed commercial feed, and it's also more active. The meat from a pastured animal will have a rich flavor and a firmer texture than that of a factory-farm animal.

"Organic." By law, the organic label means the animal was fed only organic feed with no animal by-products, that it was not treated with hormones or antibiotics, and that it had access to the outdoors at some point (though this might be very limited).

"Natural" or "All-Natural." This label is a bit deceptive. It implies healthy but may mean only that the meat itself has no added artificial flavors, colors, or other synthetic additives (some of which are prohibited by law anyway). It does not mean the animal was raised humanely, or that it had access to the outdoors, or that its diet was free of animal by-products or additives.

"Cage-Free." This term, used to describe chickens, can be misleading. It means the chickens were not individually caged, though they may still have been confined throughout their lives.

"Free-Range." For animals to be called free-range, they must have had access to the outdoors — even if they never took advantage of the open door.

190

Chicken Scallopini
with Lemon, Artichokes, and Capers

If your kids don't care for the sharp, salty flavor of capers, it's easy to push this ingredient aside.

1½ pounds boneless, skinless chicken breasts
½ cup unbleached all-purpose flour
   Salt and freshly ground black pepper
¼ cup canola oil
2 garlic cloves, minced
1 cup chicken broth
1 (15-ounce) can artichoke hearts, chopped
2 tablespoons lemon juice
1 tablespoon capers, rinsed and drained
3 tablespoons chopped fresh flat-leaf parsley

1. Place the chicken 1 piece at a time in a gallon-size ziplock bag. Set the bag on a sturdy cutting board. Using a kitchen mallet, pound the chicken to an even thickness of about ½ inch. Remove the chicken from the bag. Repeat for all the chicken pieces. (The plastic bag keeps the raw chicken off the board and from splattering in your kitchen.)

2. Mix the flour with generous pinches of salt and pepper in a shallow dish.

3. Heat half of the oil in a large skillet (*not* a nonstick skillet). Dredge 1 chicken breast in the flour, and set it in the skillet. Repeat until about half of the chicken is in the skillet. Fry for 4 minutes on medium-high heat. (Do not disturb the chicken during this time or else it will not brown evenly.) Using tongs, flip the chicken; the bottom side should be golden brown. Fry until cooked through and golden brown on both sides, about 4 minutes longer. Set the cooked chicken in a serving dish and keep warm. Repeat with the remaining oil and chicken.

4. Sauté the garlic in the same skillet until golden brown. Pour in the broth and scrape up the *fond* (crispy chicken bits) from the bottom of the skillet. Simmer until the broth is reduced by one-third, 5 to 8 minutes. Add the artichokes, lemon juice, and capers, and cook until heated through.

5. Pour the pan sauce over the chicken. Serve warm, garnished with the parsley.

Serves 6

mise en place and knife skills

ONE OF THE MOST IMPORTANT KITCHEN SKILLS in the culinary world is called *mise en place*. This oh-so-sexy French phrase means "put in place." All this means is doing your measuring, chopping, and other ingredient preparation at the start of the recipe. You should also read and understand the recipe before you begin to prepare anything. This allows you to work carefully and have all the ingredients ready. Once the burner heats up, you may not be able to juggle prep and cooking without burning your dish or forgetting something.

Mise en place allows you to work efficiently, which means a lot with kids underfoot. Or even if you just like one or two glasses of wine while you cook. Often, the prep work can be done well in advance of when the dish actually needs to be cooked, which is a real bonus when you're trying to get everything on the table at the same time.

THE BEST PIECE OF EQUIPMENT IN A KITCHEN? It's a chef's knife, otherwise known as a French knife. Buy a good one, and your *mise en place* will be a pleasure. The knife may set you back a hundred bucks or so, ouch. But it will last a lifetime, and you will wonder how you ever got along without a decent knife. It really makes that much difference. Be sure to hone your blade before each use and have your knife professionally sharpened once a year.

Chefs know how to get a vegetable chopped with the fewest cuts and in the fastest and safest way. Like *mise en place*, it's all about efficiency. The most important cuts to learn are how to cut an onion, how to dice, chop, and julienne, and how to make chiffonade. It just takes a bit of practice before you will notice drastic improvement in your prep speed.

Sizes of Cuts

| chop | large dice | medium dice | small dice | mince |

How to Chop, Dice, or Mince an Onion

 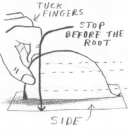 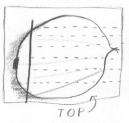 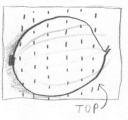

1. Cut the onion down the center. Remove the skin.

2. Lay on flat side and cut 2–3 flat slices across the onion. Stop before the root.

3. Cut down the top, through the first cuts. Stop before the root.

4. Cut down the top from side to side, crossing the last cuts

5. Voilà, a perfect dice!

How to Julienne

 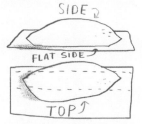  

1. Cut the end off, so the vegetable can lay flat.

2. Make slices down from the top to make sections.

3. Stack the sections and slice again, to make "fry" shapes.

4. Repeat to make thinner fries.

How to Chiffonade ("SHIFF-uh-nahd")

  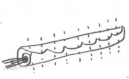 

1. Make of stack of the leaves. (This can be done with any size leaf.)

2. Roll them up like a cigar.

3. Slice down across the roll.

4. The greens will unroll into little strips.

Chicken Salad
with Red Grapes, Blueberries, and Almonds

About 1 pound boneless cooked chicken, chopped (about 1½ cups)

1 cup red grapes, sliced lengthwise

⅓ cup dried blueberries

⅓ cup canola mayonnaise

Salt and freshly ground black pepper

Pinch of cayenne pepper

⅓ cup sliced almonds

2 tablespoons chopped fresh flat-leaf parsley (optional)

Grapes, blueberries, *and* chicken? This recipe is kid nirvana in a bowl. It can be made into a one-dish lunch or dinner by the addition of either (or both) whole-grain penne or dark, leafy salad greens.

Combine the chicken, grapes, blueberries, mayonnaise, salt and pepper to taste, and cayenne in a large bowl, and stir gently. Toss lightly with the almonds added. Serve at room temperature or chilled, with the parsley sprinkled on top if desired.

Serves 6 to 8

■ Save Chicken Scraps for Broth

Get the most out of your food budget by saving your chicken scraps, bones included, for a homemade broth just like Grandma used to make.

You can even freeze the bones until you're ready to use them. To prepare, place bones and remaining meat in a large pot with some roughly chopped vegetables;

celery stalks, garlic cloves, an onion, a carrot, and any other vegetables you might choose. Cover with cold water. Bring to a boil, then reduce the heat and simmer for 5 to 6 hours. Strain the broth through a fine sieve to remove all bones and vegetables. Save any large chunks of meat for a chicken soup, and add salt and pepper for flavor. (If

you plan on using the broth in other recipes, you may want to leave out the salt and pepper, and adjust the seasonings as needed for the dish you make with the broth.) Cool the stock and remove any fat that rises and solidifies on the surface. Freeze the broth in 1-cup portions.

Lemon-Herb Roast Chicken

You can use the leftover chicken as the base of a chili, salad, wrap sandwich, or soup that will work for weeknight dinners and lunches.

1. Preheat the oven to 350°F.

2. Rinse the chickens, pat dry with paper towels, and place breast side up in a large roasting pan. Slather the chickens with the olive oil and balsamic vinegar. Sprinkle on the dried mixed herbs, salt, and pepper. Squeeze the juice from half a lemon over each chicken, then stuff a lemon rind inside each, along with about one-third of the rosemary and sage. Put the remaining herbs on the top of the chickens.

3. Roast the chickens for about 60 minutes, until the thermometer reads 170°F. *Very important:* The thermometer goes in the thickest part of the inside of the thigh, away from the bone. Cooking time will vary with the size of the chickens.

4. Remove to a cutting board and cut into pieces for serving.

Serves 6 for dinner, plus 2 pounds of meat for other recipes

2 whole chickens (about 3–4 pounds each)

¼ cup extra-virgin olive oil

2 tablespoons balsamic vinegar

2 tablespoons dried mixed herbs (*herbes de Provence* works well)

Salt and freshly ground black pepper

1 lemon, halved

1 bunch fresh or 2 tablespoons dried rosemary

1 bunch fresh or 2 tablespoons dried sage

195

Chicken Chili

This tastes even better the next day. It also freezes well. The beauty of this dish is that for prep you only have to chop an onion and shred the chicken. It takes very little time. It's also flavorful without being too spicy. (If you or the kids like spiciness, a few shakes of your favorite hot sauce will do the trick.)

2 tablespoons extra-virgin olive oil
1 large onion, chopped
2 teaspoons dried oregano, preferably Mexican
1½ teaspoons ground cumin
¼ cup ancho chile powder or mild chili powder
1 bay leaf
1 tablespoon unsweetened cocoa powder
1 teaspoon salt
½ teaspoon ground cinnamon
1 (28-ounce) can no-salt diced tomatoes, undrained
About 1½ pounds boneless cooked chicken, shredded (about 3 cups)
3 cups beef stock
1 (15-ounce) can kidney beans, rinsed and drained
1 (15-ounce) can black beans, rinsed and drained
1 (15-ounce) can pinto beans, rinsed and drained
Shredded cheddar or Monterey Jack cheese for serving

1. Heat the oil in a large pot (such as a Dutch oven) over medium heat. Add the onion and sauté until golden brown, about 7 minutes. Add the oregano and cumin; stir for 1 minute. Stir in the chile powder, bay leaf, cocoa powder, salt, and cinnamon. Add the tomatoes with their juice and the shredded chicken. Mix in the stock. Bring to a boil. Reduce the heat to medium-low, and simmer for 45 minutes, stirring occasionally.

2. Add all of the beans and simmer about 10 minutes longer. Discard the bay leaf. Serve topped with shredded cheese.

Serves 10

▬ Chile Appeal

The ancho chile powder has a smoky flavor without a lot of heat.

Beth realized chili might be a good dish for her daughter when they were smelling the spices in their cabinet. Her daughter opened the ancho powder bottle and started licking the inside. It doesn't take a rocket scientist to realize, "Hey, she might like chili!" She does. She also eats plain fennel seeds, allspice berries, and candied ginger. Then again, she also drinks her own bathwater. Go figure.

CONVERTING RECIPES FOR THE
slow cooker

Many soup, stew, and chili recipes can be easily converted for a slow cooker. Slow cookers cook foods at a relatively low temperature over many hours. Not only do slow cookers allow you to come home to a cooked meal after a long day, but the slow-cook approach also helps blend flavors nicely. Converting a standard recipe to a slow-cooker recipe does require a few tricks. These are general rules; for best results, you'll want to get to know your own make/model.

Reduce liquids. Because there's no evaporation during the cooking process, you'll want to reduce your liquids by about one-quarter to one-half. For best results, add cooked rice and pasta only at the end, or they'll get gummy.

Increase cook times. A soup recipe that on the stove top would be done in less than 30 minutes in the slow cooker will cook in 4 to 8 hours on the low setting, depending on the slow cooker. A slower recipe that would take an hour or more on the stove top will need twice as long on low. Cooking on high generally requires half the cook time as a low setting.

Brown meats first. Browning meats will enhance their flavor in slow-cooker recipes.

Sauté onions first. Onions are generally best if they're sautéed on the stove top first, so that their sugars can caramelize some.

Save tender vegetables and dairy for the end. Add tender vegetables during the last 45 minutes only, and dairy products during the last 30 minutes so that they don't curdle.

Don't overfill or uncover. Don't fill the slow cooker more than three-quarters full, or it won't cook properly. Do not remove the lid during the cooking process, or you will let too much heat escape, delaying your cooking time significantly.

197

Acorn Squash and Chicken Sausage "Cassoulet"

3 tablespoons extra-virgin olive oil

1½ cups chopped onion

½ cup chopped shallot

2 garlic cloves, minced

2 cups diced acorn squash

1 cup diced carrot

1 (28-ounce) can diced tomatoes, undrained

1 cup chicken stock

¼ cup apple cider

1 tablespoon balsamic vinegar

2 tablespoons chopped fresh flat-leaf parsley

2 teaspoons fresh thyme leaves

2 teaspoons chopped fresh basil

½ teaspoon kosher salt

½ teaspoon freshly ground black pepper

2 (15-ounce cans) white beans, rinsed and drained

1 (15-ounce) can lentils, rinsed and drained

2½ pounds precooked chicken or turkey sausage, sliced

2 cups panko bread crumbs (or regular bread crumbs)

1 cup grated Parmesan cheese

This is a great one-pot meal for fall. True cassoulet would not contain chicken, so you can call it "beanie-weenies" if that will get your kids to eat it. We just call it good.

1. Heat 2 tablespoons of the oil in a large Dutch oven, or heavy, ovenproof pot with lid, over medium-high heat. Add half the onion and all of the shallot and garlic, and sauté until golden. Add the squash, carrot, tomatoes, stock, cider, vinegar, parsley, thyme, basil, salt, and pepper. Bring to a boil. Turn down the heat and simmer until the squash and carrot are tender, about 30 minutes. Add the beans and lentils. Keep simmering gently while you prepare the onion and sausage.

2. Preheat the oven to 325°F.

3. In a large sauté pan, heat the remaining 1 tablespoon oil over medium-high heat. Add the remaining onion and the sausage (in batches) and brown. Add to the Dutch oven with the bean mixture.

4. Cover the Dutch oven and transfer to the oven; bake for 40 minutes.

5. Remove from the oven and uncover. Combine the panko crumbs with the Parmesan and sprinkle evenly over the top to make an even layer. Return uncovered to the oven for an additional 30 minutes, until the top is golden brown.

Serves 10

Golden-Crisp Chicken Nuggets

Most nuggets are anything but healthful, and only partially chicken. Most are filled with fat, and they almost always contain synthetic additives. Beth created her Golden-Crisp Chicken Nuggets recipe in an attempt to build a better nugget. It's actually based on chicken, which helps a lot. It's also delicious, especially when dipped in pesto (see page 145) or a soy-miso sauce (see page 220). Be warned; serve these to too many kids, and they might start expecting a drive-through window outside your kitchen!

1. Preheat the oven to 350°F.

2. Cut the chicken into nugget-size pieces, about 2 inches.

3. Mix the egg and yogurt together in a shallow dish. Place another shallow dish next to it with the bread crumbs, panko, Parmesan, herbs, and salt and pepper.

4. Dip a chicken piece in the egg-yogurt mixture, then transfer it to the crumb mixture and coat it thoroughly. Set on a baking sheet. Repeat until all the chicken pieces have been breaded.

5. Bake the nuggets for about 25 minutes, or until the internal temperature at the center of your thickest nugget is 180°F. Don't overbake, or the chicken will be dry.

Serves 6

DID YOU KNOW? The chicken nugget is one of the fastest-growing foods in the American diet, particularly among very young children. According to the *Wall Street Journal*, the nugget now accounts for about 5 percent of all restaurant orders — more than double what it was in 1990.

3 boneless, skinless chicken breasts (about 1½ pounds)
1 egg
2 tablespoons plain whole-milk yogurt
1 cup bread crumbs (plain or Italian-seasoned)
1 cup panko bread crumbs
½ cup grated Parmesan cheese
½ teaspoon dried Italian herb blend or pizza seasoning
Salt and freshly ground black pepper

▬ Breading Tip

If you've ever dipped a wet hand into a bread-crumb mixture, you know that fingers are just as easily coated as chicken — and it's hard to keep working with breaded fingers.

To bread chicken pieces with the least amount of mess, designate one hand for the wet dip and one for the dry. For the chicken nuggets, for example, use your "wet" hand to dip a chicken piece into the egg-yogurt mixture, and use that same hand to transfer the chicken to the crumb mixture. Use your "dry" hand to sprinkle the bread crumbs over the chicken, turning it to coat it well.

Real Turkey and Noodles

½ pound whole-grain pasta
4 tablespoons butter
1 shallot, chopped
2 tablespoons unbleached all-purpose flour
2 cups chicken stock, warmed
1 pound cooked turkey, chopped (about 1½ cups)
Salt and freshly ground black pepper
½ cup grated Parmesan cheese
½ cup panko bread crumbs

This is basic and tasty comfort food. It's a perfect way to use Thanksgiving leftovers or even leftover cooked chicken. What makes it good is using real ingredients, not processed, canned soup full of saturated fats and salt in a gluey mass. It's also quick to prepare — proof that real food doesn't always have to be real slow.

1. Cook the pasta according to the package directions. While it cooks, heat the butter in a saucepan over medium heat. When it is melted, add the shallot and sweat until translucent. Add the flour, whisking and cooking the roux until it just starts to smell nutty, or cooked, but has not yet started to brown. Slowly add the warm stock, whisking as you go to keep it smooth as it thickens, about 5 minutes. If you add the stock cold, you will have a harder time keeping the sauce lump-free. Add the chopped turkey and heat through. Season to taste with salt and pepper.

2. Heat the oven broiler to low, about 400°F.

3. Drain the pasta when it is just al dente. In a 9-inch square baking dish (not glass), combine the noodles and the turkey mixture. In a separate bowl, combine the Parmesan with the panko crumbs. Sprinkle on top of the turkey and noodles. Place the baking dish under the broiler for just a few minutes, until the crunchy topping is golden brown. Serve warm.

Serves 8

meat

We like grass-fed meat (beef, pork, and lamb). Why?

FIRST, IT'S BETTER FOR THE ENVIRONMENT than conventionally grown meat. Producing a 6-ounce steak requires about 16 times the fuel as producing 1 cup of broccoli. And one cow produces nearly 14 tons of manure per year. Worldwide, livestock production accounts for about 18 percent of all greenhouse gases — which is more than all transportation combined. That's not just a large carbon footprint, it's an entire stampede. A well-managed grass-fed beef ranch drastically decreases that footprint. Practices such as rotational grazing help maintain the health of the grassland, which creates a carbon sink that absorbs carbon dioxide from the atmosphere, offsetting much of livestock's environmental impact. Maintaining land as pasture instead of farming it to produce grain for livestock feed also reduces soil erosion.

Second, it's better for the animals. Eating a natural diet and having the space to graze keeps the animals healthy and stress-free. Grain-feeding can result in chronic diseases for the animals. Meanwhile, the close quarters of a feedlot enclosure also create stress for the animals, further increasing their chances of getting sick. To keep the animals healthy, they are fed medicines like antibiotics. Grass-fed livestock do not generally require any antibiotics, food additives, or extreme efforts to maintain their health.

And third, it's better for us. Because pasture is a rich source of omega-3 essential fatty acids, the meat from grass-fed animals contains less total fat, and more "good fats" like omega-3s and conjugated linoleic acid. Research has also shown that grass-fed meat is also higher in antioxidants like vitamin E, vitamin C, and beta-carotene.

In an industrial feedlot, thousands of animals are squeezed into a small space. On a pastured hillside? Not nearly as many. Less supply means higher prices. The following page lists some ways to enjoy economical grass-fed meat.

Here are some ways to get grass-fed meat without breaking the bank

- **Spread it out.** Use less meat by adding more vegetables, grains, legumes, and pasta to recipes to get more servings from the same amount of meat.

- **Buy direct.** Buy meat directly from a farmer. Cutting out the grocery store "middleman" — as well as the processor, packager, and distributor — can save you considerable money.

- **Buy in bulk.** The real savings come when you buy a side of beef, for example, and freeze it. This can bring your costs down to as little as $3 per pound for all cuts, including choice steaks.

■ Carbon Monoxide Meat?

As a rule, we try to live by the following principles:

Carbon monoxide = **bad**
Eating old meat = **bad**
Eating old meat that has been treated with carbon monoxide = **really bad**

That's why we were so troubled to learn that the lovely red meat we often see in the supermarket may look that pretty and red simply because it's been spiked with carbon monoxide — not necessarily because it's fresh.

The meat industry apparently loses up to $1 billion annually on meat that no longer looks fresh. Because no consumer wants to buy uncooked meat that has turned brown, food companies asked the FDA to fast-track approval of a process by which inert gases, including carbon monoxide, get blasted into meat packages. It works: Meat continues looking pink. Actually, it continues looking pink beyond all reason, for example, even if it's left

on your kitchen counter for weeks. Presumably, it might even look pink if it sat on a truck with broken air conditioning on a Texas highway in August. Not that this ever happens.

Does it kill the nasty bacteria that could be lurking in your meat? No, but it does suppress bad odors and the presence of slime, other telltale signs that your meat is spoiled.

Cooking grass-fed beef

All of the beef recipes in this book were created using lean, grass-fed beef. Here are a few tips to get the best results and the full flavor from this healthy meat source:

- Grass-fed meat tends to be **leaner** than feedlot beef. Add vegetables or a bit of olive oil to a ground meat mix to keep it moist during cooking. Look for a meat supplier that sells dry-aged beef. The process enhances the flavor and helps make the meat tender.

- Grass-fed beef takes about **30 percent less cooking time** than feedlot beef.

- Meat cuts like steaks and roasts will need to **rest for eight to ten minutes** after being removed from the heat. This allows the juices to redistribute evenly throughout. If you slice the meat before it rests, you will lose a lot of the moisture and juice.

- **"Dry" heat methods like sautéing, grilling, and roasting are best for the more-tender cuts of beef such as porterhouse and tenderloin.** When grilling, sear the meat quickly over direct heat. Finish cooking over indirect heat.

- **"Wet" heat methods, which combine heat and liquid, help keep lean grass-fed cuts from becoming dry.** These methods include steaming, poaching, stewing, and combination methods like braising (see box, page 207).

203

Food Safety:
A Primer on *E. Coli* 0157:H7

We hate fearing our foods. That's one of the reasons we work with whole ingredients wherever possible — it allows us to step away from the "food is the enemy" mind-set that seems to have denied so many people the pleasure of eating. However, there's one food-related fear that we take very seriously: *E. coli* 0157:H7.

Although there are hundreds of forms of *E. coli* out there, the 0157:H7 strain is deadly — especially for children. The bacterium releases a powerful toxin that causes hemolytic uremic syndrome (HUS), a kidney disease that can also cause damage to other organs, including the pancreas and brain. Between 5 and 10 percent of people infected with *E. coli* 0157:H7 develop HUS. Half of children diagnosed with HUS require kidney dialysis; 5 percent of them die.

Many have suggested that this strain — which had never been seen before 1977 — results from how we raise and feed cattle in this country. Cows evolved to eat grass; that's why they have four stomachs — to break down all of the cellulose in grasses. But few cattle spend much time munching grass these days; instead, they are fed staggering amounts of corn. Not only is corn inexpensive, but it also fattens the cows and creates a marbling effect. The problem is that cows can't digest corn easily, and their rumen begins to produce lots of acid as a result.

And that's what makes *E. coli* 0157:H7 so deadly: It's acid resistant. This means our own stomach acid can't kill it. Instead, it can kill us; at least 61 people die from *E. coli* each year, and another 73,000 are severely sickened.

The feeding problem is compounded by modern processing techniques. Most slaughterhouses process animals at rapid speed, making it difficult to keep manure out of the cuts of meat. Then the least expensive trimmings — including the ones closest to the cow's rear — are combined in massive grinders. A single pound of ground beef may contain parts from hundreds of cows from many locations throughout the nation and world. Through this kind of mass processing, if even one carcass was contaminated, thousands of pounds become contaminated when they are combined.

And as much as you hear about safe cooking techniques, the fact is, safe handling is not enough to kill these pathogens. A study of burgers found that not all home-cooking methods kill all *E. coli*, even when multiple temperature readings showed that burgers had been cooked to 160°F.

This information isn't included to scare you. It's just an unfortunate reality that we consumers face. Knowing about the issue, and the following tips, can help you stay safer.

- **Avoid commercially ground beef.** Sadly, that means most meat you find in the grocery store, and most premade burgers.

- **Look for smaller, local providers** producing quality, preferably grass-fed meat.

- If you don't have access to a local provider, **choose a quality butcher shop** or a grocery chain — Costco is one — that routinely tests all meat *before* it is ground.

- **Ask your butcher to give you "house-ground" meat;** this means that they take full cuts of meat and grind them on the spot for you. Quality butchers and many supermarket butcher shops will do this.

- **Cook the heck out of it.** Rare burgers are so 1975. All meat should be cooked to their safe "done" temperature (see page 206).

- **Keep meat refrigerated** when it is not actively being cooked or heated.

- **Wash your hands, and teach your kids to do the same.** *E. coli* can be spread through poor hygiene.

- Remember, too, that **many foods besides ground beef can be contaminated.** Recent outbreaks have involved eggs, spinach, apple juice, raw cookie dough, and even exposure from swimming in lake water. Take any signs of food poisoning seriously.

when is it done?

USDA food and safety standards list the following temperatures for "doneness" of each type of meat:

Type of Meat	"Doneness"	Internal Temperature
Beef, lamb, and veal	Medium	160°F
	Well done	170°F
Pork	Medium	160°F
	Well done	170°F
Ground meats including beef, lamb, pork, and veal	Medium	At least 160°F, higher for safety
Ground meats including chicken	Medium	At least 170°F, 180°F recommended
Chicken	Medium	170 to 180°F

206

Braised Beef

If you've ever been frustrated by a too-dry roast, this method will restore your faith. Braising, or cooking in liquid, is a sure way to a tender, juicy meal that's rich in iron for growing bodies (and don't worry, the alcohol in the wine evaporates). You can also make this in a slow cooker for 8 hours on low, or until the meat falls off the bone; add more liquid if necessary to make sure the beef is covered in liquid if you do.

1. Preheat the oven to 325°F.

2. Heat the canola oil in a large Dutch oven or heavy oven-proof pot with a lid, over medium-high heat. Sprinkle the meat with salt and pepper. Sear on all sides until browned, then set the meat aside on a tray. Add more oil if the pot is dry after searing. You don't want to burn the *fond* (crisy meat bits) or meat juices in the pot.

3. Add the onion and garlic to the Dutch oven and brown them, about 5 minutes. Add the tomato paste and brown it a bit. Deglaze the pan with the wine. Add the water, meat, rosemary, and thyme.

4. Bake covered for about 3 hours or until the meat reaches an internal temperature of 160°F.

Serves 12 to 14

2 tablespoons canola oil
1 (3-pound) bone-in chuck
   roast
   Salt and freshly ground
   black pepper
1 large onion, chopped
4 garlic cloves, minced
2 tablespoons tomato paste
2 cups dry red wine (Cabernet
   works well)
2 cups water
2 sprigs fresh rosemary
4 sprigs fresh thyme

▬ Braising: The Perfect Path to Tender Meat Dishes

What is the difference between braising and roasting meat?

Roasting is simply cooking meat in the oven, a dry-heat method. Higher temperatures, 375°F and above, for roasting are best suited for smaller roasts. Large roasts cook more evenly when roasted at lower temperatures, like 275 to 325°F.

Braising is a combination method. The meat is first browned on the stove top in a bit of oil. Then the meat is cooked in a liquid, such as wine or stock, in the oven. The liquid keeps the meat very moist. Traditionally, it was thought that the browning of the meat sealed in juices. It actually does not, but browning does caramelize the outside of the meat and adds a lot of flavor. Braising is an especially good cooking method for lean cuts of meat, including grass-fed beef.

Healthful Shepherd's Pie

1 tablespoon extra-virgin olive oil
1 onion, chopped
1 garlic clove, chopped
1 pound lean ground beef
¼ cup uncooked white rice
1 (28-ounce) can diced tomatoes, drained
4 cups frozen mixed vegetables (about 2 packages)
Salt and freshly ground black pepper
2 pounds sweet potatoes (about 2 large), peeled and chopped into ½-inch cubes
¼ cup milk
2 tablespoons butter
⅓ cup grated Monterey Jack cheese

This revision of an easy, classic "meat and potatoes" recipe uses sweet potatoes and extra vegetables in the meat filling to add flavor and nutrition. Sweet potatoes have a lower glycemic index than white potatoes and offer more nutrients like beta-carotene.

1. Preheat the oven to 350°F.

2. Heat the oil in a large skillet over medium-high heat. Sauté the onion and garlic until translucent, about 3 minutes. Add the ground beef and brown until no longer pink, 10 to 15 minutes. Add the rice, tomatoes, and frozen mixed vegetables. Bring to a boil, then reduce the heat and let simmer for 15 minutes. Season with salt and pepper.

3. Meanwhile, steam the sweet potatoes until fork-tender, about 20 minutes. You can do this in an electric steamer. Alternatively, put a couple of inches of water into a large pot, set a steaming basket in it, and bring to a boil. Set the sweet potatoes in the basket, cover, and let steam.

4. Let the potatoes cool slightly, then mash them in a large bowl with the milk and butter.

5. Spread the meat mixture in the bottom of a 2-quart casserole dish. Top with the mashed sweet potatoes, and sprinkle the cheese on top. Bake until the cheese melts and the top begins to get golden, 10 to 15 minutes.

Serves 8

Guinness, Cheddar, and Caramelized-Onion Burgers

These will still be juicy even when well done, thanks to sweet onions and beer and gooey dabs of cheese. Fear not; the alcohol in the Guinness evaporates during the cooking process. They pair well with coarse-grain mustard and a whole-grain bun.

⅓ cup bread crumbs

¼ cup Guinness stout

1 pound lean ground beef

2 cups (2 batches) Quick Caramelized Onions, chopped (page 65)

2 ounces cheddar cheese, finely chopped or grated (about ½ cup)

1 egg, beaten

½ teaspoon salt

½ teaspoon freshly ground black pepper

1. Preheat the oven to 350°F, or heat up the grill.

2. Place the bread crumbs in a large bowl, add the stout, and allow the crumbs to soak up the beer. Add the beef, onions, cheese, egg, salt, and pepper, and mix gently but thoroughly.

3. Shape the mixture into 3- to 4-ounce patties. If you are concerned about meat-handling safety, use food-service gloves for this step. Place on a baking sheet.

4. Bake at 350°F for about 15–20 minutes, depending on thickness, until internal temperature is 170°F. Or you can grill these 8 minutes per side for ¾-inch-thick burgers, depending on the heat level of your grill; be warned that they are juicy, and you may want to put down a layer of foil to protect the grate.

Makes 10 small, or 8 large burgers

209

Meatball Stroganoff

Double the meatball part of this recipe, and then freeze half the cooked meatballs. You can reheat them quickly with a quality jarred spaghetti sauce and add cooked pasta for a quick weeknight spaghetti-and-meatballs meal.

1 pound lean ground beef

1 egg, beaten

⅓ cup bread crumbs

⅛ teaspoon paprika

Salt and freshly ground black pepper

2 tablespoons extra-virgin olive oil

2 tablespoons butter

1 pound cremini or shiitake mushrooms, chopped

2 shallots, chopped

2 tablespoons cognac (optional)

2 tablespoons fresh thyme leaves, or 1 tablespoon dried

1 teaspoon Dijon mustard

1½ cups chicken stock

1 cup low-fat sour cream

2 tablespoons half-and-half

½ pound dried egg noodles or rotini

1. Preheat the oven to 350°F.

2. Combine the beef, egg, bread crumbs, paprika, and generous amounts of salt and pepper in a large bowl, and mix well. Form into small meatballs, about the diameter of a nickel. Place on a baking sheet. Bake the meatballs for about 15 minutes, or until the internal temperature is 170°F.

3. Heat the oil and butter in a large skillet. Add the mush-rooms and shallots and sauté about 10 minutes. Add the cognac, if desired, thyme, and Dijon, and mix well. Add the chicken stock, bring to a boil, then reduce the heat and simmer for 10 minutes. Add the sour cream and half-and-half, and stir to blend.

4. Add the meatballs. Bring to a boil, then reduce the heat and simmer for about 30 minutes, until the sauce is reduced to the point where it coats the meatballs. Season with salt and pepper.

5. Meanwhile, bring a large pot of salted water to a boil. Cook the pasta according to the package directions until al dente. Serve the sauce and meatballs over or alongside the noodles.

Serves 8

Meatloaf Florentine

This one is the absolute favorite meat dish at Beth's house. It was the first meat dish she could get her daughter to eat, and it remains one that they all love. The meatloaf makes great sandwiches the next day, and it's good enough for company.

1. Preheat the oven to 350°F.

2. Heat the olive oil in a medium skillet over medium heat. Sauté the onion and garlic until soft and light golden, about 5 minutes. Transfer to a large bowl, add all the remaining ingredients, and mix together to combine thoroughly.

3. Divide the meatloaf mixture in half. Place in two loaf pans sprayed with non-stick spray. Bake uncovered for 60 minutes, until cooked through and a meat thermometer inserted into the center reads 180°F.

Makes 2 meatloaves, 8 servings each

Variation:
Meatballs Florentine

Alternatively, shape the meat mixture into meatballs. Bake the meatballs on a baking sheet for 10 to 15 minutes, until cooked through. The meatballs freeze well and can be added to spaghetti for a hearty meal.

2 tablespoons extra-virgin olive oil

1 medium onion, chopped

1 large garlic clove, minced

3 pounds lean ground meat (beef, turkey, buffalo, pork, lamb, or a combination)

½ cup Roasted Tomatoes (page 106) or 6 ounces sun-dried tomatoes packed in oil, drained and chopped

1½ cups chopped spinach

½ cup chopped fresh herbs (primarily basil, plus some rosemary, thyme, and sage)

2 eggs, beaten

1 cup bread crumbs

½ cup grated Parmesan cheese

1 teaspoon kosher salt

½ teaspoon freshly ground black pepper

¼ cup ketchup

Pinch of red pepper flakes (optional)

Roasted Vegetables, Lamb, and Couscous

When Beth read this dish on a French preschool menu, along with cauliflower gratin and a cheese course (for toddlers!), she knew she needed to try a version of it for her own preschooler.

- 4 medium parsnips, peeled and diced into ½-inch cubes
- 3 large carrots, peeled and diced into ½-inch cubes
- 1 fennel bulb, diced into ½-inch cubes
- 1 large sweet potato, peeled and diced into ½-inch cubes
- 2 onions, 1 cut into eighths and 1 diced
- 3 tablespoons extra-virgin olive oil
- 1 teaspoon ground turmeric
- ½ teaspoon ground cumin
- ½ teaspoon salt
- 2 cups chicken broth
- 1 (28-ounce) can diced tomatoes (undrained)
- 2 garlic cloves, minced
- 1 pound ground lamb
- 1 tablespoon lemon juice
- 1 tablespoon paprika
  Pinch of cayenne pepper
- 4 ounces tomato paste
- 1 cup couscous
  Salt and freshly ground black pepper
- 2 ounces feta cheese, crumbled

1. Preheat the oven to 400°F. Spray a 9- by 13-inch roasting pan with cooking spray.

2. Combine the parsnips, carrots, fennel, sweet potato, and onion cut into eighths in the baking pan with 2 tablespoons of the olive oil and the turmeric, cumin, and salt. Toss well to coat evenly. Add ½ cup of the chicken broth and the tomatoes with their juice, and mix well. Roast in the oven, stirring occasionally, for about 1 hour, until the vegetables are tender.

3. Meanwhile, heat the remaining 1 tablespoon olive oil in a large skillet over medium-high heat. Add the diced onion and garlic and sauté. Add the lamb and brown the meat until no longer pink, 10 to 15 minutes. Add the lemon juice, paprika, and cayenne, and stir. Mix in the tomato paste. Add the remaining 1½ cups chicken broth, bring to a boil, then reduce the heat to a simmer. Add the couscous, reduce the heat to low, cover, and cook for a few minutes, until the couscous absorbs the liquid. Fluff the mixture with a fork, and season with salt and pepper.

4. Serve the lamb and couscous mixture topped with the roasted vegetables and tomato sauce. Garnish with about 1 tablespoon of feta per serving.

Serves 8

Lamburgers in Pita

good for lunch!

Herbs, olives, and yogurt with pita bread make this recipe a fun twist on the usual burger on a bun.

1. Preheat the grill, or the oven to 350°F.

2. Combine the lamb, bread crumbs, shallot, cheese, egg, mint, parsley, oregano, thyme, fennel seed, and generous pinches of salt and pepper in a large bowl. Mix well. Shape into 8 small patties about ¾ inch thick. Grill until cooked through, 6 to 8 minutes per side. The internal temperature should be at least 160°F.

3. Toss the watercress with the vinegar and oil in a medium bowl. Divide the greens among the pita halves, place a burger in each with olives and a drizzle of yogurt.

Serves 8

FOR THE BURGERS

- 1 pound ground lamb
- ¼ cup whole-wheat bread crumbs
- 1 shallot, finely chopped
- 3 ounces feta cheese, crumbled (about ¾ cup)
- 1 egg, beaten
- 2 tablespoons chopped fresh mint
- 2 tablespoons chopped fresh flat-leaf parsley
- 1 tablespoon dried oregano
- 1 tablespoon fresh thyme leaves, or 1½ teaspoon dried thyme
- 1 teaspoon fennel seed
  Salt and freshly ground black pepper

FOR THE GARNISH

- 1 cup watercress
- 2 teaspoons red wine vinegar
- 4 teaspoons extra-virgin olive oil
- 4 whole-wheat pitas, cut in half
  Kalamata olives
- ⅓ cup Greek-style yogurt

213

Spicy Asian Greens and Pork

2 tablespoons canola oil

1 1-inch length fresh ginger, peeled and chopped

2 fresh garlic scapes, or 1 garlic clove, minced

2 scallions, chopped

¼ cup Thai chili sauce, mild heat

1 tablespoon soy sauce

1 tablespoon rice wine vinegar

3 tablespoons chopped fresh cilantro

½ pound buckwheat soba noodles

½ pound ground pork

1 pound mustard greens

1 pound baby bok choy

Learning to cook with ingredients from other cultures can be a lot of fun, and it can introduce kids to new flavors. While this recipe is not true to any traditional dish, the sweet-spicy flavor with noodles is a pretty kid-safe way to begin that culinary field trip.

1. Heat 1 tablespoon of the oil in a skillet over medium heat, and sauté the ginger, garlic, and scallions until translucent, about 4 minutes. Remove to a large bowl and keep warm; set aside the skillet to use again.

2. Whisk together the chili sauce, soy sauce, vinegar, and 2 tablespoons of the cilantro, and add to the bowl with the ginger mixture. Stir together, then set aside to let the flavors blend while you prepare the pork and greens.

3. Cook the soba noodles as directed, then drain and rinse. Soba is one of the few types of noodles that do require rinsing after cooking.

4. Heat the remaining 1 tablespoon oil over medium heat in the skillet. Add the ground pork and brown the meat. Add the greens a bit at a time (as you can fit them in the skillet), and sauté until just wilted, about 3 minutes. Add the pork and greens and the noodles to the bowl with the sauce, and toss together. Serve garnished with the remaining 1 tablespoon cilantro.

Serves 6

American Cancer Society researchers did a long-term study of meat consumption by 149,000 individuals. The results showed that people who consumed the most processed meats were 50 percent more likely to develop colon cancer. A likely contributor to the increased risk is the additive sodium nitrate or sodium nitrite. Look for labels clearly marked "No nitrates," or buy your cured meats directly from a processor that does not use nitrates.

Tortellini
with Asparagus, Ham, Peas, and Parmesan-Herb Sauce

Using less of rich ingredients like half-and-half and butter keeps this dish on the lighter side and emphasizes the fresh herbs and vegetables. Using fresh, not dried, herbs is the key.

1. Cook the pasta according to the package directions. Drain and place in a large bowl.

2. Steam the asparagus for 5 to 7 minutes, until tender. You can do this in an electric steamer. Alternatively, put a couple of inches of water into a large pot, set a steaming basket in it, and bring to a boil. Set the asparagus in the basket, cover, and let steam. When done, set aside.

3. Heat the butter in a large skillet over medium heat. Sauté the scallion until golden, about 2 minutes. Add the frozen peas and water to the skillet (it will spit and bubble, so be warned and stand back). Cook for 2 minutes, stirring frequently but gently. Add the ham and cook a couple of minutes longer. Add the half-and-half. Simmer for about 5 minutes. Add all but about 2 tablespoons of the Parmesan and stir well to blend.

4. Add the sauce to the tortellini. Add the asparagus and toss gently to mix. Sprinkle with the reserved Parmesan and the chopped herbs.

Serves 6

1 pound cheese tortellini
1 pound purple (or green) asparagus, woody ends trimmed, cut into 1-inch pieces
1 tablespoon butter
1 large scallion, sliced with some of the green part (¼ cup total)
1 cup frozen baby peas
2 tablespoons water
½ pound ham, diced into ¼-inch cubes
¼ cup half-and-half
⅓ cup grated Parmesan cheese
1 tablespoon chopped fresh thyme
1 tablespoon chopped fresh basil

Ham and Broccoli Mac and Cheese

1 medium head broccoli, florets only (save the stems to use in broccoli soup or for crunch in salads)

1½ tablespoons butter

3 scallions, sliced, with 1 inch of the green parts

2 tablespoons unbleached all-purpose flour

1 cup low-fat milk

½ cup vegetable broth

1½ cups grated Monterey Jack cheese

Pinch of ground nutmeg

Salt and freshly ground black pepper

½ pound small pasta

1 pound of ham, diced into ¼-inch cubes

½ cup panko bread crumbs or regular bread crumbs

Variation: Ham and Cauliflower Mac and Cheese

Substitute cauliflower for the broccoli.

This approach adds a little bit of vegetable and meat to the usual starch and cheese in this kid favorite (if you don't eat meat, just leave out the ham and you'll still reap the extra benefits of the broccoli). Using a vegetable-flavored pasta like spinach or tomato adds color and a bit of flavor. Otherwise, the broccoli and ham are the only color in the dish. If your child is skeptical of broccoli, chop the broccoli into small pieces before adding it. The finer texture will help it all blend in.

1. Steam the broccoli for about 5 minutes, until crisp and bright green, but no longer raw. You can do this in an electric steamer. Alternatively, put a couple of inches of water into a large pot, set a steaming basket in it, and bring to a boil. Set the broccoli in the basket, cover, and let steam. Let cool.

2. Make the cheese sauce. Melt 1 tablespoon of the butter in a saucepan over medium heat. Add the scallions and sauté for a couple minutes. Add the flour and whisk. Cook this roux for a few minutes, until it smells nutty and is golden. Add the milk and the broth and heat for about 5 minutes, whisking as you add. Add the cheese and nutmeg and continue whisking until the cheese melts and the sauce is thick. Season with salt and pepper, remembering that the ham is going in, and it is salty.

3. Preheat the oven to 350°F.

4. Bring a large pot of water to a boil and cook the pasta according to the package directions. Drain.

5. Toss the pasta, sauce, broccoli, and ham in a large bowl and then transfer to a 2-quart casserole dish (oven safe). Melt the remaining ½ tablespoon of butter in a small bowl in the microwave, about 20 seconds, and toss with the bread crumbs. Sprinkle over the top of the casserole. Bake for about 15 minutes, until the bread crumbs are golden brown.

Serves 8

Winter Risotto
with Pork

Acorn squash halves make a fun serving dish and add a vegetable to this one-course meal.

1. Preheat the oven to 350°F. Coat a baking sheet with non-stick cooking spray.

2. Lightly brush 1 tablespoon of the olive oil over the squash halves. Place them cut side down on the prepared baking sheet. Bake for about 1 hour, until tender when poked with a fork.

3. Meanwhile, heat the chicken broth in a small saucepan, and keep it warm over low heat.

4. In a large pot, heat the remaining 2 tablespoons olive oil over medium-low heat and sweat the garlic and onion until translucent, about 5 minutes. Increase the heat to medium-high. Add the ground pork and brown it, breaking it up as you go. Add the carrot and heat through, about 2 more minutes.

5. Add the rice and stir until it is evenly coated with oil. Add the wine and cook, stirring often, until the rice absorbs the liquid, about 5 minutes. Stir 2 cups of the warm chicken broth into the pot. Now you're free from stirring for about 8 minutes, until the rice absorbs the liquid. After this step, you need to start stirring frequently.

6. Add another cup of the warm broth to the pot and cook, stirring frequently, until all the liquid is absorbed, about 5 minutes. Add just ¼ cup of broth next, and cook, stirring constantly, until all the liquid is absorbed, a few more minutes. Taste the rice; if it has reached al dente texture, you're done. If not, add another ¼ cup of broth and cook, stirring constantly, until all the liquid is absorbed. Repeat until the rice is done; you may not need all of the broth.

7. Mix in the Parmesan, parsley, and sage. Season with salt and pepper to taste. Serve by placing ½ cup of the risotto into each of the acorn squash halves.

Serves 6

3 tablespoons extra-virgin olive oil

3 acorn squashes, halved, seeds and stringy pulp removed

4 cups chicken broth

2 garlic cloves, minced

1 large onion, chopped

1 pound ground pork

1 cup grated carrot

1¼ cups Arborio rice

½ cup white wine

⅔ cup grated Parmesan cheese

½ cup chopped fresh flat-leaf or ¼ cup dried parsley

1 tablespoon chopped fresh or 1½ teaspoons dried sage

Salt and freshly ground black pepper

217

Black-Eyed Peas and Smoked Ham Hock

1 tablespoon extra-virgin olive oil
2 onions, chopped
2 garlic cloves, minced
6 cups water
2 pounds dried black-eyed peas, soaked overnight, rinsed, and drained
1 tablespoon dried savory
2 teaspoons dried thyme
2 bay leaves
2 tablespoons chopped fresh or 1 tablespoon dried rosemary
1 pound smoked ham hock
Salt and freshly ground black pepper

This meal is traditionally made on New Year's Day for good luck. Hey, even if it doesn't work, your family will still feel lucky to be eating it. Tastes great with cornbread.

1. Heat the oil in a large pot over medium-low heat. Add the onions and garlic and sweat until translucent, about 5 minutes. Add the water, peas, savory, thyme, bay leaves, and rosemary, and stir to mix. Add the ham hock. Bring to a boil, then reduce the heat and let simmer, covered, for about 3½ hours. Remove the lid and cook for another 30 minutes to allow the liquid to cook down and concentrate.

2. Remove the ham hock and cut the meat from it. Add the meat back to the pot and heat it. Remove the bay leaf. Season with salt and pepper to taste.

Serves 8 to 10

Variation:
Fresh Peas with Smoked Ham Hock

You can use fresh, shelled black-eyed peas or purple-hull peas for this dish. These are in season in the late summer in most climates, and you can sometimes find them frozen. For this dish, use only 4 cups water. Sweat the onions and garlic, then add the water, herbs, and ham hock and simmer, covered, for 1 hour. Add the fresh peas and simmer, covered, for 30 minutes. Remove the lid and simmer for 30 minutes longer, until the peas are al dente. Remove the ham hock and cut the meat from it, adding the meat back to the pot. Remove the bay leaf, season with salt and pepper, and serve.

Seafood

LOOK AT ANY KID'S MENU and the closest thing to seafood it lists is something that took a long swim in a deep fryer. Other popular seafood options include raw fish and shellfish, which aren't safe for young kids, and pricey items on the adult side of the menu. With so few choices when dining out, it's easy to think that kids won't like seafood if it is on the menu at home.

But kids will eat seafood, even if sometimes you don't want them to. Like the evening Beth and her spouse treated themselves to a small portion of salmon smoked on the grill. Their kiddo eyed mom and dad's treat, and said, "I want THAT!" pointing at their dinner. Did she like it? Yep. It goes to show good food really doesn't have an age minimum.

Fish offer a range of nutrients that kids need, often including the essential omega-3 fatty acids that so many Americans lack.

However, some fish are more healthful than others. Some varieties are overharvested, others are contaminated with PCBs or mercury, and some fisheries cause environmental damage. Ideally, you want what we call the "healthy fish trifecta" — high omega-3s, low contaminants, and sustainable.

If you have trouble getting your little ones to get in the swim, you can always try the "nugget" approach on page 199, simply swapping out the chicken, uh, fingers, for fish.

So, which are the types you want to eat, and which should you avoid? The good folks at the Monterey Bay Aquarium made it easy for us with their regional Seafood Watch brochures. In general, the more oily the fish, the higher the amount of omega-3s. Atlantic char, U.S. barramundi, salmon, sardines, and herring are a few of the fish that meet the bill.

Asian-Style Fish

with Greens

1 cup miso soup, prepared
½ cup honey
¼ cup soy sauce
2 teaspoons chopped fresh
   ginger
1 pound halibut (or other
   white fish)
1 tablespoon canola oil
   Salt and freshly ground
   black pepper
2 garlic cloves or 3 garlic
   scapes, chopped
1 bunch chard, spinach,
   or bok choy, chopped,
   (about 3 packed cups)

Fish should never be, well, fishy, with the exception of stronger-flavored varieties such as mackerel. Fresh fish should always smell like the sea, not like it's seen dry land one day too many. The sauce for this seafood dish is also excellent for stir-fried vegetables, such as asparagus or bok choy.

1. Combine the miso soup, honey, soy sauce, and ginger in a small saucepan. Bring to a boil, then reduce the heat and simmer until the sauce is thickened, about 15 minutes.

2. Preheat the oven to 350°F, or heat up a grill.

3. Lightly brush the fish with a teaspoon of the canola oil, and season with salt and pepper. Place on a baking sheet and bake for about 20 minutes, until the fish is firm and opaque and flakes easily. Or, grill about 6 minutes per side for 1 lb. filet, ¾ inch thick.

4. Heat the remaining canola oil in a large skillet over medium-high heat. Add the garlic and sauté for 2 minutes. Add the greens and sauté just until wilted. Serve the fish atop a bed of the greens, with the sauce drizzled over all.

Serves 4 to 6

Fish Curry

Curry does not always mean "spicy." It is actually just a term for a blend of spices. This version is a mild red curry with colorful veggies and rice.

1. Preheat the oven to 350°F. Coat a baking sheet with cooking spray.

2. Heat the oil in a large skillet over medium-high. Sauté the onion for about 5 minutes. Add the bell peppers. Sauté a couple of minutes longer, until the onion begins to turn golden brown. Add the garlic and ginger, and sauté for 2 minutes. Add the spices and tomato paste and cook, stirring constantly, for 2 minutes. Add the vegetable stock and bay leaf and bring to a simmer. Allow the sauce to simmer gently while the fish cooks.

3. Place the fish fillets on the prepared baking sheet. Bake for about 15 minutes, until the fish is flaky, firm, and no longer translucent.

4. Finish the sauce by stirring in the coconut milk and lemon juice. Adjust the seasoning with salt and pepper as desired. Bring back to a simmer.

5. Transfer the sauce to a shallow serving bowl. Remove the bay leaf. Add the fish to the bowl. Serve with the hot cooked rice.

Serves 6 to 8

1 tablespoon canola oil
1 onion, chopped
1 red bell pepper, julienned
1 yellow bell pepper, julienned
2 garlic cloves, chopped
1 teaspoon chopped fresh ginger
2 teaspoons ground cumin
2 teaspoons ground coriander
1½ teaspoons ground turmeric
½ teaspoon chili powder
1 (4-ounce) can tomato paste
1½ cups vegetable stock
1 bay leaf
2 pounds cod fillet (or other white fish)
1 (15-ounce) can coconut milk
Juice of ½ lemon
Salt and freshly ground black pepper
Hot cooked rice for serving

▬ Coconut Rice

Coconut rice is a wonderful accompaniment to Fish Curry, as well as to many other Asian dishes.

To make it, combine 1½ cups basmati rice with 1 (15-ounce) can coconut milk, 1 teaspoon ground turmeric, and 1 teaspoon sugar in a saucepan. Refill the coconut milk can with water, and add that to the saucepan. Bring to a boil, then reduce the heat and let simmer, covered, for about 20 minutes, or until the rice is done.

Turmeric, which is related to ginger, adds a nice flavor that complements the curry. Turmeric is also intriguing for its many health benefits, including anti-inflammatory and anti-cancer properties. It is most common in its ground form, although it is increasingly available in its fresh form.

Salmon Burgers

It seems somehow wrong to take fresh salmon and put it through the food processor, but these burgers, with the lemony herb dressing, are worth it. The hardest part of this recipe is pulling the pin bones and cutting the skin from the salmon fillet. A good fish market will do this for you.

2 tablespoons plus 1 teaspoon canola oil
1 shallot, chopped
1 scallion, thinly sliced
½ cup bread crumbs
2 tablespoons chopped fresh tarragon
1 tablespoon chopped fresh flat-leaf parsley
1 teaspoon Dijon mustard
¼ teaspoon salt
   Zest of 1 lemon
   Freshly ground black pepper
1 pound salmon fillet, boned and skinned
3 whole-wheat pitas, halved
   Lemon-Herb Mayonnaise (recipe follows)

1. Heat 1 teaspoon of the canola oil in a skillet over medium-high heat. Add the shallot and scallion and sauté for a couple minutes, until translucent. Scrape into a small bowl. Add the bread crumbs, tarragon, parsley, mustard, salt, and lemon zest to the bowl, along with a couple of grinds of pepper.

2. Place half the salmon in a food processor and pulse for a couple of minutes, until it begins to look like a paste. Add the crumb mixture and pulse a few times, until well combined.

3. Add the rest of the salmon and pulse for a minute or so, until the mixture is well chopped. Shape the mixture into 3-ounce patties; you should be able to make about 6 patties.

4. Heat the remaining 2 tablespoons oil in the skillet over medium-high heat. Add the salmon patties. Cook for 4 minutes on the first side, then turn and cook for 3 to 4 minutes longer. Do not overcook, but be sure the burgers are done (fish should be cooked through in the center). Serve in whole-wheat pita bread pockets with the mayonnaise.

Serves 6

¼ cup canola mayonnaise
2 tablespoons chopped fresh tarragon
1 tablespoon chopped fresh flat-leaf parsley
1 tablespoon fresh lemon juice

Lemon-Herb Mayonnaise

Combine the mayonnaise, tarragon, parsley, and lemon juice in a small bowl, and blend well. Chill before serving.

Meatless Mondays

DURING WORLD WAR I, then again during World War II, the U.S. government urged families to reduce consumption of meat to aid the war effort. The concept of "meatless Mondays" took off, and some 10 million American families enjoyed meatless meals as a form of shared sacrifice.

Today, many families throughout the United States and beyond are going meatless once a week, for new reasons. Of all foods, meats have the largest carbon footprint. Grain-fed beef has the highest "energy ratio" — the ratio of fossil fuel energy required to grow or raise that food, to energy the food provides — of all, at 54:1. Further, each kilogram of beef produced takes 100,000 liters of water to produce it. Other sources of meat have a smaller energy ratio, but they all take a far heavier toll on the environment than vegetarian foods. Studies have also shown that going meatless may reduce your risk of chronic preventable conditions like cancer, cardiovascular disease, and diabetes. On the following pages are some great ideas for your Meatless Monday Meals.

■ Loving the Leftover

We've never understood why folks don't like leftovers, especially when some items like stew and lasagna are mysteriously better the next day.

The real beauty of the leftover is that it takes minutes to reheat or reinvent for a real meal on a weeknight, saving both time and money while avoiding food waste.

A great strategy is to do most of the cooking on the weekends, and then alternate leftovers for the first few days of the week. By Thursday, a sandwich and soup or an egg dish can make for a simple, quick dinner. Friday night, try make-at-home pizza or another fun meal that can be prepared as a family.

Even restaurants leverage extra portions for soups and the next day's special. A winner of the James Beard award once confided to Beth that she serves braised meats the second day because the flavor improves overnight. So, if avoiding leftovers is your reason to eat out, think again.

Pasta with Broccoli Pesto

1 head broccoli, florets only
1 garlic clove
1 cup packed Italian flat-leaf parsley
1 cup packed basil
⅓ cup pine nuts
1 cup grated Parmesan cheese
2 teaspoon fresh lemon juice plus zest of 1 lemon
⅓ cup olive oil
Salt and pepper
½ pound pasta

If texture is the barrier to broccoli consumption around your house, this pesto variation is a spin, literally, on the traditional way to serve the nutritious green veggie. Herbs, Parmesan, and olive oil smooth out some of the bitterness, so much so that kids may not even realize it's broccoli.

1. Put a couple inches of water into a large pot, set a steaming basket in it, and bring water to a boil. Set the broccoli florets in the basket, cover, and let steam until soft, 3 to 5 minutes. You can also use an electric steamer.

2. Add the broccoli, garlic, herbs, and pine nuts to a food processor and pulse a few times to chop. Add the Parmesan and lemon juice and zest. Pulse again while drizzling in olive oil until you reach the desired texture (mixture should be very mushy). Taste and season with salt and pepper.

3. Prepare the pasta according to package directions. Drain and return to the pot. Toss the pasta with the pesto. You can use a bit of grated Parmesan as a garnish.

Serves 4 to 6

Variation:

You can use 3 cups of packed spinach leaves instead of the broccoli. Make sure they are triple-washed; no need to steam or cook before adding to the other ingredients in the food processor.

Pasta with Chard and Asparagus

in Herb-Parmesan Sauce

Beth's daughter once ate four servings, along with a pint of blueberries. We have no idea where she put it all. When she likes a recipe, she really digs in.

1. Steam the asparagus for 5 to 7 minutes, until tender. You can do this in an electric steamer. Alternatively, fill a large pot with a couple inches of water, set a steaming basket in it, and bring to a boil. Set the asparagus in the basket, cover, and let steam.

2. Bring a large pot of salted water to a boil. Add the pasta and cook according to the package directions. Drain and put back into the pot.

3. Meanwhile, melt the butter in a skillet over medium-high heat. Add the scallions and sauté until just golden, about 5 minutes. Add the flour and sauté for 3 minutes. Add the half-and-half, whisking to remove lumps, and heat through. Add the Parmesan and stir until it has melted and the sauce has a nice texture. Stir in the mixed herbs. Taste and adjust the seasoning as needed with salt and pepper. Keep warm.

4. Heat the oil in a skillet over medium-high heat. Add the chard and sauté just until it starts to wilt, about 3 minutes. Add the asparagus, and stir to combine.

5. Toss the pasta with the chard and asparagus. Pour the cheese sauce over the mixture, and stir gently to incorporate. Sprinkle the chives on top and serve.

Serves 6

1 pound asparagus, cut into 1-inch pieces

½ pound angel-hair pasta

1 tablespoon butter

2 scallions, sliced (about ¼ cup)

1 tablespoon unbleached all-purpose flour

¼ cup half-and-half

¾ cup grated Parmesan cheese

¼ cup chopped mixed fresh herbs (3 tablespoons basil, 1½ teaspoons oregano, 1½ teaspoons thyme)

Salt and freshly ground black pepper

1½ teaspoons olive oil

1 bunch chard (about 12 ounces) stems removed, chopped

1 tablespoon chopped fresh chives

1 pound eggplant (about one medium-sized), diced into ½-inch cubes

Salt

3 tablespoons canola oil

1 pound long beans, cut into 1-inch pieces

1 large onion, chopped

2 garlic cloves, chopped

1 small hot pepper (cayenne, mild jalapeño, or small Thai pepper), minced

2 tablespoons brown sugar

2 tablespoons crunchy peanut butter

2 teaspoons mild curry powder

¾ cup vegetable broth

½ cup coconut milk

Juice of 1 lime

1 bunch basil (Thai basil, if you can find it), chopped (about ⅓ cup)

Hot cooked rice for serving

Handful of chopped peanuts for garnish

Curried Eggplant and Long Beans

This curry is sweet, with a lot of flavor. It works well with eggplant, since the vegetable's spongy texture absorbs most of its flavor from the other ingredients in a recipe. You may substitute fresh green beans for the long beans.

1. Sprinkle the diced eggplant with salt, and set aside in a colander for 10 minutes. Rinse, drain, and pat dry.

2. Heat 2 tablespoons of the oil in a large skillet or wok over medium-high heat. Do not use a nonstick pan. Add the eggplant and sauté for about 3 minutes, until golden. Remove from the pan. Add the beans and sauté for a couple of minutes, until just browned a bit. Remove from the pan.

3. Heat the remaining 1 tablespoon of oil in the pan. Add the onion, garlic, and hot pepper and sauté until just golden. Add the brown sugar, peanut butter, and curry powder, and mix well. Add the vegetable broth, then stir, scraping the bottom of the pan to deglaze. Return the eggplant and beans to the skillet. Bring to a boil, then reduce to a simmer for 15 minutes. Add the coconut milk and let simmer for a couple of minutes, until slightly reduced.

4. Finish the dish with a squeeze of lime juice and half the chopped basil. Season with salt, if desired. Serve over rice, garnished with the rest of the basil and some chopped peanuts.

Serves 8

Honey-Sage Sweet Potatoes and Pasta
with Shallots

Using a whole-grain pasta with this dish adds fiber, flavor, and nutrition — which are key for a satisfying meatless main.

1. Preheat the oven to 350°F.

2. Toss the sweet potatoes, shallots, honey, brown sugar, salt, pepper, and five-spice powder with the oil in a large bowl. Spread into a single layer on a baking sheet. Bake for 15 to 20 minutes, until the sweet potatoes are tender and a bit caramelized on the outsides.

3. While the sweet potatoes are cooking, bring a large pot of water to a boil and cook the pasta according to the package directions. Drain and put back into the pot.

4. Toss the sweet potatoes with the pasta, and garnish with the sage and Parmesan.

Serves 4

1½ pounds sweet potatoes, peeled and diced into ¼-inch cubes
2 large shallots, sliced into eighths
1 tablespoon honey
1 tablespoon dark brown sugar
½ teaspoon salt
¼ teaspoon freshly ground black pepper
⅛ teaspoon Chinese five-spice powder
1 tablespoon extra-virgin olive oil
½ pound pasta (whole wheat or an oat-flax blend works well)
1 tablespoon chopped fresh sage
2 tablespoons grated Parmesan cheese

Variation:
Honey-Sage Squash with Shallots and Pasta

You can use an equal amount of winter squash like butternut or acorn here as well. Delicata squash would also be good.

227

Potato Salad
with Caramelized Onions and Vegetables

1 pound red-skinned potatoes, each about 2 to 3 inches in size

2 pounds fresh snap beans (green, yellow, purple, or Roma varieties, or a mix)

1½ pounds tomatoes (2 large), cored and seeded

1 cup Quick Caramelized Onions (page 65)

2 tablespoons capers, rinsed

3 tablespoons red wine vinegar

2 teaspoons stone-ground mustard

½ cup extra-virgin olive oil

2 tablespoons chopped fresh herbs, such as dill, basil, or parsley

Sea salt or kosher salt and freshly ground black pepper

5 cups mixed salad greens, including chopped fresh herbs like basil or dill if desired

To make this hearty salad into a perfect summer meal, add sliced, hard-boiled eggs or canned tuna. There will be leftovers, so store the salad greens separately from the other vegetables and dressing, combining the salad on the plate when ready to eat. If the greens are stored mixed with the dressing and vegetables, they will get wilted and dark.

1. Bring a large pot of water to a boil. Add the potatoes, and boil until the potatoes are fork-tender, about 20 minutes. Remove with tongs and let cool. Do not turn off the heat. Put the green beans in the still-boiling water, and let cook for 4 minutes to blanch. Remove with tongs and place into an ice-water bath to stop the green beans from cooking more (they will get mushy and continue cooking if left hot).

2. Cut the cooled potatoes into wedges. Core the tomatoes by cutting the top and tough white core away. Gently squeeze to seed the tomatoes, removing the gel and seeds, leaving the flesh. Cut the tomatoes into similar-size wedges as the potatoes. Place the tomatoes, potatoes, green beans, onions, and capers in a very large serving bowl.

3. Whisk the vinegar and mustard in a small bowl. Continue whisking, drizzling in the olive oil to make a dressing. Add the herbs and salt and pepper to taste. Drizzle the dressing over the cooked vegetables. Add more salt and pepper, if needed. Just before serving, add the salad greens to the bowl and toss with the vegetables and dressing.

Serves 10

Carrot-Quinoa "Biryani"

To make this vegan, use vegetable stock in this recipe. The earthy spice and sweet and nutty flavors will please both vegans and nonvegans alike. Just be sure to rinse the quinoa well, so it isn't bitter.

¾ cup quinoa, rinsed and drained

¼ cup green lentils, rinsed and drained

2 cups chicken or vegetable stock

2 bay leaves

1 tablespoon extra-virgin olive oil

1 onion, chopped

1 garlic clove, minced

1½ teaspoons grated fresh ginger

2 large carrots, peeled and grated

½ cup frozen peas

½ teaspoon garam masala spice blend

¼ teaspoon ground turmeric

¼ cup slivered almonds

Salt and freshly ground black pepper

1 cup raisins, currants, or Craisins

1. Combine the quinoa and lentils in a large saucepan with the chicken stock and bay leaves. Bring to a boil, then reduce the heat and simmer until all the broth is absorbed, the lentils are al dente, and the quinoa is cooked, about 20 minutes.

2. Heat the oil in a large skillet over medium-high heat. Add the onion, garlic, and ginger and sauté until the garlic is just golden, about 2 minutes. Add the carrots, peas, garam masala, and turmeric, and sauté for a couple of minutes, until heated through. Add the almonds and season with salt and pepper.

3. Remove the bay leaves from the lentil-quinoa mixture. Mix the mixture with the vegetables. Add the raisins and stir gently to combine.

Serves 6

229

the anti-diet

There's no magic pill. They can't fool us anymore. Or make us give up bread. You were a cruel man, Dr. Atkins.

So, here's our anti-diet. Take a normal-size plate. Top with food. Do not overload it or mound the servings to the rim. Have three of these a day, with half the plate holding fruit and veggies, a fourth holding a lean meat or other protein source, and the other fourth holding a whole grain. Avoid sugary beverages and lots of butter.

That's all there is to it. Really. No long diet book to read. No stepping on the scale.

Try to eat most, not all, of your meals like this. There will be adjustments for things like pasta dishes and other combination dishes. Between meals, if you get hungry, have a healthful snack. Aim for five to nine servings of vegetables and fruits every day, with more vegetables than fruit. Try to make sure that most, if not all, of the fats you consume are healthy fats like olive or canola oil, nuts, and fatty fish like salmon.

It won't work every day. Holidays and parties will happen, or just the kind of day where you really, really want a cookie. Aim for eating well for most meals, most days. And remember portion sizes. Observe the portion sizes in the illustration above.

Surprised? Portions really aren't as big as what we think. They are certainly not what's packaged in the store or served to us in a restaurant.

Ketchup? It does not count as a vegetable — unless you plan to eat half a cup of ketchup (and even then, about a third of it would just be sugar). Fries count as a starchy vegetable, not a vegetable. Ready for this? You only get 10 to 15 fries per serving. That's like one tiny corner of the supersize

One serving of vegetables =
½ cup cooked or 1 cup raw

One serving of meat =
3 ounces (this is not even
a quarter-pounder)

One serving of dairy =
1 cup skim milk or 3 to
4 ounces yogurt

One serving of fruit =
1 small apple, 1 cup berries,
or ¼ cup dried fruit

One serving of grains/legumes/starches =
⅓ cup cooked pasta, ½ cup mashed potato,
½ cup legumes, or 1 slice whole-grain bread

package. Or, perhaps just licking the grease off the bottom of
the carton.

Confused? No crazy all-cabbage fasting or pharma-foods?
These are basic, healthful eating guidelines and actual food.
Good food. No diet. We hate diets. Almost as much as we hate
sit-ups.

Because we also hate to count servings (and don't have
time), we will just stick to the plate approach, eat a lot of different colors of fruits and veggies, and try to exercise some.
And, yeah, sometimes, we're going to eat ice cream.

231

Pumpkin Gnocchi

*with Walnut Cream Sauce
and Balsamic Reduction*

1 cup extra-fine semolina
flour, plus extra for dusting
work surface

1 cup pumpkin purée

1 egg

¼ teaspoon pumpkin pie spice
(optional)

4 ounces mascarpone cheese

½ cup heavy cream

1 cup walnut pieces

¼ teaspoon ground nutmeg
Salt

½ cup balsamic vinegar

Yes, you can make gnocchi. It's easy and fun if you have a bit of time to spare. Get the kids to help roll out the long dough for cutting and shaping the gnocchi, like they're having fun with Play-Doh. Just make sure they don't eat this dough — it has raw eggs.

1. Dust a work surface with some flour. Mound the pumpkin purée on the work surface, and make a well in the center. Crack the egg into the well, and top it with ½ cup of the flour and the pumpkin pie spice, if desired. Mix with your hands, gently turning and folding the flour in. Add the rest of the flour a bit at a time, until the texture is no longer sticky. You may not need all of the flour.

2. Cut the dough in half. With your hands, roll one half into a long cylinder, about ¾ inch in diameter. Cut the cylinder into ½-inch-thick segments. You may need a touch of flour to keep things workable. Using the tines of a fork, roll each little piece along the back of the tines, pressing the center in with your thumb and rolling the dough piece

---

Rolling Gnocchi

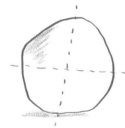

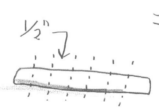

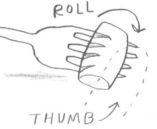

1. Divide your dough ball into quarters.

2. Roll it out like a clay snake to ¾" diameter. Cut into ½" pieces.

3. Roll the little pieces down the tines of a fork using the ball of your thumb.

4. After some practice, you'll get little corduroy pillows!

off the tips of the tines. You should end up with an oval that has ridges on one side and a fold along the back. No worries if it is not perfect — the ridges are to hold sauce, not for show. Repeat the process with the other half of the dough.

3. Place the fresh gnocchi in a single layer on a baking sheet, and chill in the freezer for at least 20 minutes. You can now freeze the gnocchi in a bag or container without them sticking together, or you can bring a pot of salted water to a boil and cook them for dinner. I make two batches and do both.

4. For the sauce, combine the cheese and cream in a small saucepan over low heat and heat slowly until warm. Stir in the walnuts and nutmeg, and heat to a near simmer. Season with salt to taste.

5. For the balsamic reduction, heat the vinegar in a small saucepan over medium-low heat until it is reduced by two-thirds and has a syrupy texture.

6. To serve, bring a large pot of salted water to a boil, add the gnocchi, and cook at a full boil until the gnocchi floats to the top, about 12 minutes. Drain, and set the gnocchi on a serving platter. Spoon the walnut sauce over the top and drizzle with the balsamic reduction.

Serves 6

Vegetable Parmigiano

This dish is among the easiest ways to introduce kids to eggplant, leveraging "pizza" ingredients like mozzarella cheese and tomato sauce.

1 egg
2 cups panko bread crumbs
1 cup plus ¼ cup grated Parmesan cheese
1 teaspoon garlic powder
1 teaspoon dried oregano
½ teaspoon salt
¼ teaspoon freshly ground black pepper
2 small or 1 medium eggplant
1 medium zucchini
2 small tomatoes
1 cup part-skim ricotta cheese
⅓ cup part-skim mozzarella cheese
¼ cup chopped fresh basil
1 tablespoon chopped fresh flat-leaf parsley
1½ cups tomato sauce

1. Preheat the oven to 400°F, and grease a baking sheet (preferably with raised edges).

2. Beat the egg in a flat dish. Combine the panko, 1 cup of the Parmesan, garlic powder, oregano, salt, and pepper in another flat dish, and blend well.

3. Slice the eggplant and zucchini about ¼ inch thick. Core and seed the tomatoes, and cut them into 1-inch-thick slices.

4. Set the tomatoes on the prepared baking sheet. Dip the eggplant and zucchini slices into the egg mixture and then dredge in the panko mixture, making sure they are well coated. Set the breaded slices on the prepared baking sheet. When you're done, press any remaining panko mixture onto the tomato slices.

5. Bake the vegetables for 15 minutes, then carefully turn each slice over and bake for 15 minutes longer.

6. Meanwhile, combine the ricotta, mozzarella, basil, and parsley in a medium bowl, and mix well.

7. When the vegetables are done baking, remove them from the oven, but leave the oven on. Spread about 1½ teaspoons tomato sauce over each slice of eggplant and zucchini. Spread about 2 teaspoons of cheese filling onto each of those slices, as well as on top of the tomato slices. Dust all the sliced vegetables with the remaining ¼ cup Parmesan. Bake for about 20 minutes, until the tops are light golden brown.

Serves 6

CHAPTER FIVE

SNACKS & SWEETS

taking the fight out of kids' favorite foods

Snack foods are BIG BUSINESS in America...

Packaged snacks are currently worth about $68 billion, and an estimated 3,000 new snack products are released every single year — most of them mere clever rearrangements of simple starches, salt, sugar, oil, and artificial flavorings.

Snacks are essential for kids. With their high metabolism and small bellies, children require a pick-me-up between meals. The American Academy of Pediatrics actually recommends that young children eat four to six times daily, and we've all seen the results of a toddler who has gone too long without refueling: The child collapses into a wailing, tear-stained puddle on the floor.

By the time they're school-age, children need snacks to stay alert in school and to have sufficient energy for after-school homework, sports, and other activities.

Yet most nutrition experts agree that kids' snacking habits undermine good health rather than contribute to it. There seem to be a few reasons for this:

- **Kids are snacking more than ever.** Between 1977 and 1996, kids' snacking increased 30 percent. Today, a full 25 percent of children's calories comes from between-meal foods.

- **Most snack foods are gross.** All that increased snacking might not be so bad if the quality of most snack foods wasn't so appalling. Today, the most popular snack foods among kids are soft drinks, cookies, chips, and candy.

■ **Snack foods that look healthful can be the opposite.** Even snacks that appear healthful are often not much better than candy; many of the leading granola bars on the market are higher in sugar than cookies. Don't even get us started about fruit snacks, which nutrition expert Marion Nestle has called "candy disguised as fruit."

With a little advance planning, though, snacks can boost children's health rather than detract from it. Here are a few tips for better snacking:

■ **Be prepared.** Packaged snacks are everywhere: in vending machines, at gas stations, in school hallways, and even in fitness centers. Every time your child sees them, they will serve as a reminder to "eat, eat, eat." Nearly half of all snack purchases are made on impulse. Be prepared with a healthful alternative.

■ **Consider snacks as you would a meal.** Since snacks are responsible for a full quarter of children's energy intake, it's a good idea to plan them much as you would a meal, with an eye on their overall nutrition.

■ **Location, location, location.** At home, keep snacking to a specific locale. Encourage kids to eat snacks at the table instead of mindlessly grazing on snacks while doing homework, watching television, or doing other activities.

Consistency is key. The more you can feed kids meals and snacks according to a predictable schedule, the less likely they are to harass you for unhealthful snacks throughout the day.

■ **Make the healthful stuff more convenient.** Keep healthful snacks — like vegetable slices with dip, fresh fruits, nuts, and cheese slices — someplace where kids can reach them. Keep less-healthful options out of sight.

237

dips & chips

OUTSIDE OF SUGARY TREATS, salty chips probably get top billing in the roster of irresistible junk foods. Scoop on a heap of creamy, cheesy dip, and you have the mother lode of saturated fat in one bite-size morsel. Still, "chips" and dip can stay on the snack bar, and even offer some nutrition. Check out these healthful recipes.

FACT: A 2004 study showed that teens served a fast-food lunch ate an average of 1,652 calories in a single setting — more than 60 percent of their recommended daily energy intake.

Source: Ebbeling C. B., Sinclair K. B., Pereira M. A., et al. Compensation for Energy Intake From Fast Food Among Overweight and Lean Adolescents. JAMA. 2004; 291: 2828–2833.

Lima Bean Hummus

We know, it's lima beans. But, really, it's good.

1. Bring the vegetable broth and frozen lima beans to a boil in a medium saucepan. Reduce the heat, cover, and simmer for 15 minutes, until the lima beans are soft.

2. Peel the garlic cloves. Put the bean mixture, garlic cloves, lemon juice, and salt and pepper to taste in a food processor. Pulse until it is a nice purée.

3. Add the olive oil with processor running until the hummus is the desired texture. Serve with pitas or any good bread.

Makes about 2 cups

1 cup low-sodium vegetable broth
1 (16-ounce) package frozen lima beans
2 garlic cloves
3 tablespoons lemon juice
  Salt and freshly ground black pepper
⅓–½ cup extra-virgin olive oil
  Pita bread or other bread wedges

Hummus Toppings

For a spicy Asian flair, garnish the hummus with:

- 1 tablespoon chopped fresh mint
- 1 tablespoon chopped fresh basil
- 1 teaspoon Asian hot sauce
- Zest from 1 lemon, chopped

For a more traditional Middle Eastern style, garnish the hummus with:

- 1 tablespoon chopped fresh flat-leaf parsley
- Zest from 1 lemon, chopped

FACT: Between 1977 and 2006, the span of a single generation, the amount of snack calories consumed by children of all ages increased by an average of 168 calories per day to a total of 586 calories. Children aged 2 to 6 consumed an extra 181 calories per day during snack time.

Source: Piernas, Carmen and Popkin, Barry M. "Trends In Snacking Among U.S. Children," Health Affairs, 29, no. 3 (2010): 398–404.

White Bean–Pesto Dip

1 (15-ounce) can cannellini
   beans, rinsed and drained
¼ cup Basil Pesto (page 145)
½ teaspoon salt
   Freshly ground black pepper

Fast and light, this dip goes great with sliced raw veggies or good, crusty bread.

Blend the beans, pesto, salt, and pepper to taste in a food processor until smooth.

Makes about 1 cup

Fresh Tomatillo Salsa

5 medium tomatillos
1 small yellow onion
1 green bell pepper
3 scallions
2 garlic cloves
1 jalapeño pepper, or other
   small pepper with medium
   heat, seeds removed
   Juice of ½ lime
½ teaspoon salt
1 tablespoon olive oil
3 tablespoons chopped fresh
   cilantro

Kids love salsa and chips. We don't have to tell them salsa is just loads of chopped vegetables, do we? Here's a green salsa that is best made in late summer, when tangy tomatillos are at their peak. In other months, you can make it with canned tomatillos; the result will be more liquidy, but still tasty.

1. Chop the tomatillos, onion, bell pepper, and scallions into small pieces. Mince the garlic and hot pepper. Mix all the vegetables together in a large bowl, and then add the lime juice, salt, and olive oil. Stir.

2. Add the chopped cilantro just before serving. The salsa can be served right away, but its flavor improves slightly if it can sit for an hour.

Makes about 1½ cups

Pita "Chips"

4 whole-wheat pita rounds
1 tablespoon olive oil
½ teaspoon kosher salt

Whole grain pita chips are a great way to get all the crunch of chips without the fat.

1. Preheat oven to 400°F.

2. Cut each pita round into eight triangles. Brush olive oil on the pita wedges and place on a baking sheet.

3. Sprinkle with the salt. Bake for about 7 minutes, or until crisp.

Serves 6

Salt and Vinegar Kale Chips

These chips were inspired by a tip from Ali's friend, Shannon Toye. We've made them on many occasions, and they are a surprising hit with kids and even adults who say they do not like greens. In both our homes, the kids have been known to run off with the whole bowl — so get a good first helping! With this recipe, you want the chips to be both crispy and bright green. If they start to brown, they can taste burned. If you find that the chips are browning before the kale is crispy, reduce the oven temperature.

1 bunch kale, 6 to 8 stems or 12 ounces
2 tablespoons olive oil
2 teaspoons balsamic vinegar (optional)
Kosher salt

1. Preheat oven to 350°F.

2. Wash the kale, dry thoroughly in a salad spinner, and tear into bite-size pieces. Toss in a large bowl with the olive oil and balsamic vinegar, if desired. Rub the leaves to make sure each gets a coating of oil so they crisp up well. Oil a baking sheet.

3. Place the kale in a single layer on the baking sheet. Sprinkle with kosher salt to taste. Bake for about 6 minutes, then stir and turn the kale and bake for 6 to 9 minutes longer. Remove crisp pieces as they get done to prevent burning and to allow the remaining kale chips to get even heat.

Serves 4

▬ Kale Chips Appeal to Kids

A University of Wisconsin extension project involved 201 elementary school students in making and tasting this recipe themselves. According to the study, 99 percent of the kids had never heard of kale before. After they made the kale chips, all but one of the kids tasted them. And 99 of them (just under half) liked the taste on the first try. Okay, not all of them liked them right off the bat. But half? On the first try? We're talking about kale here, folks. Those odds make it seem worth a try.

Make-Your-Own Microwave Popcorn

¼ cup popcorn kernels
1 small brown paper bag
   (such as a lunch bag)
Extra-virgin olive oil or
   melted butter
Salt

▬ Reasons to Pop Your Own

We were crushed to learn that many commercial brands of microwave popcorn use perfluorooctanoic acid (PFOA) in their packaging.

The Environmental Protection Agency considers PFOA potentially carcinogenic based on animal studies. Until recently, most commercial brands also used diacetyl, a flavoring agent that caused lung damage in the people who worked in popcorn manufacturing facilities. We also just kind of hate shelling out our money to giant food corporations — especially when some of the leading brands of microwave popcorn are owned by companies with spotty records for food safety.

Who can deny the convenience of microwave popcorn? It's fast, it's inexpensive, and it makes a perfect afternoon snack for the kids . . . or yourself. But many commercial brands are suspect (see the sidebar), health-wise. Fortunately, we don't have to depend on the commercial brands. For a fraction of the cost, we can make our own microwave popcorn . . . and so can you.

1. Place the popcorn kernels in the brown paper bag. Fold over the top of the bag two or three times (do not staple or tape) and place on its side in the microwave.

2. Cook on HIGH for 1½ to 2 minutes (varies by microwave), or until there are about 2 seconds between each pop.

3. Remove from the microwave, add the olive oil and salt to taste, and shake until the popcorn is coated. Pour into a serving bowl. It's really that simple. So simple a child could do it.

Makes 8 cups popped corn

Popcorn Seasonings

To step it up, try adding your own seasoning blends to the popcorn in place of the olive oil and salt.

Cinnamon-sugar popcorn: Mix 1 tablespoon sugar with ½ teaspoon ground cinnamon. Sprinkle onto buttered popcorn.

Herbed popcorn: Mix ½ teaspoon dried basil, ¼ teaspoon dried oregano, a pinch of cayenne pepper, and 1 tablespoon grated Parmesan cheese. Sprinkle over buttered popcorn or over popcorn coated with olive oil.

Nacho-flavored popcorn: Mix 1 teaspoon paprika, ½ teaspoon crushed red pepper flakes, ½ teaspoon ground cumin, and ½ cup grated Parmesan cheese. Sprinkle over buttered popcorn.

NEGATIVE about ADDITIVES

You know how your child sometimes has those . . . uh . . . moments? The three-hour tantrum? The inability to put shoes on, even though you've asked 17 times? The insane, can't-stop-jumping-on-the-bed-sorry-but-I-just-can't-stop hyperactivity? Turns out some common food additives could be making these moments worse.

A study from the United Kingdom lends support to the idea that common food additives could influence a host of behavior issues in children, including temper tantrums, poor concentration, and hyperactivity. Researchers at Southampton University tested combinations of synthetic colorings and preservatives that a typical child might consume in a day. They studied the effect in groups of healthy three-year-olds and eight- and nine-year-olds. In both groups, the study results linked key additives to an array of behavior problems. While several of the additives they studied are banned in the United States, others are widely used, including FD&C Yellow 5, FD&C Yellow 6, FD&C Red 40, and sodium benzoate. Similar studies have been published in the past.

Although parental absolution might feel like a relief temporarily — *Aha! It's the food, not your parenting! You're off the hook!* — after a while, you might weary of the mood swings. And since the food manufacturers aren't exactly offering to babysit after your child consumes these additives, you might consider moving toward foods that don't include chemical cocktails in their ingredient lists.

Source: D. McCann, A. Barrett, A. Cooper, et al., "Food additives and hyperactive behaviour in 3-year-old and 8/9-year-old children in the community: a randomised, double-blinded, placebo-controlled trial," *Lancet* 370 (9598): 1560–7.

the ten best snacks to have around

Walk down the grocery aisle labeled "snacks" and you realize that food manufacturers have hijacked this category so effectively that most consumers can only comprehend a snack as something that comes in a brightly colored package, often with licensed characters. The actual food variety in that package is generally limited to the four "c's;" chip, cookie, candy, crap.

It's time to take back the snack. With all of those colorful packages screaming at your kid, it's easy to forget that nature itself has provided a number of perfect portion-size individually wrapped snacks. Take apples, for example; the wrapper is edible and you can even compost the core and plant the seeds. All for pocket change. Here are some other "new" old ideas when it comes to snacks to keep handy and say "Yes!" to:

1. Vegetables
With or without a healthy dip. But kids do love to dip.

2. Fruit
Bring back the fruit bowl, front and center. It's not just decoration anymore. Dried is second best to fresh.

3. Nuts
We're crazy about them.

Popcorn
Good old-fashioned popcorn, the favorite, crunchy whole-grain snack of kids everywhere. (To learn how to make your own microwave popcorn, see page 242.)

Cheese
Cheese just tastes so good, even the healthier, lower-fat options. Calcium and protein are an added bonus. Also consider low-fat cottage cheese mixed with fruit or yogurt sweetened with honey or fruit.

Edamame in the pods
If popcorn were a legume, well, it would be edamame. Plus, it's just plain fun to squirt the beans out of the pod to eat them.

Low-sugar, whole-grain cereals and crackers
Sometimes it's all about the crunch. Look for options made with healthy oils and limited sweeteners.

Hard-boiled egg
Cook up a bunch at a time, and you'll always have a filling, protein-rich snack on hand.

Make-your-own trail mix
Let kids mix their own trail mix using favorite dried fruits, whole-grain pretzels, nuts, seeds, and dried cereals. Keep in an airtight container.

Milk with honey
Funny how adding just a touch of honey turns regular old milk into a treat. If you're near a microwave, add a few drops of vanilla extract, and then heat it until steaming warm. Yum.

245

Yogurt

Yogurt is simply fermented milk; healthy bacteria (probiotics) are introduced, and they curdle the milk and release lactic acid. The bacteria help boost your immune system in impressive ways. Homemade yogurt is inexpensive and delicious, and combined with fresh or dried fruit, it makes an excellent snack.

4 cups milk

Yogurt starter (either a commercial brand, or ¼ cup plain yogurt with live cultures)

1. Heat the milk until it froths (185°F). A double boiler is recommended so that your milk doesn't burn. If you don't have one, just stand there and stir. Avoid using ultra-pasteurized milk, as it won't taste nearly as good.

2. Cool milk to around 110°F (lukewarm, slightly warmer than body temp). This takes an hour or so, with occasional stirring to maintain an even temperature.

3. Place the yogurt starter in a sterilized bowl, and pour in your warm milk. *Note:* It's important to sterilize the bowl, so unfriendly bacteria don't grow alongside yogurt's friendly bacteria; a single dishwasher cycle will do the trick.

   You can either use a commercial starter, like Yogourmet, or take a large dollop of plain yogurt with active cultures. You simply need enough live cultures to get the whole process moving. If you use yogurt, select plain yogurt that is as fresh as you can find, so that you have a good quantity of active live cultures.

   Be sure your milk is neither too hot nor too cold. If you add milk that is too hot to the starter, you will kill the cultures; if your milk is too cool, you might not kick-start the culture growth.

4. Keep warm, let sit, let it happen. If you don't have a yogurt maker, maintaining the correct level of warmth is the only challenging part. The process works best if the bowl of milk and starter sits at a temperature of about 110°F for many hours. An electric yogurt maker guarantees that temperature. Other methods include:

- Let the bowl sit on an electric heating pad.
- Let it sit in the oven with the pilot light on.
- Let it sit in an insulated cooler with jars of hot water.
- Wrap the bowl in a down vest or heavy blanket.

The process generally takes at least 8 hours, sometimes longer, and the yogurt often doesn't begin to thicken until the last couple of hours. Don't panic; just wait it out.

5. Once thickened, chill, and then serve. Serve with fresh fruit, granola, a touch of honey, or whatever strikes your fancy.

Note: Homemade yogurt is thinner than commercial yogurt. Most commercial yogurts are thickened with pectin or other thickening agents. If you find homemade yogurt too thin, you can thicken it with some powdered milk.

DID YOU KNOW? Many common children's food products that in the United States contain artificial food dyes are sold in the United Kingdom with natural versions of those same colors.

sweets & desserts

LET'S FACE IT: MOST OF US LIKE SWEET THINGS. We're born with a taste for sweetness, and the first food that most of us ever consume — breast milk — is plenty sweet. Got a sweet tooth? Or have kids with one? Don't feel bad. A sweet tooth, like opposable thumbs and a tendency to gossip, simply means you are human.

The truth is, there's nothing wrong with a spoonful of sugar now and then. But what about 31 spoonfuls? That's what the average American eats each day. For teens, it's a whopping 34 teaspoons. Every single day. We'll go ahead and do the math for you: That's more than 12,000 teaspoons during a single year.

In moderate amounts, food manufacturers are quick to assure you, sugar is not a problem. And we agree with them. The problem is simply that it's everywhere, in copious amounts, often crowding out healthier foods in a child's diet, spiking blood sugar, and leaving kids in a vicious cycle of craving and binging.

Think about it: When you're running errands — taking the kids to dance classes, picking up a prescription, purchasing a roll of paper towels — how many times do you pass a vending machine or display filled with candy bars and soda? How easy is it to pick up a dozen doughnuts? And in all those hours, precisely how often do you come across a bowl of fresh fruit or vegetables? Exactly.

Research indicates that kids often crave sugar during peak growth spurts. Beyond that, some children simply appear to have more affinity for the stuff than others. Some kids can take sugar or leave it, enjoying it when it's offered to them but otherwise giving it no thought whatsoever. Others are crazy for the stuff — we mean literally crazy

— constantly jonesing for their next hit like a junkie on the edge of withdrawal.

There doesn't seem to be any rhyme or reason in determining which kids are crazed sugar fiends, either. Parents whose first child throws regular tantrums over sugary foods sometimes marvel at how little their second child cares about the stuff. Or the opposite happens: Parents note with pride that little Johnny doesn't care for sugary treats, then suddenly find themselves with a second child who scoops heaps of granulated sugar straight out of the bag with bare hands.

Because every kid is different, there is no one-size-fits-all solution. Believe us, we wish there were. In talking with parents about sweets, we heard an array of potential solutions. We talked with parents who have a weekly "dessert night" to satisfy cravings. We spoke with parents who made a policy of eating only handmade sweets (which eliminates most of them), or who give the child a small sugary treat daily, but just one. We talked with a mother who believed that the key to moderation was handing her daughter a cookie in the middle of the day, unasked. We even talked with one mother who reported in a chipper manner that she once allowed her son to eat so many candy bars that he threw up — "that did the trick for a long time," she offered helpfully.

Avoid the sugar struggle

Never soothe with sweets. It can sometimes be tempting to squelch a nasty tantrum with a big hunk o' sugary goodness. Resist that urge, unless you want tantrums to become more frequent instead of less.

Start with fruit. When your child begins rummaging the cabinets in hopes of mainlining sugar, offer her some fruit instead. Oh, sure, she might protest, hoping for something with a quicker hit. But you both might find that the natural sugar in fruit is enough to satisfy the craving.

- **If not fruit, try fruit salad.** Kids who groan about an individual piece of fruit are often delighted to have a fruit salad. Need to call in the big guns? Try smoothies.

- **Play.** Have you ever noticed that the more you exercise, the more healthful your cravings become? Kids are the same way. Get them moving.

- **Keep it out of sight. Or better yet, out of the house.** An array of studies show that the more people see a given food, the more likely they are to eat it. Candy in clear dishes is consumed 71 percent more than candy in opaque dishes. Ice cream presented in an open cooler is eaten more than twice as often as ice cream in a closed cooler. Similar effects might be at work in your house: Keep it out of sight, and it is more likely to stay out of mind.

- **Serve big, healthful lunches.** Most people start craving sugar and empty carbohydrates after lunch. Make lunches big, and healthful, and you might find your kids craving sugar a little less as the day goes on.

- **Eat regularly.** Make sure your children are eating healthful meals regularly. This can help them avoid spikes in blood sugar, which then lead to low blood sugar and cravings.

- **Lose the anxiety.** Even kids who don't find Oreos in the kitchen cabinet are going to find them outside the house. That's okay. Remember that the goal — to raise a child with healthy overall attitudes toward food — is a long-term one. Counting every cookie they eat won't help with that goal, and it likely could hurt.

fruit desserts

FRUIT ALONE IS A GREAT SNACK OPTION, and it stands in for dessert pretty well, too. But, if you want something special after a meal that offers a sweet reward with a bit less guilt, try these fruit desserts. They're worth eating your veggies for.

Granola Bar? Or Simply Candy?

It's tempting to give kids "fruit snacks" and granola bars as a healthful snack option. But here's how leading brands of a dehydrated fruit snack and yogurt-flavored "nutrition" bar stack up when compared to sweet treats:

Product	Sugar Content per 37 Grams
Strawberry-kiwi "fruit snack"	19 grams
Twizzlers	15 grams
Oreo cookie	14 grams
Yogurt multigrain bar	13 grams
Milk shake–flavored Pop-Tart	12 grams

Perfect Peach Summer Side

3 peaches, halved, pit removed
2 ounces mascarpone cheese
⅓ cup fresh blueberries
¼ cup Fig Balsamic Vinaigrette (page 95)

Easy, elegant, and healthy. Use peaches fresh from the farmers' market and this dish will be pure heaven. You can brush the peaches with some olive oil and grill them for a couple minutes, cut side down, to add some smoky flavor to the mix. This is not necessary, though. You can also make this a salad course by simply adding mixed greens as the base, and perhaps a few walnuts on top.

Place the peaches cut side up on a plate, add a dollop of mascarpone to each, and sprinkle the blueberries over them. Drizzle with the dressing.

Serves 6

Rhubarb Crumble
with Rosemary and Thyme

3 pounds rhubarb, diced
⅓ cup plus 1½ cups sugar
¼ cup cornstarch
Juice of 1 lemon
½ cup (1 stick) butter, softened
1 cup unbleached all-purpose flour
2 sprigs fresh rosemary, chopped
1 tablespoon chopped fresh thyme leaves

Herbs pair remarkably well with fruit, adding complexity to the sweetness. If you are not a rhubarb fan, you can substitute an equal amount of strawberries or other berries. In this recipe, fresh herbs are best. Dried versions will lend a bitter taste.

1. Preheat the oven to 350°F.

2. Combine the rhubarb, ⅓ cup of the sugar, cornstarch, and lemon juice in a large bowl, and toss to mix. Scrape the mixture into a 9- by 13-inch baking dish.

3. Combine the butter, remaining 1½ cups sugar, flour, rosemary, and thyme in a medium bowl. Use a fork to cut in the butter until the mixture resembles coarse cornmeal. Sprinkle the topping evenly over the rhubarb. Bake for about 50 minutes, until golden brown on top and bubbly in the center. Serve warm.

Serves 12

Apple Cider Applesauce

good for lunch!

You can put this through the food mill, but why? The old-school chunky texture is great. If your family does not like things spicy or is not fond of the flavor of anise, omit the cardamom and star anise. For kids who are not used to spice, try adding just a little bit and let them get used to the new flavor. Over time you can build up the spice profile.

4½ pounds apples (we recommend Gala), peeled, cored, and sliced

2 cups no-sugar-added apple cider

1 cinnamon stick

1 star anise (optional)

2 tablespoons lemon juice, plus more if desired

¼ cup sugar

¼ teaspoon ground cinnamon

¼ teaspoon ground cardamom (optional)

1. Combine the apples, cider, cinnamon stick, star anise, if desired, and lemon juice in a large Dutch oven. Bring to a boil, then reduce the heat and simmer, covered, for 25 minutes, until the apples are tender.

2. Remove the star anise and cinnamon stick. Mash to the desired consistency with a potato masher, then simmer, uncovered, for 10 to 15 minutes longer, until the mixture is the desired thickness.

3. Remove from the heat and mix in the sugar, ground cinnamon, and cardamom, if desired. Adjust the level of tartness with additional lemon juice if desired.

Serves 12. Freezes well also

Sauce Variations:

Early-season apples are tarter than late-season apples, and some varieties are sweeter than others. You may want to add the sugar gradually, tasting as you go to decide how much you'll need.

Also, you can skip peeling the apples for this recipe if you like. Use a stick blender at the end to incorporate the peels. Much of the apple's nutrition is just under the peel, so this variation will bump up the fiber, nutrition, and flavor of the applesauce. Both versions are good. If you go with the stick blender in the hot applesauce, keep it immersed. Or else. Ouch.

Ginger-Vanilla Cherry-Berry Cobbler

3 cups cherries and/or other berries

¼ cup plus 2 tablespoons sugar

2 teaspoons cornstarch

½ cup unbleached all-purpose flour

1 tablespoon chopped crystallized ginger

1 teaspoon baking powder

¼ teaspoon salt

½ teaspoon ground Ceylon or regular cinnamon

⅛ teaspoon ground mace

2 tablespoons butter, softened

¼ cup cream

1 tablespoon milk

1 teaspoon vanilla extract

Beth created this dessert especially for a friend whose little girl likes baked goods and desserts but has an egg allergy. The biscuits come out very light and fluffy.

1. Preheat the oven to 400°F.

2. Combine the fruit, ¼ cup of the sugar, and cornstarch in a saucepan over medium heat. Bring to a boil, stirring often, and then reduce the heat and let simmer slowly to thicken while you mix the biscuit topping.

3. Combine the flour, remaining 2 tablespoons sugar, ginger, baking powder, salt, cinnamon, and mace in a large bowl, and stir to mix. Use a fork to cut in the butter until the mixture resembles coarse meal. Add the cream, milk, and vanilla and stir until the batter just comes together. Do not overmix.

4. Pour the fruit filling into a 9-inch square glass dish. Drop the biscuit batter by tablespoonfuls on top. Bake for 20 to 25 minutes, until a toothpick inserted in a biscuit comes out clean. Serve warm.

Serves 12

Popstickles

At Beth's house, homemade ice pops are loaded with fruit and even some herbs for a more healthful treat. Just be sure to call them popSTICKles, as her daughter reminds Beth, because of the stick.

Peaches and Herb Popstickles

Combine the peaches, honey, thyme, and mint in a blender and purée. Pour into reusable ice-pop molds. Freeze for at least 4 hours.

5 large or 8 small peaches, peeled, pit removed, and diced
½ cup honey
   Leaves from 1 sprig fresh thyme
6 fresh mint leaves

Pineapple-Cilantro Popstickles

Combine the pineapple, lime juice, and agave nectar in a blender, and purée. Stir in the cilantro (if you purée the cilantro with the rest of the ingredients, you will end up with green pops). Pour into reusable ice-pop molds and freeze for at least 4 hours.

½ pineapple, peeled, cored, and diced
   Juice of 1 lime
2 tablespoons agave nectar or honey
1 tablespoon chopped fresh cilantro

Berry Balsamic Popstickles

Combine the berries, honey, rosemary, vinegar, pepper, lemon juice, and lemon zest in a blender and purée. (Trust us on the pepper and vinegar.) Pour into reusable ice-pop molds and freeze for at least 4 hours.

Fills about 6 large popstickle molds

5 cups fresh strawberries, blackberries, or a mix
¾ cup honey
   Leaves from 1 sprig of fresh rosemary
2 tablespoons balsamic vinegar
2 grinds black pepper
1 tablespoon lemon juice
   Zest of 1 lemon

255

breads, cakes, and cookies

FOR MANY OF US, our first memories of cooking are making baked goods — mixing up cookie batter, or peeking through the oven to see if a homemade cake had risen. Baking doesn't just fill the kitchen with treats and tantalizing aromas, though; it's also a chance for kids to develop some important life skills. By learning how to bake, children also learn about patience, precision, and pride in one's work. Observing the effect of ingredients like baking soda can cultivate scientific curiosity, and measuring and cutting can enhance basic math skills. The fact that the end result is a delicious treat transforms the activity from mere education to sheer delight.

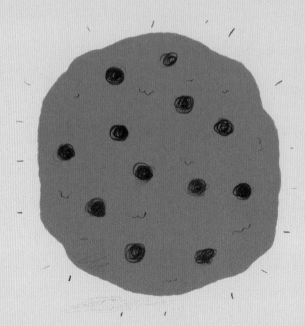

Chocolate-Walnut Zucchini Bread

In a good season, zucchini are abundant, like the kudzu vine of vegetables. This recipe is a good way to get all that extra summer bounty eaten as fast as it grows. The end result is rich, moist, and chocolatey without being overly sweet. Take it to your next PTA bake sale, and you'll delight the children *and* their parents. You can also make these as muffins, adjusting the baking time to 25 minutes.

1. Preheat the oven to 350°F.

2. Place zucchini in colander and press to drain excess moisture. Combine the flours, cocoa powder, baking powder, baking soda, and salt in a medium bowl, and mix well.

3. In a separate large bowl, combine the granulated sugar, brown sugar, oil, eggs, and vanilla. Cream with an electric mixer. Slowly add the dry ingredients to the sugar mixture, mixing just until blended. Fold in the zucchini, chocolate chips, and nuts.

4. Scrape the batter into a 10- by 5-inch loaf pan, sprayed with nonstick cooking spray. Bake for 1 to 1½ hours, until a toothpick inserted in the center comes out clean.

Makes 1 loaf

3 cups grated zucchini
1 cup unbleached all-purpose flour
¾ cup whole-wheat flour
¼ cup unsweetened cocoa powder
1½ teaspoons baking powder
½ teaspoon baking soda
½ teaspoon salt
½ cup granulated sugar
½ cup brown sugar
½ cup canola oil
3 eggs
1 teaspoon vanilla extract
1 cup dark chocolate chips, 60 percent cocoa content
⅔ cup chopped walnuts or pistachios

FACT: Vending machines filled with unhealthful snacks and soda are present in 43 percent of elementary schools, 73 percent of middle schools, and 98 percent of high schools.

Source: Centers for Disease Control and Prevention (CDC), Atlanta, Georgia.

257

Dark Chocolate– Honey Ganache

8 ounces bittersweet
   chocolate, chopped
½ cup plus 2 tablespoons
   heavy cream
¼ cup honey
2 tablespoons unsalted butter
1 teaspoon orange extract
   (optional)
   Pinch of ancho chile powder
   (optional)

Ah, frosting. That grocery store pure-sugar-and-shortening stuff is nasty, and you deserve better. This is a great topping for the Beet Brownies on the next page, and you can also use this to top Bundt cakes, pound cakes, or ice cream. Store it in the refrigerator (well hidden), and warm it up before serving.

Put the chocolate in a medium bowl. Bring the cream, honey, and butter to a boil in a small saucepan. Pour the hot liquid over the chocolate. Whisk until smooth. Add the orange extract and ancho powder, if desired. Let cool before using.

Makes about 1 cup

▬ Stealth Nutrition: Where We Stand

Many parents have embraced the concept of "stealth" nutrition: surreptitiously adding vegetables to cakes, cookies, and other treats so that kids don't notice they're eating these veggies.

We like a good slice of zucchini bread as much as the next person, and we enjoy figuring out how to make a single kind of vegetable into a side, a main dish, a snack, and even a dessert, too. But we offer a few words of caution. Eating vegetables is not some sleazy gastronomic affair to be carried on in a dark pantry. Treating them like this only reinforces the concept of "vegetable equals yuck" when you are discovered. (If it's good, why would you need to hide it?)

When kids' primary exposure to spinach comes in the form of brownies, they're no more likely to reach for salads when they get the chance. And most of the brownies they find in the world will decidedly not contain spinach. Not to mention, most of these recipes offer pretty limited quantities of the vegetables — not enough that you can feel confident they're getting what they need.

If you feel like adding carrots to cookies, by all means, go for it. Just do so as a supplement, not as a substitute.

You Can't Beet Brownies

Actually, you can. The beets here give the brownies a deep, "red velvet" chocolate hue. Their flavor does not stand out at all, but it complements the dark chocolate flavor well. Take one bite and ask yourself: Is it beet? Is it brownie? Deliciously, it's both.

1. Preheat the oven to 350°F.

2. Combine the butter and oil in a large skillet over low heat, and cook until the butter is melted. Add the chocolate chips, and heat until the chocolate is melted, stirring frequently. Remove from the heat and let cool a bit. Add the sugar, vanilla, and eggs, mixing well.

3. Combine the flour, cocoa powder, five-spice powder, if desired, and salt in large bowl, and mix well. Fold in the chocolate mixture, followed by the beets and pecans, if desired.

4. Pour into a 9- by 13-inch baking pan sprayed with nonstick cooking spray. Bake for about 30 minutes, testing after 25 minutes. If you like fudgy brownies, remove the brownies from the oven when a toothpick inserted in the center comes out nearly clean. If you like firmer brownies, wait until the toothpick comes out completely clean. Let cool, then frost with ganache.

Makes 16 brownies

¾ cup (1½ sticks) butter
¼ cup canola oil
8 ounces bittersweet or semisweet chocolate chips
2 cups sugar
1 teaspoon vanilla extract (or ½ teaspoon vanilla extract plus ½ teaspoon orange extract)
5 eggs
⅔ cup whole-wheat pastry flour
⅓ cup unsweetened cocoa powder
1 teaspoon Chinese five-spice powder (optional)
½ teaspoon salt
1½ cups cooked, peeled, and shredded beets (or beet purée)
1 cup chopped pecans (optional)
Dark Chocolate–Honey Ganache (page 258)

▬ Customizing Baking Recipes

Beth likes dark, fudgy, spicy brownies and prefers the beets to be noticeable. Ali prefers a more cakelike texture and a lighter touch with the spice. Her kids also prefer the beets to be puréed smooth. You can adjust recipes, like this one, for your own family's tastes. With baked goods, you just need the moisture-to-flour ratio to stay consistent with the original recipe. Don't be afraid to play with the spice or the type of chocolate, adding nuts or not. It's easy to customize recipes for your family's preferences.

Ginger-Carrot-Raisin Cupcakes

1½ cups plus 1 tablespoon whole-wheat flour
1½ teaspoons baking powder
1 teaspoon ground cinnamon
½ teaspoon baking soda
½ teaspoon salt
1 cup brown sugar
½ cup canola oil or applesauce
3 eggs
1 teaspoon orange extract
3½ cups shredded carrots
1 cup raisins
2 tablespoons chopped crystallized ginger
Cream Cheese Frosting (recipe follows)

Carrot cake is one of our favorite cakes ever. Unlike a lot of purchased versions, this recipe has more carrot than any other ingredient. And it still tastes great.

1. Preheat the oven 350°F.

2. Combine the flour, baking powder, cinnamon, baking soda, and salt in a medium bowl, and mix well.

3. In a separate large bowl, combine the brown sugar, oil, eggs, and orange extract. Cream with an electric mixer. Slowly add the dry ingredients, mixing just until blended. Fold in the carrots, raisins, and ginger.

4. Spoon the batter into 12 muffin cups with liners. Bake for about 30 minutes, until a toothpick inserted in the center comes out clean. Let cool. Frost with Cream Cheese Frosting.

Makes 12 cupcakes

Cream Cheese Frosting

4 ounces low-fat cream cheese, softened
4 tablespoons butter, softened
1 teaspoon orange extract
2 cups confectioners' sugar

Combine the cream cheese, butter, orange extract, and confectioners' sugar in a medium bowl. Cream with an electric mixer on medium-high speed until fluffy.

Pumpkin Molasses Cookies

These cookies are somewhere between pumpkin pie and gingerbread, between Thanksgiving and Christmas, kind of like a store shelf on the first of November. But better.

1. Preheat the oven to 350°F.

2. Combine the flour, baking powder, cinnamon, ginger, mace, salt, and cloves in a medium bowl, and mix well.

3. Cream together the butter, brown sugar, molasses, egg, and vanilla in a large bowl. Stir in the pumpkin, mixing well. Slowly add the dry ingredients, mixing until just blended. Fold in the raisins.

4. Spoon onto a cookie sheet, about 1½ tablespoons of batter for each cookie, and bake for 12 to 14 minutes until just golden on the bottom but still soft. Let cool, then glaze.

Makes about 2 dozen cookies

2¼ cups unbleached all-purpose flour
1½ teaspoons baking powder
1 teaspoon ground cinnamon
½ teaspoon ground ginger
½ teaspoon ground mace or nutmeg
½ teaspoon salt
¼ teaspoon ground cloves
½ cup (1 stick) butter, softened
¾ cup brown sugar
¼ cup molasses
1 egg
1 teaspoon vanilla extract
1 cup pumpkin purée
⅔ cup raisins
Orange Glaze (recipe follows)

Orange Glaze

Combine the sugar, cream, butter, and orange extract in a medium bowl, and mix well. Drizzle over the cooled cookies.

1 cup confectioners' sugar
1 tablespoon cream
1 tablespoon butter, melted
½ teaspoon orange extract

Whole-Grain Chocolate Chunk Cookies

1½ cups whole-wheat pastry flour
1 cup quick-cooking oats
1 teaspoon baking soda
1 teaspoon salt
¼ cup canola oil
2 tablespoons butter
¾ cup granulated sugar
¾ cup brown sugar
¾ cup chunky natural peanut butter
2 eggs
1 teaspoon vanilla extract
12 ounces bittersweet or semisweet chocolate chunks

Dark chocolate, less butter, and whole grains take the edge off guilt for this version of "monster cookies." Use natural peanut butter, with no added fats or sugars.

1. Preheat the oven to 375°F.

2. Combine the flour, oats, baking soda, and salt in a medium bowl, and mix well.

3. Cream the oil, butter, granulated sugar, and brown sugar in a large bowl with an electric mixer, starting on low speed and finishing with a couple of minutes on high speed. Add the peanut butter, eggs, and vanilla, and mix well.

4. Slowly beat the dry ingredients into the peanut butter mixture, with the mixer on low. Scrape down the sides as needed. The dough will be very thick. Fold in the chocolate chunks.

5. Form cookies, with hands, in 3-inch rounds on a baking sheet; you will have to press the dough together a bit to shape the cookies. Bake for 12 to 14 minutes, until just a hint of brown on the bottom.

Makes about 2½ dozen cookies

DID YOU KNOW? The amount of food dyes allowed for daily consumption per capita has increased to almost five times since 1955, according to FDA data.

Crispy Rice and Almond Squares

good for lunch!

By trading out the simple carbohydrates of white rice and marshmallows, these squares gain whole-grain heft, protein from the nut butter, and a lot more flavor.

¾ cup sugar

1 cup brown rice syrup

1 cup natural almond butter or peanut butter

¼ teaspoon salt

6 cups crispy brown-rice cereal

1. Heat the sugar and brown rice syrup in a saucepan over low heat. Add the nut butter and salt and stir until smooth. Pour the brown rice cereal into a large bowl. Pour the hot mixture over the cereal, folding to combine.

2. Press the mixture into a 9- by 13-inch pan sprayed with nonstick cooking spray, and allow to cool before cutting.

Makes 16 squares

FACT: Research suggests that kids most crave sugar during peak growth. A study conducted at the University of Washington gave children age 11 to 15 increasingly sweet solutions to drink and rate. The children who preferred the sweeter drinks also showed a high level of a chemical associated with bone growth. The cravings were the body's way of telling them that their bones need more calories for fuel.

Source: Susan E. Coldwell, Teresa K. Oswald, and Danielle R. Reed, "A marker of growth differs between adolescents with high vs. low sugar preference." *Physiology and Behavior*, March 2009. Volume 96, Issues 4–5, 23. 574–580 Authors: S. E. Coldwell, T. K. Oswald, Danielle R. Reed.

263

Soda: a dose of something no one needs

Let's say someone was trying to slip your kid a pill that dramatically increased his or her risk for type 2 diabetes, early kidney disease, heart disease, obesity, and tooth decay. There's no particular reason for this pill, no benefits that couldn't be obtained from, say, ordinary tap water. You'd probably say something like, "*Back off, buster. Don't peddle that stuff around my kid.*" Yet as a society, we're actually paying $66 billion of our hard-earned dollars for this kind of product every single year. It's just that instead of paying for it in pill form, we're buying it in liquid form: soda.

At the risk of alienating some folks, we'll come right out and say it: We are not fans of soda. Not the brand-name kinds, not the fancy organic varieties. Not the kind that comes in more-for-your-money three-liter bottles, and not even the ironic holiday-edition versions produced by one manufacturer in flavors like Brussels sprout and green bean casserole.

We don't care for soda in part because we just don't like the taste of it. But we also don't like it for all the same reasons that all those physicians, dietitians, and public health researchers don't like it: because it destroys teeth, appears to leach calcium from bones, contributes to type 2 diabetes, and dramatically increases a child's risk of being obese. Dr. David Ludwig, director of the Obesity Program at the Children's Hospital Boston, has done more than 40 research studies on childhood obesity. His research shows that for every daily soda a child drinks, the risk of obesity increases by 60 percent.

> " You do not need to add sugars to fruit concentrates. To make 'juiced' products, food chemists process fruit juice until it is basically fruit-flavored sugar, and then reconstitute it. 'Fruit concentrate,' according to the U.S. Dietary Guidelines, is a euphemism for sugars. "
>
> Marion Nestle, *What to Eat*, North Point Press, 2007.

Yet kids are guzzling it more than ever before. In the 1950s, children had three cups of milk for every one cup of soda. Now that has reversed, says Dr. Ludwig. Most children in the United States have three cups of soda for every one cup of milk.

And that's the final reason we don't like it: because it wholly confounds us. Why exactly are so many people drinking so much of it? Sure, soda is cheap. But it's not nearly as inexpensive as not drinking soda in the first place.

Don't get us wrong: We live in the real world. Our kids go to school, to parties, to play dates, picnics, baseball games, restaurants, and carnivals. By kindergarten, Ali's daughter had attended her first party where soda was the only available beverage — no water, no milk, no juice boxes. Just soda. It's certainly not like our kids don't know what soda is.

But we have both drawn a line in the sand, and that line forms a big radius around our homes: We don't serve soda in the house. We accept that there will be times that kids drink soda outside the home. But at the kitchen table? *Back off, buster.*

That's not to say we haven't found some use for soda. After scouring the Internet, we've found a couple good uses for the stuff. It turns out a piece of crumpled aluminum foil dipped in soda does a pretty good job at removing rust from chrome. And if you've got a lime scale–stained toilet bowl that could use a good cleaning, a can of cola left to sit for an hour can often do the trick. Beyond that, though? We'll go without.

265

the real scoop on sugar

LIFE WITH KIDS IS SWEET. Sometimes, in fact, it's a little too sweet, as sugar gets hurled at children from seemingly every direction. How much sugar is too much? And is it really that bad for your kids? Here's the scoop on children's favorite taste sensation.

Is Sugar Addictive?

YOU HEAR PEOPLE say it all the time: "I'm addicted to sugar." But is sugar actually addictive? Scientists haven't agreed on that. However, researchers at the Penn State College of Medicine analyzed how rats respond to sugar, and they have found similarities to how the animals react to addictive drugs like cocaine. Specifically, when humans and rats eat sugary treats, their levels of dopamine, a neurotransmitter that is active in many addictive behaviors, increases.

Another study, conducted at Princeton University, found that rats who are deprived of food for 12 hours and then given food and sugar water tend to binge on the sugary drink. In yet another trial, rats given sugar water after being without it for two weeks tended to drink more than ever before. All this behavior is consistent with the way rats — and humans — respond to other addictive substances.

Okay, so in several of these studies, the rats were given unusually large amounts of sugar — up to 46 percent of their total caloric intake. By contrast, sugar makes up 15 to 28 percent of total energy in the typical American person's diet. On the other hand, we can point to plenty of kids' cereals, snacks, and beverages that are 46 percent sugar or more.

Even the researchers who conducted these studies feel that the word *addictive* seems alarmist. Rebecca L. Corwin, Ph.D. and

Snack Attack

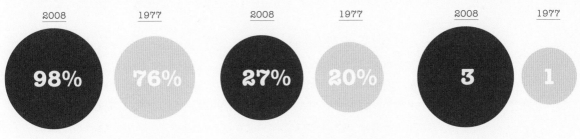

2008	1977	2008	1977	2008	1977
98%	76%	27%	20%	3	1

Kids ages 2–18 who snacked **Daily calories from snacks** **Snacks per day**

Think today's kids snack less than they did a generation ago? Think again. Today, children are consuming more snacks overall, and getting more of their total calories from snacks, than they were 30 years ago. The quality has changed, too, and not for the better. During snack time, children consume fewer fruits and fewer dairy products. What exactly are kids snacking on? No surprise here: They're downing greater quantities of juice, sweetened beverages, and sugary and salty foods.

Source: "Trends in Snacking Among U.S. Children," Carmen Piernas and Barry M. Popkin, Health Affairs 29, No. 3 (2010): 398–404.

researcher in the Penn State Study, notes that people shouldn't be scared away from sugar altogether. "Like all foods," Dr. Corwin was quoted as saying, "sugar in moderation is perfectly okay."

Ahh, there's that word again: *moderation*.

High-Fructose Corn Syrup: Spare Yourself, Spare Your Health

PICK UP RANDOM ITEMS IN THE GROCERY STORE. Soft drinks, sure. Even things like juice "cocktails." And while you're at it, try tomato sauce. Ketchup. Cookies. Crackers. Soups. Yogurt. Bread. High-fructose corn syrup is in lots of these items, perhaps most.

These days, a remarkable number of products contain high-fructose corn syrup. Is that a problem, you wonder. Maybe. Actually, what we mean is, "Yes, definitely, but it may or may not be for the reasons some think."

High-fructose corn syrup (HFCS), this thing that Americans eat an average of 63 pounds of each year, is a corn-based sweetener. It's heavily processed using various mechanical procedures and the addition of at least three enzymes. The end product has a slightly higher fructose content than table sugar.

But wait. First the "why?" Why so much HFCS? Food manufacturers love the stuff because it mixes easily with other ingredients, extends the shelf life of processed foods, helps prevent ice crystals and freezer burn, helps breads to brown, and keeps foods soft. It also traditionally has been cheaper than other sweeteners, as a result of U.S. agricultural subsidies and tariffs and highly mechanized manufacturing processes.

So, what's the problem? Many experts say that the problem isn't HFCS itself, but rather the added calories that would come from any sweetened foods. Marion Nestle, for example, says, "I view corn sweeteners as an especially inexpensive and ever present form of sugar(s), but nothing more sinister . . . if corn sweeteners have anything to do with obesity, it is surely because processed foods are loaded with them, and lots of people are eating lots more of such foods."

Dr. Mehmet Oz, author of *You: The Owner's Manual*, has suggested that the higher fructose content means that our bodies process HFCS differently than other sugars. Lots of organizations, from the Weston A. Price Society to the AARP, have said similar things, noting the very strong correlation between HFCS and obesity. The research is spottier there, although one small-scale study at Princeton demonstrated that rats with access to high-fructose corn syrup gained significantly more weight than those with access to table sugar, even when their overall caloric intake was the same. The same study also found that the HFCS led to abnormal increases in body fat, especially in the abdomen, and a rise in circulating blood fats called triglycerides.

So the problem may be that there's something inherently wrong with HFCS and with how a body processes it. But it may be simply that this otherwise harmless ingredient is associated with empty, low-nutrition foods that people eat in huge amounts.

Our take on it: Who cares? Let's just not eat it. Seriously. Let's stop consuming things with high-fructose corn syrup. Let's just swear it off. We can almost promise you that you'll feel better. It's possible that this is because there's something inherently evil about the stuff. Or maybe — even more likely — it's simply because by ruling out HFCS, you will eliminate many low-nutrition foods that otherwise might have ended up in your cart.

If nothing else, think of high-fructose corn syrup as a giant red flag that says, "I'm heavily processed! You don't want to eat me!"

Okay, sure, if you replace HFCS-free cookies with an equal quantity of cookies made with cane sugar, you might not find much benefit at all. But if you use HFCS as a guide to the *types* of food you want to eliminate, there's a good chance you'll avoid a boatload (or rather, a cartload) of highly processed, unhealthful things.

Are Artificial Sweeteners the Solution?

NOT IN OUR OPINION. Not only are most artificial sweeteners made from chemicals by people wearing safety goggles and long white lab coats, they also don't seem to offer any kind of long-term benefit.

Throughout human history, a sweet taste meant that calories were coming in, which meant that the body was taking in energy. It was a pretty simple formula: Sweet equals energy. Every time. Today, with artificial sweeteners, the relationship between sweet taste and energy has been broken. Sweet *might* equal energy, but it also might equal nothing whatsoever. Some researchers worry that this confusion of signals can interrupt the body's delicate feedback loops that regulate appetite, causing people to lose their ability to regulate weight. Perhaps this is why some research studies actually show a weight *gain* in people who regularly drink diet sodas.

For example, Purdue University researchers demonstrated that rats eating food sweetened with saccharin took in *more* calories and gained *more* weight than rats that ate foods sweetened with regular old table sugar. Another study, of nearly 3,700 residents of San Antonio, Texas, showed that people who drank three or more artificially sweetened diet beverages a day were more likely to have gained weight over an eight-year period than those who never drank diet beverages.

We have no way of knowing whether the diet beverages actually caused the weight gain, of course. But these studies sure don't sell us on those colorful packets of sweetness that we see in coffee shops and on tables in diners.

Not to mention, artificial sweeteners taste pretty awful. They may or may not be "safe" — the National Cancer Institute says they are, by the way — but they sure are an assault to the taste buds. Can feeding children something that tastes terrible and ultimately doesn't seem to improve health instill a lifelong love of real food and healthy eating? We doubt it.

■ Know Your Sugars

When you do pick up a snack food item at the store, don't forget to read the label ... perhaps even more carefully than you think.

Ingredients must be listed by quantity, and manufacturers are conscious of this. If the first item on the list is a whole-grain flour, great, but keep reading. You may see up to three or more different types of sugars or sweeteners. Using different types of sweeteners prevents sugar from showing up as the main ingredient. Sugars can show up listed as recognizable sources, such as brown rice syrup, corn syrup, and cane sugar. But beware of "ose" words that are also sugars, such as glucose, sucrose, dextrose, lactose, and fructose. Other hidden sugar ingredients are "ols" or sugar alcohols, which include sorbitol, maltitol, xylitol, and mannitol.

whole-food SUGAR SUBSTITUTES

White sugar can often be replaced with whole-food alternatives. While they are typically no lower in calories, many of these alternatives have the advantages of a higher mineral content and they can often be purchased from local suppliers. Be aware that replacing white sugar with natural alternatives can affect the taste of finished dishes, and sometimes it will require reducing other liquids in the recipe or making other adjustments. Following are guidelines for each sweetener.

When substituting alternative sweeteners for white sugar, it's a good idea to record the amount of sweetener that was used, the amount of liquid you decreased in the recipe, any change to oven temperature, and any other adjustments you made to the recipe. Write it down before you forget. Then record your experience of the final product. This will allow you to make adjustments as needed in future recipes.

271

Agave nectar

replace 1 cup sugar with: ⅓ cup
reduce liquid by: ⅓ cup

Made from the sap of a slow-growing succulent plant, agave nectar is smooth and mild tasting, with floral undertones. It has a syrupy consistency. Light varieties have a neutral flavor; darker varieties contain more minerals and a stronger flavor. It will brown faster than sugar; when baking, reduce oven temperature by 25°F.

Barley malt

replace 1 cup sugar with: 1⅓ cups
reduce liquid by: ¼ cup

A thick, malty syrup used most frequently in beer making, but also in bread baking and for other baked goods. Barley malt releases its sugars more slowly than refined sugar and is less likely to cause sugar crashes. Add ¼ teaspoon baking soda per 1 cup barley malt.* Refrigerate after opening and discard if it has an off smell.

Brown rice syrup

replace 1 cup sugar with: 1–1¼ cups
reduce liquid by: ¼ cup

A mild-tasting, naturally processed liquid sweetener made from sprouted brown rice, it has the consistency of honey and a high protein content and is good for baking. Like molasses, it is good in spice cakes and baked beans. Its complex sugars are released more slowly into the bloodstream than white sugar. Baked goods made with rice syrup tend to be hard and very crisp. Add ¼ teaspoon baking soda per 1 cup rice syrup.*

Date sugar

replace 1 cup sugar with: ⅔ cup
reduce liquid by: none

A powder made from dried, ground dates. It does not dissolve well and can burn easily, but it works well in crisps or as a topping ingredient. Although not a complex sugar, date sugar does contain minerals, including folic acid. Store in a tightly closed jar.

Fruit juice concentrates

replace 1 cup sugar with: ¾ cup
reduce liquid by: ¼ cup

Fruit juice concentrates are simply juices from which most of the water and fiber have been removed. Do not reconstitute before using in recipes. Store in freezer.

Whole-Food Sugar Substitutes (cont.)

Honey

replace 1 cup sugar with: ¾ cup
reduce liquid by: ¼ cup

Do not give to children younger than one year, as honey can contain spores that are dangerous for babies. Darker honey contains more minerals and also has a stronger flavor than lighter honey. Store unrefrigerated. If crystals form, place the opened jar in a pan of hot water over low heat for 10 to 15 minutes. Prevent overbrowning by lowering your oven temperature by 25°F. Add ¼ teaspoon baking soda per 1 cup honey.*

Maple sugar

replace 1 cup sugar with: 1 cup
reduce liquid by: none

Granulated maple sugar is simply maple syrup that has been boiled until the liquid has disappeared. It has a strong maple flavor. Add ⅛ teaspoon baking soda per 1 cup maple sugar.*

Maple syrup

replace 1 cup sugar with: ¾ cup
reduce liquid by: ¼ cup

Made from the sap of maple trees, maple syrup should not be confused with processed "maple-flavored" syrups, which are generally highly processed corn syrups. Darker maple syrup, or grade B, has a stronger flavor than lighter maple syrup, grade A. Add ¼ teaspoon baking soda per 1 cup maple syrup*, and reduce oven temperature by 25°F. Store refrigerated.

Molasses

replace 1 cup sugar with: 1⅓ cups
reduce liquid by: 5 tablespoons

Has a distinct taste that asserts itself nicely in foods like gingerbread, baked beans, and rye bread. Light molasses is the sweetest and mildest version. Dark molasses is more flavorful and should be used if a recipe calls for simply "molasses." Blackstrap molasses has a strong, bitter flavor and isn't really suitable as a sugar substitute for most recipes. Molasses is a good source of minerals like iron, calcium, copper, manganese, potassium, and magnesium.

*This step is not necessary if you are using sour cream, sour milk, or buttermilk.

Stevia

replace 1 cup sugar with: 1 teaspoon, powdered or liquid forms
reduce liquid by: none

Made from a shrub native to Paraguay, stevia is about 300 times sweeter than sugar, with an aftertaste. Stevia is not absorbed by the body and does not have calories. Although it has been consumed by humans for more than 1,000 years, the FDA warns that there are no long-term safety studies on stevia, and it can currently be sold only as a dietary supplement.

Brown sugar

replace 1 cup sugar with: 1 cup, tightly packed
reduce liquid by: none

Brown sugar can be either natural, meaning unrefined sugar that naturally maintains its molasses, or it can be simply a white sugar that has had molasses added for color. Most grocery store brown sugars are the latter. Store brown sugar in an airtight container. If your brown sugar becomes hardened, place it in a tightly sealed container with an apple wedge, or with several drops of water, for several days.

Sucanat, Rapadura

replace 1 cup sugar with: 1 cup
reduce liquid by: ¼ cup

These sugars are pure dried sugarcane juice, which maintain their full molasses content. Crystals are large, brown, and uneven. They have a deep flavor that is reminiscent of caramel, which pairs nicely with chocolate recipes.

Turbinado

replace 1 cup sugar with: 1 cup
reduce liquid by: none

Turbinado sugar comes from the first pressing of the sugarcane. It has larger crystals and a higher moisture content than table sugar. It retains a trace amount of natural molasses, giving it a light caramel color and a delicate hint of molasses flavor. Because of its higher moisture content, it is good for baked goods, but be careful using turbinado sugar in recipes that call for great accuracy. The larger crystals will not measure the same as sugar. Store in an airtight container.

EPILOGUE:

WHAT'S NEXT

a road map for the journey

You've met your vegetables and you are on a first-name basis with the produce guy...

You've witnessed the miracle of your kids eating leafy greens and enjoying them. What's more, you've realized you're ready to join the Cleaner Plate Club by making more conscious food choices for yourself, your family, and heck, even the planet. If you're feeling ready for the journey back to real food, here are some things to keep in mind for the ride.

Knowledge Is Power

SOMETIMES IT SEEMS THAT the more you know about the food industry, the more overwhelming this knowledge feels. We remember only too well our own early lessons about food processing, safety, additives, and the environmental costs of our food system — we were like textbook cases of the Kübler-Ross emotional stages: denial, shock, anger, bargaining, depression . . .

Then, finally, we realized something valuable, something that brought more relief than anxiety: As consumers, we have the ultimate power over what is stocked on our grocery-store shelves. Simply by picking up this book, you've already leveraged the most important tool we all have: choice.

It's true that too often food manufacturers sacrifice consumer safety and health in the quest for easy profits. When that happens, the counteraction is simple: Don't buy that product. Put something else in your cart instead. While you're just one consumer, the truth is, it takes only a small number of vocal consumers to drive enormous change. Within the past few years, most of the nation's largest food retailers ceased buying milk from dairies that used a synthetic growth hormone — effectively eliminating the market for that hormone — at the request of a relatively small percentage of customers.

Staying informed, and then speaking your mind, has never been easier. A vast number of online resources track food safety issues and can put you directly in touch with policy makers and manufacturers. (Many are listed in the resources section of this book starting on page 292.) When corporations make unethical choices, we can find out about it faster than their highly paid PR firms can say "retainer."

Baby Steps Take You Far

REMEMBER WHEN YOUR CHILDREN took their first steps? It required all their concentration and every single muscle in their body. They probably fell down after the first step, or the second. But it wasn't too long before they were dashing away from you on the playground like

277

wildebeests escaped from the zoo. Changing food habits is kind of like that.

Sure, it would be nice to say that everyone can improve their family's eating habits overnight, simply because they want to. But change is hard, and you're working against an entire industry whose systems are designed to support food that is cheap, ready-made, and of low nutritive value. If you find that making changes to your family's eating habits is difficult, that's okay. It's normal, in fact. Just take a cue from your kids: Keep trying.

The World Beyond Your Dining Table

ONE OF THE MAIN CRITIQUES of eating whole, local foods — "voting with your fork" — is that it is an elitist act, because not all people can afford to exercise this voting right. There's truth to that; in our current system, it is much harder for some people to access good food than it is for others. But that's not a reason to dismiss good food; it's a reason to fight for it.

Food justice is the rallying cry of a growing movement to ensure that everyone has access to healthful foods. Most food justice initiatives have an element of self-reliance, as they empower communities to develop their own solutions.

Call it good karma, social responsibility, or simply a chance to shape the world your children will inherit. But the truth is, we gained a richer understanding of our food system only when we started volunteering for food justice. Among other efforts, Beth volunteers with an urban agriculture center and Ali serves meals at a free lunch program, often with her older daughter. The need is great, and growing. Best of all, you can use whatever skills and interests you have. Like to cook? Consider hosting a fund-raising dinner in your own home featuring local foods and asking friends to donate healthful foods or funds for a local agency or food bank. Or help teach a food and nutrition cooking class for at-risk kids in your community.

Want to learn to garden? Try helping out at a community or charity garden, learning valuable skills as you help others. If you are an experienced gardener, you can donate your extra produce to a local food pantry or help build a local urban agriculture project or community garden.

Maybe you are better suited to organizing, writing, and forging a business strategy. Well, we've never met a social organization that didn't need help with fund-raising and grant writing. Advocating for more equitable food distribution is something all of us can do on our own, employing our own particular skill sets. In our resources, we list many websites that provide more information about food issues and actions you can take to further food justice.

The Road Less Traveled

THERE'S NO DOUBT that choosing whole foods over processed foods requires more effort. But whenever you do it, you can accomplish some incredible things.

First, you protect your family from most of the hazards of highly processed foods, like additives and trans fats, instantly improving their long-term chances of good health.

Second, you contribute to the demand for real food, thus increasing the likelihood that supply — more fresh produce, more responsible production — will follow.

Third, you create a real food culture for your family, tying daily sustenance to the memories and shared experiences at a family table. Your children will grow up with more healthful food habits and a stronger understanding of nutrition choices — something that will make it easier for them to become healthy adults. You might even help them make their own children healthy ... a generational legacy if ever there was one.

If you can take the next step and purchase your food locally, you support economic development in your community and enable small family farms to flourish. Survival of these farms preserves farmland, helps increase the richness and variety of your local foodshed, connects you to your food and community, and encourages the growth of new farms and farmers' markets . . . ultimately creating a more healthful world for your kids in the long term.

Challenge Yourself to Eat Local

YOU HAVE PROBABLY HEARD PLENTY about the benefits of reducing your "food miles." Food miles refers to the number of miles food travels before reaching your plate. Imagine a plate with carrots from the Midwest, salad from California, grapes from Chile, and fish from China. Depending on where you live, your dinner has racked up enough frequent-flier miles for a free first-class trip.

Or, consider an apple in the Big Apple. About 75 percent of the apples sold in New York City are shipped all the way from the West Coast, and some are shipped from as far away as New Zealand. Meanwhile, the state of New York produces more apples annually than city residents consume.

Food miles are an important part of a meal's carbon footprint, but they aren't the only factor. An accurate measure of a food's carbon footprint would consider the total energy picture of food production: water use; harvesting techniques; fertilizer, pesticide, and herbicide inputs; types of feed for livestock; renewable energy applications; and means of transportation, packaging, and storage. It gets rather complicated.

Fortunately, food miles are just one of the reasons for eating local, and arguably not even the most compelling reason. Supporting sustainable, local agriculture boosts your local economy, supports family farms in your community, and shapes an environment where it's easier to be healthy.

That all sounds quite noble, but eating local is a rewarding pursuit in itself. The food is simply better: There are more unique varieties, flavors are stronger, nutritional benefits are greater, and you have the added comfort of knowing where the food came from, who produced it, and how it was raised.

Interested in eating more local foods? Consider participating in the Eat Local Challenge. It's not difficult, and you can set your own goals. You could challenge yourself to eat one meal of local ingredients each week, or a few local items for a month, or a season, or even just for your Thanksgiving dinner. Whatever you decide, it's a chance to participate in a culinary adventure that's both exciting and educational. See the Eat Local Challenge in the resources on page 292 to learn more.

Don't Leave the Kids Behind

THE JOURNEY TO REAL FOOD IS A FAMILY TRIP. Just like every outing with kids, it all goes a lot easier if everyone wants to be along for the ride — and there's no extra baggage. Research on children's garden and "seed to table" programs have demonstrated that involving kids in food production, selection, and preparation results in more healthful eating habits, increased consumption of vegetables, and a greater willingness to try new foods. There's no need to wait for one of these programs to reach your school. You can do all of these activities as a family.

Even if you lack space for a garden, you and your kids can start vegetables in pots and put them on a balcony or walkway. Start small and grow your efforts — and your family garden — over time.

Kids as young as three or four can help with simple kitchen tasks like shelling peas, peeling garlic, pouring measured ingredients, and mixing. Older kids can help measure and prepare ingredients, and eventually help with culinary tasks that require hot stoves and sharp blades. By helping in the kitchen, kids not only become more likely to try the food they prepare, but they may also improve their math and reading skills. Kid-size kitchen gadgets are more widely available, but no special equipment is needed other than your patience and enthusiasm.

Sometimes, just giving kids the power to choose new fruits and vegetables is enough to encourage more healthful eating and avoid the dinnertime power struggles. Take your kids with you when you go to the farmers' market. Let them pick which vegetables and fruits they want to try and offer some options for how to prepare them. If your child voted for an item, it pretty much guarantees that she will eat it at dinnertime.

281

10 ways to embrace positive change

WE ARE REAL PARENTS, with real kids, and we assure you: There is nothing perfect going on at our households. We wage the same wars over sugar instead of spinach, TV instead of quality family time, and why the Tinker Bell outfit cannot be worn to school during a blizzard. We face the same crazy schedules and parenting battles as everyone else. Other than a slight bend toward National Public Radio and a greater-than-average affinity for kale, we are, relatively speaking, pretty normal. Here are some of the ways we've tried to make better food possible in our own families.

1. Limit Commercials.

Children watch an average of four hours of television per day. Sure, we can debate the intellectual merits of *SpongeBob SquarePants*, but to our minds, the biggest problem with all this screen time is that it translates to some 15,000 to 20,000 junk-food ads per year. There are a lot of things we can do to minimize this influence: choose DVDs, "zap" the commercials in prerecorded shows, turn to channels like PBS, or just aim to watch a little less TV overall.

2. Eat a Family Meal More Often Than Just Thanksgiving.

It's not going to happen every day, but it could happen more than once a year. If you need help getting it all done, teach kids kitchen skills. It's not only helpful for you, but it's also great for them. And there's no reason why they can't help with the dishes too!

3. Teach Your Kids Not to Listen to Strangers.

One of the most insidious facts about marketing to kids — on the TV, online, and elsewhere — is that so much of it is targeted to children too young to understand the difference between a commercial and the regular program. They simply absorb this message along with everything else. We can teach our kids to identify marketing messages and why these messages are often not serving their best interests.

4. No Skipping School.

Many kids rely on that school lunch program as their main source of nutrition daily. Fortunately, there is a lot of exciting change going on with school lunch programs. Now is a great time to get involved; perhaps you want to organize a school garden, or set up a farm-to-school program. Don't forget to educate yourself; there are so many issues to learn about, including key legislature like the Childhood Nutrition Act, food safety bills, and the latest farm bill — all of which directly affect your food supply.

5. Choose Characters Wisely.

Here's the reality: We can't escape marketing and character licensing. There are going to be movies and books, toys and games, and some TV in our lives. Choose the ones that are giving your kids the right messages and not selling unhealthful foods on the side. If your child must have a licensed character, try pencils, socks, notebooks, or other items that aren't edible.

283

6. Teaching Nutrition Is Just as Important as Teaching Reading.

Ideally, we would like to avoid the food fights altogether. Of course, we'd also like to avoid wrinkles, turning forty, and root canals. But when your child insists that it must be jelly beans for dinner, it's time for a lesson in nutrition. Before you get out the laser pointer and the new food-pyramid diagram, don't bother. We can't even decipher that thing.

This lesson is so simple that even a three-year-old can understand it. It's called "Anytime Foods and Sometimes Foods." *Anytime* foods are the ones that you always say "yes" to. They are the ones about which we might say, "This is what we eat every day to grow big muscles like Supergirl." *Sometimes* foods, on the other hand, might taste good and be fine in moderation, but they "won't help you run fast like an apple would." Continue teaching why healthful foods are important. Those whys are important, since your child will one day — sooner than you might expect — be making a fair number of independent nutrition decisions daily.

7. Learn the Difference Between Hunger and Habit.

When our kids say, "I'm hungry," they sometimes mean just that. Other times, though, they mean something else. Sometimes they're bored. Sometimes they don't want to go to bed. Other times, it's plain old habit. If they typically get a snack every time they get in the car, then they'll be "hungry" every time they get in the car. Helping them understand the difference between hunger and habit is an important way of helping them develop a healthy relationship to food.

8. Drive Past the Drive-Through.

There are meals we can prepare in less time than it takes us to order a "biggie with fries." We can make a sandwich on whole-grain bread, slice some fruit, and heat a few frozen veggies in five minutes flat. When it comes to fast food, let's go cold turkey — on wheat with canola mayo.

9. Wage Peas.

Depending on who you are, this will either be the most welcome change or the most difficult one: giving up the battle over broccoli. Just let go and work toward the long-range goal of healthful eating without the daily struggle. If it gets to be too much, limit all the options at home to healthy ones. That way, all choices are good ones.

10. Pay It Forward.

Find your inner locavore by taking a field trip to the field — or at least the farmers' market. Find ways to support sustainable agriculture and lower your food miles and carbon footprint while getting the best food you've ever tasted. And don't do it just for yourself. One in every eight Americans — more than 37 million Americans, many of them children — are experiencing hunger and poverty. Other families struggle with access to better food choices. If we can help all kids have better food, we help our fellow citizens succeed in school and in life, and we point the way toward a brighter future for our nation's next generations.

to everything there is a season: rediscover seasonal eating

ONE OF THE MOST AMAZING PARTS of this real food journey for us has definitely been rediscovering seasons for food. In the first year, we admit, there was a weekly element of surprise at seeing what was in the CSA box and at the farmers' market, surprise accompanied by a bit of panic — *what am I going to make with that?* Or sometimes, what *is* that?

If you are new to seasonal eating, cooking with what is fresh might seem limiting. Bear with it. As you get more familiar with the process, you will find that it is more of an adventure and exploration than a limitation. Not only do you begin to learn how best to cook each item, but you also taste each at its finest, its peak. There is no substitute, we have learned, for a tree-ripened peach or a juicy just-picked heirloom tomato. The abundance, particularly noticeable with items like zucchini, is also a chance to explore more than one way to cook each item.

After your first few seasons of buying and cooking this way, you might wonder how you ever did things differently. You'll begin to see the first asparagus as a sign of warmer days, and the first tomato as the start of summer, and apples and pumpkins as synonymous with cool fall days and holidays ahead. For us, it adds a kind of rhythm, a pacing, to an otherwise frenzied world.

The following list is a general guide to when certain crops are in season for most climates. The weather will vary, which is an understatement! And the seasons will blend as well. There is a magical week in September when all of summer's bounty is available right alongside the first winter squash and a short second burst of greens, cole crops, and lettuces. Southern and temperate areas have year-round abundance, of course, which we envy during the coldest winter days where we live. But then the first sun-ripened strawberries, fresh from the plant, taste a thousand times better when you have been without for a little while.

We've also organized the recipes from this book by season. Many of the recipes in this book rely on using fresh, seasonal ingredients for the best flavor. While your corner megamart will likely carry all of these ingredients year-round, this index will help you find recipes that are based on the items you will find in season at your farmers' market — with a few recipes for late in the year when little is available in the way of seasonal produce.

> "It is wonderful to see that this good food revolution has become so mainstream and so inclusive. . . . We have won over the hearts and minds of the public: all generations, all cultures and all classes. Now we have to win over the food industry and the government, to see that supplies of better food meet this growing demand. And we have to ensure that this occurs equitably, so that it is no longer just a lifestyle choice for some but a life necessity for all."
>
> Will Allen, food activist.

Spring

In-Season Produce

Alliums: scallions, leeks, garlic scapes, chives

Cole crops: broccoli, cauliflower

Greens: cabbages, chard, kale, spinach

Herbs: borage, chervil, lovage

Lettuces: leaf lettuce, mâche, miner's lettuce, spring mix

Root vegetables: beets, radishes, turnips

Others: artichokes, asparagus, mushrooms, peas and pea shoots, rhubarb, sorrel

Spring Recipes

Side Dishes

- Asian Slaw, page 138
- Baby Kale and Garlic-Mustard Dressing, page 132
- Better-Than-Takeout Egg Drop Soup, page 182
- Braised Red Cabbage with Blueberries, Raisins, and Goat Cheese, page 75
- Broccoli and Cauliflower Salad, page 71
- Garlicky White Beans and Kale, page 90
- Honey-Lemon Spring Vegetable Sauté, page 131
- Honey-Spice Roasted Cauliflower, page 79
- Marinated Broccoli, page 133
- Red Cabbage Slaw with Dried Fruit and Savory Praline, page 134
- Red, Gold, and Orange Salad, page 69
- Roasted Asparagus, page 67
- Roasted Beets with Mixed Herbs and Shallots, page 132
- Spinach Sautéed in Butter and Parmesan, page 108

Main Dishes

- Asparagus and Spinach Frittata, page 164
- Chicken Scallopini with Lemon, Artichokes, and Capers, page 191
- Ham and Broccoli Mac and Cheese, page 216
- Hash Brown, Chard, Tomato, and Ham Frittata, page 165
- Lamburgers in Pita, page 213
- Lemon-Herb Roast Chicken, page 195
- Meatball Stroganoff, page 210
- Meatloaf Florentine, page 211
- Pasta with Broccoli Pesto, page 224
- Pasta with Chard and Asparagus in Herb-Parmesan Sauce, page 225
- Shirred Eggs, page 166
- Tortellini with Asparagus, Ham, Peas, and Parmesan-Herb Sauce, page 215

Summer

■ In-Season Produce

Alliums: garlic, onions

Beans: green beans, pole beans, field peas, lima beans

Berries: blackberries, blueberries, gooseberries, raspberries, strawberries

Cole crops: cabbages, collard greens, kohlrabi

Greens: amaranth, arugula, collards, mustard greens

Herbs: basil, cilantro, lemongrass, marjoram, mint, oregano, parsley

Melons: cantaloupe, honeydew, watermelon

Peppers: bell peppers, hot peppers

Root vegetables: potatoes

Squashes: summer squash (yellow, zucchini, pattypan, and so on)

Stone fruits: apricots, cherries, nectarines, peaches, plums

Others: corn, cucumber, eggplant, fennel, figs, okra, tomatillos, tomatoes

■ Summer Recipes

Side Dishes

- Basic Vinaigrette, page 95
- Basil-Mint Cucumbers, page 83
- Blackberry Balsamic Vinaigrette, page 95
- Cantaloupe and Honey Salad, page 94
- Fig Balsamic Vinaigrette, page 95
- Green Beans Sautéed with Roasted Tomatoes and Shallot, page 106
- Lemony Couscous Salad, page 145
- Panzanella, page 116
- Potato Salad with Caramelized Onions and Vegetables, page 228
- Quick Caramelized Onions, page 65
- Roasted Ratatouille, page 86
- Roasted Summer Vegetables, page 97
- Roasted Tomatoes, page 106
- Soyccatash, page 144
- Squaghetti, page 144
- Stone-Ground Mustard Vinaigrette, page 95
- Summer-Squash Fritters, page 141
- Sun-Dried Tomato Pesto, page 97
- Tangy Kohlrabi Slaw, page 138
- Tarragon, Red Grape, and Ricotta Salata Salad, page 88
- Thai Summer Salad, page 139
- Vegetable Parmigiano, page 234
- Zucchini-Bacon Fritters, page 110

Main Dishes

- Asian-Style Fish with Greens, page 220
- Bread and Tomato Soup, page 186
- Breakfast Panini, page 167
- Curried Eggplant and Long Beans, page 226
- Fish Curry, page 221
- Guinness, Cheddar, and Caramelized-Onion Burgers, page 209
- Health Rounds, page 169
- Pan-Seared Chicken with Roasted Tomatoes, Pesto, and Goat Cheese, page 189
- Salmon Burgers, page 222
- Spicy Asian Greens and Pork, page 214
- Summer Vegetable Soup, page 180

Snacks and Desserts

- Banana–Peanut Butter Smoothie, page 168
- Berry Balsamic Popstickles, page 255
- Chocolate-Walnut Zucchini Bread, page 257
- Fresh Tomatillo Salsa, page 240
- Ginger-Vanilla Cherry-Berry Cobbler, page 254
- Peaches and Herb Popstickles, page 255
- Perfect Peach Summer Side, page 252
- Pineapple-Cilantro Popstickles, page 255
- Pita "Chips," page 240
- Rhubarb Crumble with Rosemary and Thyme, page 252
- White Bean–Pesto Dip, page 240

Fall

■ In-Season Produce

Cole crops: Brussels sprouts, broccoli, cabbages

Fruits: apples, grapes, pears, persimmons, pomegranates

Greens: kale, mustard greens, spinach

Herbs: rosemary, sage, savory, thyme

Nuts: chestnuts, hickory nuts, pecans, walnuts

Root vegetables: beets, carrots, horseradish, parsnips, sweet potatoes, rutabaga, turnips

Squashes: pumpkin, winter squash

■ Fall Recipes

Side Dishes

- Black Beans and Winter Squash, page 121
- Caramelized Onions and Chard Sauté, page 136
- Carrot-Orange Soufflé, page 135
- Carrot-Raisin Slaw, page 76
- Cider-Braised Brussels Sprouts, page 73
- Delicata-Chard "Side-or-Sauce," page 81
- Golden Roasted Potatoes, page 100
- Greens Gratin, page 140
- Honey-Chipotle Mashed Sweet Potatoes, page 146
- Honey-Glazed Turnips with Shallots, page 103
- Orange-Basil Sweet Potatoes, page 146
- Sautéed Red Chard with Clementines, Feta, and Balsamic Reduction, page 134
- Sweet Potato–Parmesan "Fries," page 113

Main Dishes

- Acorn Squash and Chicken Sausage "Cassoulet," page 198
- Carrot-Quinoa "Biryani," page 229
- Cauliflower-Cheese Soup with Carrots and Greens, page 187
- Chicken Salad with Red Grapes, Blueberries, and Almonds, page 194
- Fall Vegetable Soup, page 181
- Fennel, Potato, and Leek Soup, page 182
- Healthful Shepherd's Pie, page 208
- Hearty Kale-Potato Soup, page 183
- Pumpkin–White Cheddar Soup, page 185
- Roasted Vegetables, Lamb, and Couscous, page 212
- Squash, Carrot, and Lentil Soup, page 184

Snacks and Desserts

- Apple-Cider Applesauce, page 253
- Dark Chocolate–Honey Ganache, page 258
- Ginger-Carrot-Raisin Cupcakes, page 260
- Pumpkin Molasses Cookies, page 261
- Salt and Vinegar Kale Chips, page 241
- You Can't Beet Brownies, page 259

Winter

▬ In-Season Produce

Some farms may have greenhouses for production, but with the exception of southern regions and areas with temperate climates, such as California, most growing seasons are over. In these warmer regions, the following are in season:

Fruit: grapefruits, lemons, limes, oranges
Others: avocados, pistachios

▬ Winter and Not-Seasonal Recipes

Main Dishes

- Black-Eyed Peas and Smoked Ham Hock, page 218
- Braised Beef, page 207
- Chicken Chili, page 196
- Ginger-Banana-Oatmeal Pancakes, page 168
- Golden-Crisp Chicken Nuggets, page 199
- Honey-Sage Sweet Potatoes and Pasta with Shallots, page 227
- Pumpkin Gnocchi with Walnut Cream Sauce and Balsamic Reduction, page 232
- Real Turkey and Noodles, page 200
- Slow-Cooker Oatmeal, page 161
- Winter Risotto with Pork, page 217

Snacks and Desserts

- Lima Bean Hummus, page 239
- Crispy Rice and Almond Squares, page 263
- Make-Your-Own Microwave Popcorn, page 242
- Whole-Grain Chocolate Chunk Cookies, page 262

> " Focus too intently on hunger, and you'll lose sight of its cause. Devote yourself too narrowly to agriculture, and you'll forget about the consumer. Care too much about your own food, and you'll forsake food justice. There are larger purposes in life when all our interests come together. Closing the food gap is one of them."
>
> — Mark Winne, *Closing the Food Gap: Resetting the Table in the Land of Plenty.* Beacon Press, 2008.

resources

We both look to the following resources as a constant source of information for this book and for our own real food journey. If you're interested in food issues, take a moment to check out some of these resources.

Food Sustainability, Security, and Safety Issues

Organizations

American Farmland Trust
202-331-7300
www.farmland.org
Nonprofit organization dedicated to policies and programs that conserve farmland, support family farmers, and create sustainable agricultural systems. Website allows consumers to take action, including sending messages to political representatives.

Center for Rural Affairs
402-687-2100
www.cfra.org
Advocates for sustainable agriculture, keeping our food system in the hands of family farms, and other policies that support rural

America. Website includes a smart blog about rural issues.

Center for Science in the Public Interest
202-332-9110
www.cspinet.org
A nonprofit created to educate the public, advocate government policies that are consistent with scientific evidence on health and environmental issues, and counter industry's powerful influence on public opinion and public policies. Includes helpful charts on dangerous food additives and is notable for lobbying efforts for truth in food marketing and getting trans fats eliminated from fast foods.

Eat Local Challenge
www.eatlocalchallenge.com
Information on local food, food policy, and guidance on the benefits and resources for eating locally. Offers the opportunity to participate in a nationwide Eat Local Challenge.

The Ethicurean
www.ethicurean.com
Resource for information about food policy, safety, and legislation that affects our food supply.

Feeding America

800-771-2303

http://feedingamerica.org

Our nation's leading domestic hunger-relief charity. Feeding America's network provides food to more than 25 million low-income people facing hunger in the United States, 9 million of which are children and 3 million of which are seniors. You can find volunteer and advocacy opportunities in your own community at their site.

Food & Water Watch

www.foodandwaterwatch.org

Advocates policies that guarantee safe, wholesome food produced in a humane and sustainable manner and public, rather than private, control of water resources, including oceans, rivers, and groundwater.

Food First/Institute for Food & Development Policy

510-654-4400

www.foodfirst.org

Devoted to issues of food justice, food security, and food access.

GovTrack.us

www.govtrack.us

Site that allows users to easily subscribe to updates about the status of a piece of legislation and track its progress through Congress.

Grist

206-876-2020

www.grist.org

One of the top environmental issue websites, with a section dedicated to food issues.

Local Harvest

831-515-5602

www.localharvest.org

Searchable database for sourcing farmers' markets, CSAs, and local ingredients near you.

Sustainable Table

212-991-1930

www.sustainabletable.org

Celebrates local sustainable food, educates consumers on food-related issues, and works to build community through food.

Publications and Productions

Kenner, Robert. *Food, Inc.* DVD. 2009.

A documentary that covers "what we eat, how it's produced, who we have become as a nation and where we are going from here."

Kingsolver, Barbara, Steven L. Hopp, and Camille Kingsolver. *Animal, Vegetable, Miracle: A Year of Food Life.* New York: Harper-Collins, 2007.

A memoir of the year Kingsolver's family spent eating locally, with simple recipes and information about our food system.

293

McGinnis, J. Michael, Jennifer Appleton Gootman, and Vivica I. Kraak, eds. *Food Marketing to Children and Youth: Threat or Opportunity?*. Washington, DC: National Academies Press, 2006.
Twenty years of research and studies examining the tactics and impact of food marketing on children's health, including statistics and trends of current food-related diseases in children.

Nestle, Marion. *What to Eat: An Aisle-by-Aisle Guide to Savvy Food Choices and Good Eating*. New York: North Point Press, 2006.
A guide to making healthy and safe food choices in the supermarket and beyond.

Pollan, Michael. *In Defense of Food: An Eater's Manifesto*. New York: Penguin Press, 2008.
The most sensible, well-researched, common-sense book on diet and nutrition issues we have read.

———. *The Omnivore's Dilemma: A Natural History of Four Meals*. New York: Penguin Press, 2006.
An ethical, political, and ecological investigation of our food system. Examines four meals down to their literal roots and contrasts industrial production with more-sustainable food systems. Considered a galvanizing exploration of all the factors driving the Eat Local food movement . . . and a fascinating read, as well. A companion book for children is available as well: *The Omnivore's Dilemma: The Secrets Behind What You Eat*, Young Readers Edition. New York: Dial Books, 2009.

Schlosser, Eric. *Fast Food Nation: The Dark Side of the All-American Meal*. New York: Hougton Mifflin, 2001.
Groundbreaking book that exposes all of the impacts, from the environmental to the cultural and human toll, by the fast-food industry.

Sustainable Table. *The Meatrix*. DVD. 2003
Critically acclaimed short films on the grim reality of factory-farmed meats. Visit their website at: www.themeatrix.com.

Wansink, Brian. *Mindless Eating: Why We Eat More Than We Think*. New York: Bantam, 2006.
A fascinating, easy-to-read resource that examines the hidden persuaders that encourage people to eat more, or less, with tips for shaping the environment to be healthier . . . without the stress.

Our Favorite Cookbooks

There are many terrific cookbooks available; here are some of the ones that are most frequently used — and dog-eared and food splattered — in our homes.

Bittman, Mark. *How to Cook Everything: 2,000 Simple Recipes for Great Food,* **2nd ed. Hoboken, NJ: John Wiley & Sons, 2008.**
A relaxed, comprehensive, and straightforward guide to food from one of the nation's most admired food writers.

Chesman, Andrea. *Serving Up the Harvest.* **North Adams, MA: Storey Publishing, 2007.**
Organized according to the season's harvest, this book offers more than 100 recipes that can be made quickly with minimal ingredients.

Kafka, Barbara, and Christopher Styler. *Vegetable Love.* **New York: Artisan, 2005.**
A well-organized, encyclopedic approach to vegetables featuring great information and recipes.

Labensky, Sarah R., and Alan M. Hause. *On Cooking: A Textbook of Culinary Fundamentals,* **4th ed. Upper Saddle River, NJ: Prentice Hall, 2010.**
A textbook for culinary students, this book is also a great reference for home cooks. It covers all the cooking fundamentals: food safety, nutrition, tools and equipment, staples, ingredients, and presentation, as well as recipes.

Lind, Mary Beth, and Cathleen Hockman-Wert. *Simply in Season,* **2nd ed. Scottdale, PA: Herald Press, 2009.**
Delivers simple recipes that can be made with seasonal ingredients. There is a colorful companion children's cookbook by Mark Beach and Julie Kauffman. *Simply in Season Children's Cookbook.* Scottdale, PA: Herald Press, 2006.

Madison Area Community Supported Agriculture Coalition. *From Asparagus to Zucchini: A Guide to Cooking Farm-Fresh Seasonal Produce.* **Madison, WI: Jones Books, 2004.**
Originally written for Madison, Wisconsin, CSA members, the book now has national distribution. Organized by ingredient; each entry contains recipes, storage/preservation information, cooking tips, and nutritional information.

Blogs

Ali's Clean-er Plate Club
www.cleanerplateclub.com
Ali's blog.

The Ex-Expatriate's Kitchen
http://expatriateskitchen.blogspot.com
Beth's blog.

School Lunches

Chef Ann Cooper:
The Renegade Lunch Lady
631-697-0844
www.chefann.com
Ideas, strategies, tips, and recipes to help build a better school lunch program. Chef Ann's book, *Lunch Lessons*, offers great insights into starting a healthful lunch program at your child's school.

Farm to School
www.farmtoschool.org
Program to help schools source local produce for lunch programs and to help educate students on food sources and nutrition.

School Nutrition Association
301-686-3100
www.schoolnutrition.org
National, nonprofit association for school nutrition professionals.

Marketing to Children

Campaign for a Commercial-Free Childhood
857-241-2028
www.commercialexploitation.org
Campaign for a Commercial-Free Childhood (CCFC) is a national organization that includes health care professionals, educators, advocacy groups, parents, and individuals. Its goal is to limit negative impacts of marketing on our children.

The Henry J. Kaiser Family Foundation
650-854-9400
www.kff.org
Nonprofit foundation that provides research and communications on major health issues impacting our country. Site includes a Media and Health section with studies regarding the impact of food marketing and media exposure on children's health.

Page references in *italics* indicate photos or illustrations.

A

Acorn Squash and Chicken Sausage "Cassoulet," 198
additives, 243
alliums, 62–65, *63*
almonds/almond butter
    Chicken Salad, 194
    Crispy Rice and Almond Squares, 263
    Health Rounds, 169
anthocyanins, 74
anti-diet, the, 230–31
Apple Cider Applesauce, 253
artichokes/artichoke hearts
    Chicken Scallopini, 191
    Roasted Summer Vegetables, 97
arugula, 92, *93*
Asian Slaw, 138–39
Asian-Style Fish, 220
asparagus, *48*, 66–67, *67*
    Asparagus and Spinach Frittata, 164
    Honey-Lemon Spring Vegetable Sauté, 131
    Pasta with Chard and Asparagus, 225
    Roasted Asparagus, 67
    Tortellini, 215

B

Baby Kale and Garlic-Mustard Dressing, 132
bacon
    Panzanella, 116
    Shirred Eggs, 166
    Zucchini-Bacon Fritters, 110

baking recipes, customizing, 259
bananas
    Banana-Peanut Butter Smoothie, 168
    Ginger-Banana-Oatmeal Pancakes, 168
barley, 40
basil
    Basil-Mint Cucumbers, 83
    Basil Pesto, 145
    Curried Eggplant and Long Beans, 226
    Orange-Basil Sweet Potatoes, 146
beans, 41. *See also* snap beans
    Acorn Squash and Chicken Sausage "Cassoulet," 198
    Chicken Chili, 196
    Curried Eggplant and Long Beans, 226
    Garlicky White Beans and Kale, 90
    Lima Bean Hummus, 239
    Thai Summer Salad, 139
    White Bean–Pesto Dip, 240
béchamel, 178
beef, 207–11
    Braised Beef, 207
    cooking grass-fed, 203
    Guinness, Cheddar, and Caramelized-Onion Burgers, 209
    Healthful Shepherd's Pie, 208
    Meatball Stroganoff, 210
    Meatloaf Florentine, 211
beets, *68*, 68–69
    Red, Gold, and Orange Salad, 69
    Roasted Beets, 132
    You Can't Beet Brownies, 259

berries
    Berry Balsamic Popsickles, 255
    Braised Red Cabbage with Blueberries, Raisins and Goat Cheese, 75
    Chicken Salad, 194
    Ginger-Vanilla Cherry-Berry Cobbler, 254
    Perfect Peach Summer Side, 252
Better-Than-Takeout Egg Drop Soup, 182–83
"Biryani," Carrot-Quinoa, 229
Black Beans and Winter Squash, 121
Blackberry Balsamic Vinaigrette, 95
Black-Eyed Peas and Smoked Ham Hock, 218
bok choy
    Honey-Lemon Spring Vegetable Sauté, 131
    Summer Vegetable Soup, 180
Braised Red Cabbage with Blueberries, Raisins and Goat Cheese, 75
braising, basics of, 207
bread
    Bread and Tomato Soup, 186
    Breakfast Panini, 167
    Chocolate-Walnut Zucchini Bread, 257
breakfast, 159–69
    importance of, 159
    quick/easy options, 160
Breakfast Panini, 167

broccoli/broccolini, 70–71, *71*
  Asian Slaw, 138–39
  Broccoli and Cauliflower Salad, 71
  Ham and Broccoli Mac and Cheese, 216
  Marinated Broccoli, 133
  Pasta with Broccoli Pesto, 224
Brownies, You Can't Beet, 259
Brussels sprouts, 72–73, *73*
  Cider-Braised Brussels Sprouts, 73
bulgur, 41
bulk foods, 33, 40–44
burgers
  Guinness, Cheddar, and Caramelized-Onion Burgers, 209
  Lamburgers in Pita, 213
  Salmon Burgers, 222

C

cabbage, 74–75
  Asian Slaw, 138
  Braised Red Cabbage with Blueberries, Raisins and Goat Cheese, 75
  napa cabbage, 74, 75
  Red Cabbage Slaw, 134
  Tangy Kohlrabi Slaw, 138
cancer prevention, 70, 214
Cantaloupe and Honey Salad, 94
Caramelized Onions and Chard Sauté, 136
carrots, 76–77, *77*
  Carrot-Orange Soufflé, 135

Carrot-Quinoa "Biryani," 229
Carrot-Raisin Slaw, 76
Ginger-Carrot-Raisin Cupcakes, 260
Squash, Carrot, and Lentil Soup, 184
"Cassoulet," Acorn Squash and Chicken Sausage, 198
cauliflower, 78–79, *79*
  Broccoli and Cauliflower Salad, 71
  Cauliflower-Cheese Soup, 187
  Honey-Spice Roasted Cauliflower, 79
celeriac/celery root, 101, *102*
chard, 80–81, *81*
  Caramelized Onions and Chard Sauté, 136
  Delicata-Chard "Side-or-Sauce," 81
  Fall Vegetable Soup, 181
  Hash Brown, Chard, Tomato, and Ham Frittata, 165
  Honey-Lemon Spring Vegetable Sauté, 131
  Pasta with Chard and Asparagus, 225
  Sautéed Red Chard, 134–35
cheese, 61. *See also* parmesan cheese
  Asparagus and Spinach Frittata, 164
  Braised Red Cabbage with Blueberries, Raisins and Goat Cheese, 75
  cheese-based soup, 179
  Guinness, Cheddar, and Caramelized-Onion Burgers, 209
  Ham and Broccoli Mac and Cheese, 216

Hash Brown, Chard, Tomato, and Ham Frittata, 165
  Pumpkin-White Cheddar Soup, 185
  Red, Gold, and Orange Salad, 69
  Tarragon, Red Grape, and Ricotta Salata Salad, 88
  Vegetable Parmigiano, 234
Cherry-Berry Cobbler, Ginger-Vanilla, 254
chicken, 188–200
  Acorn Squash and Chicken Sausage "Cassoulet," 198
  Chicken Chili, 196
  Chicken Salad, 194
  Chicken Scallopini, 191
  Golden-Crisp Chicken Nuggets, 199
  Pan-Seared Chicken, 189
  scraps for broth, 195
Chili, Chicken, 196
chips/popcorn, 238–47
  Make-Your-Own Microwave Popcorn, 242
  Pita "Chips," 240
  Salt and Vinegar Kale Chips, 241
chocolate, 257–59
  Chocolate-Walnut Zucchini Bread, 257
  Dark Chocolate-Honey Ganache, 258
  Whole-Grain Chocolate Chunk Cookies, 262
  You Can't Beet Brownies, 259
Cider-Braised Brussels Sprouts, 73
"clean fifteen" fruits/vegetables, 129
Cobbler, Ginger-Vanilla Cherry-Berry, 254

Community Supported Agriculture (CSAs), 4, 53–55
control game, avoiding, 25–26
cookies and bars, 261–63
Crispy Rice and Almond Squares, 263
Pumpkin Molasses Cookies, 261
Whole-Grain Chocolate Chunk Cookies, 262
co-ops, 36, 54
corn, 122–23
on the cob, microwaved, 123
Soyccatash, 144
Summer-Squash Fritters, 141
coupons, use of, 36
couscous, 41
Lemony Couscous Salad, 145
Roasted Vegetables, Lamb, and Couscous, 212
Crispy Rice and Almond Squares, 263
cruciferous vegetables, 70
Crumble, Rhubarb, 252
cucumber, 82–83, *83*
Basil-Mint Cucumbers, 83
Thai Summer Salad, 139
Cupcakes, Ginger-Carrot-Raisin, 260
curry
Curried Eggplant and Long Beans, 226
Fish Curry, 221

D

daikon radish, 101, *102*
Dark Chocolate-Honey Ganache, 258

Delicata-Chard "Side-or-Sauce," 81
desserts & sweets, 248–50. *See also* fruit desserts
"dilution effect," nutrition and, 56
dinner, 174–77
family dinners, 174–75, 283
faster-than-drive-thru, 176–77
dips and spreads, 60, 239
Fresh Tomatillo Salsa, 240
Lemon-Herb Mayonnaise, 222
Lima Bean Hummus, 239
White Bean–Pesto Dip, 240
"dirty dozen" fruits/vegetables, 129
diseases, diet and, 14
doubling recipes, 46
dressings
fat-free, 94
make-your-own, 95

E

E. coli, 49
safety primer on, 204–6
tips, safety and, 205
eating habits, 8, 11, 17, 277–78
edamame (soybeans), 122, 124, *127,* 245
Asian Slaw, 138
Soyccatash, 144
eggplant, 84–86, *85*
Curried Eggplant and Long Beans, 226
Roasted Ratatouille, 86
eggs, 162–67
Asparagus and Spinach Frittata, 164
Better-Than-Takeout Egg

Drop Soup, 182–83
Breakfast Panini, 167
Hash Brown, Chard, Tomato, and Ham Frittata, 165
Shirred Eggs, 166
exercise, 22

F

fall produce/recipes, 290
Fall Vegetable Soup, 181
farmers' markets, 46–52
appeal of, 47–49
consumption habits, 52
shopping at, 49–51
value and, 51–52
farm-to-consumer venues, 45–55, 285
CSAs, 53–55
farmers' markets, 46–52
fats, 147–53
almond oil, 151
avocado oil, 153
butter, 150
canola oil, 152
corn oil, 152
extra-virgin olive oil, 151
flaxseed oil, 150
ghee (clarified butter), 153
hazelnut oil, 152
lard, 151
margarine, 153
oils, tips for use of, 149–50
olive oil, 153
palm kernel oil, 153
palm oil, 152
peanut oil, 152
pumpkinseed oil, 150
safflower oil, 152
sesame oil, 151

fats (*continued*)
soybean oil, 153
sunflower oil, 152
types of, 147–48
walnut oil, 151
fennel bulb
Fennel, Potato, and Leek
Soup, 182
Red, Gold, and Orange
Salad, 69
Fig Balsamic Vinaigrette, 95
fighting over food choices,
18–19
fish. *See* seafood
food additives, 243
food justice, 278–79
food miles, 280–81
food preferences, 12–17
abnormal norms, 14–17
cultural influences, 15–16
exposure to foods, 13, 15
modeling and, 16
food safety, 49, 204–6
"doneness" of meat, 206
pesticide residues, 129
resources for, 292–93
tips for, 205
fresh vs. frozen produce, 125
Frittata, Asparagus and
Spinach, 164
Frittata, Hash Brown,
Chard, Tomato, and
Ham, 165
Fritters, Summer-Squash,
141
Fritters, Zucchini-Bacon, 110
frozen vs. fresh produce, 125
fruit, dried. *See also* raisins
Red Cabbage Slaw, 134
fruit desserts, 251–55
Apple Cider Applesauce,
253

Ginger-Vanilla Cherry-
Berry Cobbler, 254
Perfect Peach Summer
Side, 252
Popstickles, 255
Rhubarb Crumble, 252

G

Ganache, Dark Chocolate-
Honey, 258
garlic/garlic scapes, 62, *63*
Baby Kale and Garlic-
Mustard Dressing, 132
Garlicky White Beans and
Kale, 90
ginger
Ginger-Banana-Oatmeal
Pancakes, 168
Ginger-Carrot-Raisin
Cupcakes, 260
Ginger-Vanilla Cherry-
Berry Cobbler, 254
Gnocci, Pumpkin, *232,*
232–33
Golden-Crisp Chicken
Nuggets, 199
Golden Roasted Potatoes, 100
grapes
Chicken Salad, 194
Tarragon, Red Grape, and
Ricotta Salata Salad, 88
grass-fed meat, 202, *203*
green beans. *See* snap beans
greens, leafy, 137. *See also*
specific vegetable
Asian-Style Fish, 220
Cauliflower-Cheese Soup,
187
Greens Gratin, 140
Spicy Asian Greens and
Pork, 214
Guinness, Cheddar, and
Caramelized-Onion
Burgers, 209

H

ham
Black-Eyed Peas and
Smoked Ham Hock, 218
Ham and Broccoli Mac
and Cheese, 216
Hash Brown, Chard, To-
mato, and Ham Frittata,
165
Shirred Eggs, 166
Tortellini, 215
Hash Brown, Chard,
Tomato, and Ham
Frittata, 165
Healthful Shepherd's Pie,
208
Health Rounds, 169
Hearty Kale-Potato Soup,
183
heirloom vegetables, 115
herbs, 87–88, *88. See also*
basil
Honey-Sage Sweet Pota-
toes and Pasta, 227
Lemon-Herb Mayonnaise,
222
Lemon-Herb Roast Chick-
en, 195
Popstickles, 255
Rhubarb Crumble, 252
Tarragon, Red Grape, and
Ricotta Salata Salad, 88
high-fructose corn syrup
(HFCS), 267–69
honey, 61, 273
Cantaloupe and Honey
Salad, 94
Dark Chocolate-Honey
Ganache, 258
Honey-Chipotle Mashed
Sweet Potatoes, 146
Honey-Glazed Turnips
with Shallots, 103
Honey-Lemon Spring
Vegetable Sauté, 131

Honey-Sage Sweet Pota-
toes and Pasta, 227
Honey-Spice Roasted
Cauliflower, 79
Hummus, Lima Bean, 239
hunger and habit, 284
hydrogenated oils, 148

K

kale, *89,* 89–90
Baby Kale and Garlic-
Mustard Dressing, 132
Fall Vegetable Soup, 181
Garlicky White Beans and
Kale, 90
Hearty Kale-Potato Soup,
183
Honey-Lemon Spring
Vegetable Sauté, 131
Salt and Vinegar Kale
Chips, 241
kids, involving, 281
knife skills. See *mise en
place*/knife skills
knowledge is power, 277
Kohlrabi Slaw, Tangy, 138

L

lamb, 211–13
Lamburgers in Pita, 213
Roasted Vegetables, Lamb,
and Couscous, 212
leeks, 62, *63*
Fennel, Potato, and Leek
Soup, 182
leftovers, 46, 171, 223
lemon
Chicken Scallopini, 191
Honey-Lemon Spring
Vegetable Sauté, 131
Honey-Spice Roasted
Cauliflower, 79

how to zest a, 79
Lemon-Herb Mayonnaise,
222
Lemon-Herb Roast Chick-
en, 195
Lemony Couscous Salad,
145
lentils, 42
Squash, Carrot, and Lentil
Soup, 184
lettuces, *48,* 92–95, *93*
Cantaloupe and Honey
Salad, 94
fat-free dressings on, 94
Potato Salad, 228
local foods, 49, 279, 280–81.
See also farm-to-
consumer venues
lunch/lunch-box, 170–73
easy favorites, 172–73
recipes for, 173
strategies for, 170–71
school lunches, 154, 296

M

mâche, 92, *93*
Marinated Broccoli, 133
marketing of food, 11
to children, 282, 283, 296
in stores, 30, 32
Mayonnaise, Lemon-Herb,
222
meat, 188–99. *See also* beef;
lamb; pork
carbon-monoxide spiked,
202
grass-fed, 202, 203
meatless Mondays, 223–34
micronutrients, 5, 94
millet, 42
mirepoix, 179
mise en place/knife skills,
192–93
chiffonade, how to, 193

julienne, how to, 193
onion, chop/dice, 193
sizes of cuts, 192
mushrooms, 126, *127*

N

nutrition, 23–24
nutritional dilution, 56
"stealth" nutrition, 258
teaching about, 284
nuts. *See also* almonds/
almond butter
Cantaloupe and Honey
Salad, 94
Chocolate-Walnut Zuc-
chini Bread, 257
Pumpkin Gnocchi, 232,
232–33
Red Cabbage Slaw, 134
Thai Summer Salad, 139

O

oats/oatmeal, 44
Ginger-Banana-Oatmeal
Pancakes, 168
Slow-Cooker Oatmeal, 161
oils, 149–53
tips for, 149–50
types of, 150–53
okra
Roasted Ratatouille, 86
omega-3 essential fatty
acids, 148
in eggs, 163
fresh, not cooked, 150
in meat, 201
omega-6 essential fatty
acids, 148

onions, 64–65
  Caramelized Onions and Chard Sauté, 136
  Guinness, Cheddar, and Caramelized-Onion Burgers, 209
  Potato Salad, 228
  Quick Caramelized Onions, 65
oranges/orange juice/orange extract
  Carrot-Orange Soufflé, 135
  Orange-Basil Sweet Potatoes, 146
  Red, Gold, and Orange Salad, 69
  Sautéed Red Chard, 134–35
organic vs. conventional produce, 128–29

P

Pancakes, Ginger-Banana-Oatmeal, 168
Pan-Seared Chicken, 189
pantry, 32, 34
  lunch box and, 172–73
  well-stocked, 35
Panzanella, 116
parmesan cheese
  Acorn Squash and Chicken Sausage "Cassoulet," 198
  Basil Pesto, 145
  Cauliflower-Cheese Soup, 187
  Greens Gratin, 140
  rinds, for soup, 181
  Spinach Sautéed in Butter and Parmesan, 108

Sweet Potato-Parmesan "Fries," 113
  Vegetable Parmigiano, 234
parsnips, 101
  Roasted Vegetables, Lamb, and Couscous, 212
pasta
  Ham and Broccoli Mac and Cheese, 216
  Honey-Sage Sweet Potatoes and Pasta, 227
  Pasta with Broccoli Pesto, 224
  Pasta with Chard and Asparagus, 225
  Real Turkey and Noodles, 200
  Tortellini, 215
peaches
  Peaches and Herb Popstickles, 255
  Perfect Peach Summer Side, 252
peanut butter
  Banana-Peanut Butter Smoothie, 168
  Crispy Rice and Almond Squares, 263
  Health Rounds, 169
  Whole-Grain Chocolate Chunk Cookies, 262
peas, 126, 127
  Black-Eyed Peas and Smoked Ham Hock, 218
  split peas, 43
  Tortellini, 215
peppers, bell, 96–97, 99
  Fish Curry, 221
  Roasted Summer Vegetables, 97
peppers, chipotle
  Honey-Chipotle Mashed Sweet Potatoes, 146

Perfect Peach Summer Side, 252
pesto
  Basil Pesto, 145
  Pasta with Broccoli Pesto, 224
  Sun-Dried Tomato Pesto, 97
  White Bean–Pesto Dip, 240
phytonutrients, 59, 91
Pineapple-Cilantro Popstickles, 255
Pita "Chips," 240
Popcorn, Make-Your-Own Microwave, 242
Popstickles, 255
pork. See also bacon; ham
  Spicy Asian Greens and Pork, 214
  Winter Risotto, 217
portions. See serving sizes
positive change, embracing, 282–85
potatoes, 98–100, 99. See also sweet potatoes
  Fennel, Potato, and Leek Soup, 182
  Golden Roasted Potatoes, 100
  Hash Brown, Chard, Tomato, and Ham Frittata, 165
  Hearty Kale-Potato Soup, 183
  Potato Salad, 228
poultry, 188–200
prep time, 3, 188
processed foods, six simple words and, 38–39
produce. See also seasonal eating
  fresh vs. frozen, 125
  organic vs. conventional, 128–29
pumpkin, 119

Pumpkin Gnocchi, 232, 232–33
Pumpkin Molasses Cookies, 261
Pumpkin-White Cheddar Soup, 185

Q

Quick Caramelized Onions, 65
quinoa, 42
Carrot-Quinoa "Biryani," 229

R

raisins
Braised Red Cabbage with Blueberries, Raisins and Goat Cheese, 75
Broccoli and Cauliflower Salad, 71
Carrot-Quinoa "Biryani," 229
Carrot-Raisin Slaw, 76
Ginger-Carrot-Raisin Cupcakes, 260
Pumpkin Molasses Cookies, 261
Slow-Cooker Oatmeal, 161
Real Turkey and Noodles, 200
Red, Gold, and Orange Salad, 69
Red Cabbage Slaw, 134
Rhubarb Crumble, 252
rice, 42–43
Coconut Rice, 221
wild rice, 44
Winter Risotto, 217
roasting foods, 142–43, 207
Roasted Asparagus, 67
Roasted Beets, 132

Roasted Ratatouille, 86
Roasted Summer Vegetables, 97
Roasted Tomatoes, 106
Roasted Vegetables, Lamb, and Couscous, 212
root vegetables, 101–3, 102. See also specific vegetable
Honey-Glazed Turnips with Shallots, 103
roux, 3, 178
rutabaga, 101, 102

S

salads
Asian Slaw, 138–39
Broccoli and Cauliflower Salad, 71
Cantaloupe and Honey Salad, 94
Carrot-Raisin Slaw, 76
Chicken Salad, 194
Lemony Couscous Salad, 145
Potato Salad, 228
Red, Gold, and Orange Salad, 69
Red Cabbage Slaw, 134
Tangy Kohlrabi Slaw, 138
Tarragon, Red Grape, and Ricotta Salata Salad, 88
Thai Summer Salad, 139
Salmon Burgers, 222
Salsa, Fresh Tomatillo, 240
Salt and Vinegar Kale Chips, 241
sandwiches. See also burgers
caramelized onions in, 65
saturated fats, 147
sauces. See also pesto
Delicata-Chard "Side-or-Sauce," 81
Sautéed Red Chard, 134–35

sautéing, basics of, 143
scallions, 62, 63
seafood, 219–22
Asian-Style Fish, 220
Fish Curry, 221
Salmon Burgers, 222
seasonal eating, 286–91
spring, 288
summer, 289
fall, 290
winter, 291
serving sizes
anti-diet and, 230–31, 231
consumption and, 20–21, 21, 37
shallots, 62, 63
Green Beans Sautéed with Roasted Tomatoes and Shallot, 106
Honey-Glazed Turnips with Shallots, 103
Roasted Beets, 132
Shepherd's Pie, Healthful, 208
Shirred Eggs, 166
shopping strategies, 27–56
bulk foods, 40–44
farm-to-consumer venues, 45–55
pantry goods/staples, 34, 35
six simple words, 38–39
for supermarket, 30–37, 31
tips, healthful/frugal, 32–34
six simple words, 38–39
slow cooker
recipe conversions, 197
Slow-Cooker Oatmeal, 161
"Smart Choices," 37

Smoothie, Banana-Peanut Butter, 168
snacks & sweets, 235–74
  best snacks, 244–45
  as big business, 236–37
  breads, cakes, cookies, 256–63
  dips & chips, 238–47
  fruit desserts, 251–55
  soda, 264–65
  sweets & desserts, 248–50
  trends and, 267
snap beans, *104,* 104–6
  Green Beans Sautéed with Roasted Tomatoes and Shallot, 106
  Honey-Glazed Turnips with Shallots, 105–6
soda, 264–65
soup, 178–87
  basic techniques, 179
  Better-Than-Takeout Egg Drop Soup, 182–83
  Bread and Tomato Soup, 186
  Cauliflower-Cheese Soup, 187
  chicken scraps for broth, 195
  Fall Vegetable Soup, 181
  Fennel, Potato, and Leek Soup, 182
  Hearty Kale-Potato Soup, 183
  Pumpkin-White Cheddar Soup, 185
  soup definitions, 178
  Squash, Carrot, and Lentil Soup, 184
  Summer Vegetable Soup, 180
soybeans. *See* edamame

Spicy Asian Greens and Pork, 214
spinach, 107–8, *108*
  Asparagus and Spinach Frittata, 164
  Meatloaf Florentine, 211
  Spinach Sautéed in Butter and Parmesan, 108
  Thai Summer Salad, 139
spring produce/recipes, 288
Squaghetti, 144
squash. *See* summer squash; winter squashes
Stone-Ground Mustard Vinaigrette, 95
Stroganoff, Meatball, 210
sugar. *See* under sweeteners
sugar substitutes, whole food, 272–74. *See also* sweeteners
  agave nectar, 272
  barley malt, 272
  brown rice syrup, 272
  brown sugar, 274
  date sugar, 272
  fruit juice concentrates, 272
  honey, 273
  maple sugar/syrup, 273
  molasses, 273
  stevia, 274
  sucanat, rapadura, 274
  turbinado sugar, 274
summer produce/recipes, 289
summer squash, 109–11, *111*
  Chocolate-Walnut Zucchini Bread, 257
  Squaghetti, 144
  Summer-Squash Fritters, 141
  Zucchini-Bacon Fritters, 110
Summer Vegetable Soup, 180
Sun-Dried Tomato Pesto, 97

supermarket strategies, 30–37
  battle plan for, 31, 31
  coupons, use of, 36
  downside of 30 percent more, 34, 36–37
  pantry goods/staples, 34, 35
  "Smart Choices," 37
  tips, healthful/frugal, 32–33
"sweating" vegetables, 178
sweeteners. *See also* sugar substitutes, whole food
  artificial, 269–70
  consumption of, 19
  high-fructose corn syrup, 267–69
  label reading and, 270
  sugar, addictiveness and, 166
  sugar struggle, avoiding, 249–50
sweet potatoes
  Fall Vegetable Soup, 181
  Healthful Shepherd's Pie, 208
  Honey-Chipotle Mashed Sweet Potatoes, 146
  Honey-Sage Sweet Potatoes and Pasta, 227
  Orange-Basil Sweet Potatoes, 146
  Sweet Potato-Parmesan "Fries," 113
sweets. *See* desserts & sweets; fruit desserts; snacks & sweets
Swiss chard. *See* chard

T

Tangy Kohlrabi Slaw, 138
Tarragon, Red Grape, and Ricotta Salata Salad, 88

Thai Summer Salad, 139
30-minute meals, 188
Tomatillo Salsa, Fresh, 240
tomatoes, 114–18, *116, 117*
   Bread and Tomato Soup,
     186
   Chicken Chili, 196
   Green Beans Sautéed with
     Roasted Tomatoes and
     Shallot, 106
   Hash Brown, Chard, To-
     mato, and Ham Frittata,
     165
   Healthful Shepherd's Pie,
     208
   Lemony Couscous Salad,
     145
   Pan-Seared Chicken, 189
   Panzanella, 116
   peeling, coring, seeding,
     118
   Roasted Ratatouille, 86
   Roasted Summer Veg-
     etables, 97
   Roasted Tomatoes, 106
   Squaghetti, 144
   Summer Vegetable Soup,
     180
   Sun-Dried Tomato Pesto,
     97
Tortellini, 215
trans fats, 147
Turkey and Noodles, Real,
   200

Turnips with Shallots,
   Honey-Glazed, 103

U

unsaturated fats, 147
"un-vegetables," the, 122–27,
   127
   corn, 122–23
   edamame (soybeans), 122,
     124, 127, 245
   fresh vs. frozen, 125
   mushrooms, 126, 127
   peas, 126, 127

V

vegetables. *See also* specific
   vegetable
   tips, vegephobia and,
     60–61
   Vegetable Parmigiano, 234
velouté, 179

W

watercress, 92, *93*
wheat berries, 44
whole foods, 5, 38–39
Whole-Grain Chocolate
   Chunk Cookies, 262

"whys" parable, 158
winter produce/recipes, 291
Winter Risotto, 217
winter squashes, 119–21,
   120, 121
   Acorn Squash and Chick-
     en Sausage "Cassoulet,"
     198
   Black Beans and Winter
     Squash, 121
   Delicata-Chard "Side-or-
     Sauce," 81
   Fall Vegetable Soup, 181
   Squash, Carrot, and Lentil
     Soup, 184
   Winter Risotto, 217

Y

Yogurt, 246–47
You Can't Beet Brownies,
   259

Z

zucchini. *See* summer
   squash

Other Storey Titles You Will Enjoy

Fix, Freeze, Feast, by Kati Neville and Lindsay Tkacsik.
Great recipes that start with a warehouse club tray pack of meat and end
with a freezer full of delicious meals, ready for thawing anytime.
256 pages. Paper. ISBN 978-1-60342-726-5.

Ghoulish Goodies, by Sharon Bowers.
A colorful collection of creepy treats for celebrating Halloween or
any frightful occasion.
160 pages. Paper. ISBN 978-1-60342-146-1.

The Good-to-Go Cookbook, by Kathleen Cannata Hanna.
Hundreds of recipes to feed busy families, from weeknight dinners that
take to 15 minutes to prepare to relaxed suppers for the weekend.
336 pages. Paper. ISBN 978-1-60342-076-1.

The Locavore Way, by Amy Cotler.
Tips and strategies to buy, cook, and eat close to home!
256 pages. Paper. ISBN 978-1-60342-453-0.

Put 'em Up, by Sherri Brooks Vinton.
A comprehensive guide to creative preserving: bright flavors,
flexible batch sizes, modern methods.
304 pages. Paper. ISBN 978-1-60342-546-9.

Raw Energy, by Stephanie Tourles.
More than 100 recipes for delicious raw snacks: unprocessed,
uncooked, simple, and pure.
272 pages. Paper. ISBN 978-1-60342-467-7.

**These and other books from Storey Publishing are available
wherever quality books are sold or by calling 1-800-441-5700.
Visit us at www.storey.com.**